The Animal-To-Come

Animalities

Series Editor
Matthew Chrulew, Curtin University

Editorial Advisory Board
Brett Buchanan, Laurentian University
Vinciane Despret, Université de Liège
Donna Haraway, University of California, Santa Cruz
Jean Langford, University of Minnesota
Dominique Lestel, École normale supérieure
Stephen Muecke, Flinders University
Stephanie Posthumus, McGill University
Isabelle Stengers, Université libre de Bruxelles
Thom van Dooren, University of Sydney
Cary Wolfe, Rice University

Books available
Deborah Bird Rose, *Shimmer: Flying Fox Exuberance in Worlds of Peril*
Robert Briggs, *The Animal-To-Come: Zoopolitics in Deconstruction*

Forthcoming books
Dominique Lestel, *Animality: An Essay on the Status of the Human*, translated by Brett Buchanan, together with *Animalities* by Matthew Chrulew

Visit the series website at
edinburghuniversitypress.com/series-animalities

The Animal-To-Come
Zoopolitics in Deconstruction

Robert Briggs

EDINBURGH
University Press

For Nic, Noah and Chloe

Edinburgh University Press is one of the leading university presses in the UK. We publish academic books and journals in our selected subject areas across the humanities and social sciences, combining cutting-edge scholarship with high editorial and production values to produce academic works of lasting importance. For more information visit our website: edinburghuniversitypress.com

© Robert Briggs, 2021, 2023

Edinburgh University Press Ltd
The Tun – Holyrood Road, 12(2f) Jackson's Entry, Edinburgh EH8 8PJ

First published in hardback by Edinburgh University Press 2021

Typeset in 10/14pt Warnock Pro and Gill Sans
by Cheshire Typesetting Ltd, Cuddington, Cheshire

A CIP record for this book is available from the British Library

ISBN 978 1 4744 9394 9 (hardback)
ISBN 978 1 4744 9395 6 (paperback)
ISBN 978 1 4744 9396 3 (webready PDF)
ISBN 978 1 4744 9397 0 (epub)

The right of Robert Briggs to be identified as the author of this work has been asserted in accordance with the Copyright, Designs and Patents Act 1988, and the Copyright and Related Rights Regulations 2003 (SI No. 2498).

Contents

Zoopolitics in Deconstruction?	1
1. Following the Animal-To-Come...	11
2. Specifically Cultural	35
3. Zoopower	62
4. Political Animals	92
5. Responding (After Anthropos)	121
What Hope for the Animal-To-Come?	156
Notes	168
Bibliography	219
Index	234

To name is not to say what is true but to confer on what is named the power to make us feel and think in the mode that the name calls for.

Isabelle Stengers, *In Catastrophic Times*

Zoopolitics in Deconstruction?

> The relations between humans and animals *must* change. They *must*, both in the sense of an 'ontological' necessity and of an 'ethical' duty. I place these words in quotation marks because this change will have to affect the very sense and value of these concepts (the ontological and the ethical).
>
> Jacques Derrida[1]

As little as twenty years ago, research monographs dedicated to exploring 'the question of the animal' from the perspective of contemporary continental philosophy were few and far between. While discussions of animal rights and reflections on environmental ethics multiplied over the last two or three decades of the twentieth century, these studies tended to develop and circulate within fields grounded predominantly in Anglo-American traditions of moral philosophy that had little time for post-Kantian continental thought.[2] Even in those traditions, moreover, philosophical engagement with questions of animality was sectional and seen as marginal to the proper concerns of philosophy.[3] Since the turn of the century, however, 'the question of the animal' has become a major theme in theoretically and philosophically informed research, to the point that some scholars have taken to speaking of 'the animal turn' in humanities inquiry.[4] Such research can be found not only in work that explicitly identifies as 'animal studies' but also in a range of disparate disciplines that have to varying degrees drawn some impetus and inspiration from post-Heideggerian thought or 'theory': philosophy, literary and cultural studies, art criticism and practice, social theory, history, geography and anthropology.

Trailing, as it does, in the wake of these developments, this book sets out to formulate a thought of 'the animal-to-come' both as an emblem heralding recent humanities work on 'the animal question' and as a means for reflecting on and further developing this work in new directions. A significant portion of that recent work has been critically focused, in the sense that it proposes to identify and dispel the 'anthropocentric' prejudice that pervades humanities (even post-humanities) thinking. Here the targets are a mechanistic view of animality inherited from Descartes; the reductionism inherent in the use of a singular noun to identify an uncountable diversity of species and individuals; and a prevailing presumption of human exceptionalism, which arguably infects the thought even of those great critics of humanism and metaphysics, Friedrich Nietzsche, Martin Heidegger, Emmanuel Levinas, Giorgio Agamben and Jacques Derrida, among others.[5] Indeed, Derrida's own *The Animal That Therefore I Am* may be said to have been, if not the catalyst for this critically charged work, then certainly one of its most influential sources.[6]

In the following discussion, I pursue a speculative engagement with such inquiry. In particular, I develop a reading of Derrida's deconstructive interrogation of the human-animal distinction in the context of his 'quasi-messianic' logic of 'the future-to-come' with a view to inducing 'the animal-to-come'. Based on a series of lectures originally presented in 1997, the text of *The Animal That Therefore I Am* was written at a time when Derrida's thought had often turned towards the motif of 'to-come' or 'future-to-come' (*à-venir*), as in 'justice-to-come' and 'democracy-to-come'. Yet the possible relations between the two themes were not explored in any great detail at the time, nor in the years since.[7] In Chapter 1, then, I reflect on what a reinterpretation of Derrida's engagement with 'the animal' in terms of the logic of 'to-come' may offer to critical engagement with the question of animals and animality. In so doing, I explicitly develop this formulation of 'the animal-to-come' as a means for engaging human-animal difference less as a matter of ontological difference (whether or not there is one) and more as an institutional field or problem, whose essential openness and transformability derives from the eventness of the event, from the fact of events remaining irreducibly to come. 'The' human-animal distinction is thereby recast as an effect of what Derrida calls 'writing': the iterative reinscription of a certain form or force of 'human exceptionalism' within a broader textual field of animality, where 'textual' is to be read in Derrida's sense of the term as encompassing both institutional inscription and quasi-transcendental differentiation and deferral.

Such a move undoubtedly provides some support for the injunction increasingly sounded within interdisciplinary humanities inquiry to attend to the interests and welfare of animals. In affinity with such work, the notion of 'the animal-to-come' implies a form of analysis that can critically reflect on the multiple and diverse sites, practices and events that continue to sustain the limits between human and nonhuman animals. However, in line with this book's speculative – as distinct, in a sense, from critical – orientation, my primary aim is to pursue the more 'hauntological', non-normative task of reviewing inherited concepts of power, politics and culture in such a way as to enable alternative understandings of 'animal politics'.[8] What happens to political thought, for example, if we take the problematic – or, after Derrida, 'limitrophic'[9] – nature of 'the' human-animal distinction not so much as something to be demonstrated or reasserted in the face of all anthropocentrisms, whether explicit or unwitting, but rather *as a given*? What sorts of animal-existential possibilities may be derived from tracking not the animal but the animal-*to-come* through the inherited traditions and discourses that continue to shape prevailing concepts of culture and politics?

In this sense, my approach contrasts in a number of ways with many of the studies that take up the animal question from a position informed specifically by Derrida's work. In the first place, where much of that recent work identifies in Derrida's *The Animal That Therefore I Am* certain philosophical resources for speculating on the nature of 'our' ethical relation to the 'animal other', I pursue a markedly different set of questions and in so doing attempt to lay out a relatively novel interpretation of certain landmark features of Derrida's argument. One of the book's points of departure from such conventional readings lies precisely in this attempt to follow Derrida's account of the 'limitrophic' nature of human-animal differences as a question of institutionality. The perhaps more significant divergence, however, relates to my reading of Derrida's remarks on the 'nonpower at the heart of power'. Where these remarks are frequently taken to isolate the vulnerability of the animal other as a basis for thinking through the possibility (or, indeed, justice) of affirming a compassionate ethics of response in the face of the vulnerability or suffering of the 'animal other',[10] in Chapter 3 I use this thought of nonpower as a starting point for speculating on a 'concept' of power – what I nickname 'zoopower' – geared towards the task of identifying and analysing the arenas, operations and stakes of an alternative 'zoopolitics' (as distinct, in a sense, from an animal ethics).

Put differently, this book is not a work of moral philosophy, seeking to establish or insist upon the necessity (or difficulty) of recognising ethical obligations towards animals. Although there are obviously ethical dimensions to the project and its conclusions, the discussion refrains (as far as possible) from making normative claims: it has no particular case to press with regard to the 'need' to grant individual animals ethical standing, and indeed eschews (again, as far as possible) the language both of prescription ('should', 'must', 'ought') and of ethico-political ideals. When I do work with ostensibly ethical concepts or conditions – such as vulnerability, in Chapter 3, and responsibility, in Chapter 5 – I attempt to engage them in ways that diverge from moral philosophy's conventional concerns with questions of justice, obligation and the like. The reflections on zoopolitics that unfold across the course of this book do not take as their departure point any in-principle arguments regarding what ought to be, therefore, but simply respond to the mundane fact (as it were) that animals – particular animals, at least – already *are* granted certain ethical standing, which is to say, up to a point and under specific circumstances. This is not to argue that the ethical claims that animals might make on us do not or cannot exceed or complicate present forms of recognition, protection and response. It is simply to say that, today, the ethical status of animals is *routinely* both given and denied, posited and contested, and such ambivalent standing is 'granted' as much by contemporary social conditions (such as animal cruelty legislation) and cultural practices (animal companionship, for example) as by a body of philosophical arguments. To the extent that the latter might nevertheless be considered by some as paramount, such arguments have for some time now been developed and debated by others – as well, on occasion, by me[11] – and I have nothing much to add to those debates here.

A second key point of difference between the argument laid out here and many Derridean reflections on the animal question is that the insights of two other, relatively less canonical, thinkers – Dominique Lestel and Vinciane Despret – play a crucial role in the explorations to follow. Pioneers of a new mode or field of inquiry dubbed 'philosophical ethology', Despret and Lestel have each made several fertile contributions to the question of the animal that merit broader recognition and, I would argue, purposeful investigation under the rubric of the animal-to-come.[12] While the French publications of these two figures have earned some recognition across continental Europe, the English translation of their respective essays and monographs has begun only in the last few years, such that their impact on animal studies in the English-speaking world, particularly in the case of Lestel, is less pronounced. The inclusion of their work here serves other purposes, however, beyond merely advertising the insights of relatively unheralded researchers. For Lestel's and Despret's various investigations are frequently grounded in empirical studies of animal behaviour and often proceed via analyses of specific, material sites in which different modes or moments of animal existence are inscribed. In that sense, their investigations arguably possess a 'concreteness' that might be felt to be lacking from Derrida's more expressly philosophical approach. While their studies warrant being read in their own right, therefore, I call on their observations at strategic points as a means of parlaying Derrida's thought into more 'applied' investigations of the possibilities of the animal-to-come, particularly insofar as those observations help to illustrate what I characterise as the institutionality of various forms, modes and sites of animality and human-animal difference(s).

Such appeals to Despret and Lestel should make it clear, moreover, that 'the animal-to-come' as I deploy the term here is not reducible to a neo-deconstructive neologism, but hopes to capture or indicate a less disciplined, less sectarian mode of taking up the question of the animal. Derrida, that is, features as but one of a number of figures whose insights inform the book's various investigations, with the argument unfolding through discussions of ideas developed by Lestel and Despret, but also via engagements with Thomas Hobbes, Hannah Arendt, Michel Foucault, Giorgio Agamben, Donna Haraway, Isabelle Stengers and a number of contemporary theorists of 'the posthuman'. At the same time, the analysis is 'interdisciplinary' to the extent that it supplements reflections on post-Kantian philosophy with references to research in ethology, sociology and a certain kind of cultural studies, in addition to the empirically grounded work of Lestel and Despret. The overarching figure in the argument is not 'Derrida', in other words, nor even 'deconstruction', but 'the animal-to-come', and it is the latter 'who' invokes and organises the conceptual contributions of the various critics and theorists engaged along the way.

The phrase which constitutes the subtitle of this book ('zoopolitics in deconstruction') is therefore not intended to signal a concern with 'deconstructing' animal studies, in the sense of pursuing a critical reading of the various arguments for affirming animal rights or an animal ethics. Rather, the objective is to investigate the deconstructive thematics of 'to-come' and its hauntological potential to respond to, and perhaps to shed new light on, questions of animal existence and the place of animality in (post)humanist conceptions of history, culture and politics. The task is thus to explore the capacity of prevailing concepts of history, culture and politics to enable novel images of zoopolitics – *notwithstanding* the apparent 'anthropocentrism' of such concepts. What might be meant by 'zoopolitics' is, in that sense, precisely the issue that drives the following discussion, with the focus being on the question of what thought has to become to confront the challenges posed by 'the posthuman',[13] rather than on the ways that historical forms of thought, culture or politics have sought to marginalise or delegitimise 'animal interests'. The term 'zoopolitics' thus functions as a marker of the potential for inherited concepts or contexts of 'politics' – as well as related concepts such as 'institution', 'culture', 'power', 'action', 'responsibility', and so forth – to accommodate questions of animality and animal existence.

For this reason, and to the extent that it responds to a body of work that already treats the figure of 'man' and the human-animal distinction as thoroughly suspect, my argument does not revolve around producing a simple critique of political and philosophical anthropocentrism. The logics of anthropocentrism and of human exceptionalism (though these are perhaps not quite the same thing) are key issues in much work on 'the animal question', and it is understandable that attempts to engage this question seek routinely to demonstrate and denounce the operation of these logics in the history of ideas. I am wary, however, of the extent to which the critical hunt after 'anthropocentrism' perhaps can proceed only by turning tail on the thought of the animal-to-come. Certainly, this retreat seems clear in the kinds of 'critique' that follow a trail laid by discourses and practices that have never felt obliged to challenge modern forms of thought or existence in the name of animals. As a question of reading or interpretation, that is, the desire to expose and condemn anthropocentric tendencies that are, more often than not, virtually self-confessed operates more in the name of a *given* idea of 'man', hence of human-animal difference, hence of animality, than in the name of any thought of what may come 'after' such concepts. In the form of a moral complaint, moreover, charges of anthropocentrism effectively downplay the force of tradition (and the metaphysical system which animates it) over attempts to change forms of thought about animals and animality. Against this temptation to engage anthropocentrism as a simple axiological system – against the tendency to depict it, that is, as a mere value and prejudice which one ought to disown as a matter of principle – the thought of the animal-to-come calls for renewed attention to what Derrida has referred to as the 'eschato-teleological situation' in which 'the name of man has always been inscribed'.[14] Accordingly, when I do turn to the problem of anthropocentrism (in Chapter 5), I pursue it in the context of the apparent return of the figure of 'man' – in the themes of anthropogenesis, on the one hand, and the Anthropocene, on the other – with a view to considering the role that recent reimaginings of the human as a biological being first and foremost may play in attending to the *question* of the animal.

A final remark concerns the role or status of my appeals to Derrida or deconstruction in the following discussion. Derrida plays a major role in shaping the argument here to the extent that it emerges not only from engagement with his insights into (animal) being and time, as it were, but also from a way of thinking that is heavily indebted to his writing (in all senses of that term) and to deconstruction generally. But my aim is not to provide a close and faithful, exegetical reading of Derrida's work, be it on animals or anything else. While I strive to provide some of the requisite interpretation and justification for leading Derrida's philosophemes perhaps elsewhere than towards those destinations where his work has been taken by others, elucidation of that work is not my ultimate goal here. As a consequence, my commentaries perhaps lack the rigour and philosophical sophistication of the best readers of Derrida today.[15] Indeed, at times I undoubtedly overlook possible connections with the most philosophically consequential conclusions reached by Derrida (as well as by his readers) in favour of drawing on relatively minor points or passages – but always with a view to exploring *other* consequences and making *other* connections. Unfortunately, the English translation of Derrida's *Life Death* seminars was published only after this investigation was completed, preventing me from drawing on that text in any substantive way.[16] I would suggest, nevertheless, that Derrida's explicit move in those seminars to connect a thinking of life with the thematics of the institution lends some support to my interpretation (particularly as it is laid out in Chapter 1) both of Derrida's 'concept' of writing and of what's at stake in how he formulates the animal question. At various points across the following discussion, moreover, I engage with *Life Death* indirectly when I make occasional reference to the recent work in 'biodeconstruction' that has arisen specifically in response to the questions that Derrida raises in those seminars.

At any rate, while Derrida features as a key reference point throughout, it is not my intention to present an authoritative account of his work or to argue its merits over any other 'approach', let alone suggest its 'superiority'. The discussion's mode is, again, more speculative than corrective, aiming to multiply possibilities rather than closing them down. In saying that, I do not mean to raise up a non-normative, 'non-corrective' approach as the very model of good, productive philosophy. After all, critical commentary has undoubtedly played its part in creating the intellectual and social conditions that have allowed the question of the animal to be taken seriously. What's more, performances in critical distinction can be thoroughly engaging (just ask Bruno Latour!) and I have no interest in playing the role of killjoy in this regard. But in the wake of the possibility of 'the animal-to-come' we are left with a continuing challenge, one which drives the remainder of the book: *how* to follow 'the animal' in philosophy, in history, in political thought, if we are no longer prepared to take 'the' distinction between human and animal as unproblematic? What comes 'after' the critique of human exceptionalism and the problematisation of conventional understandings of 'the animal'? How to *follow* what is still to come?

How to follow 'the animal-to-come', that is, such that 'it' *remains* always to come?

In the course of developing such questions I have had the good fortune of being able to test my arguments before a number of readers. A preliminary discussion of the book's key concept has previously been published as 'Following the animal-to-come', *Derrida Today* 12, 1 (2019): 20–40, passages from which have been reproduced throughout this book, most notably in Chapters 1 and 5 as well as in this preface; an extract from Chapter 3 appeared as 'Derrida's Nonpower – From Writing to Zoopower', *SubStance* 149 (2019): 23–40; and parts of Chapter 5 are based on 'geo-: What's a Species to Do?', *Ctrl-Z: New Media Philosophy* 7 (2017). I thank the journal editors and the anonymous referees for their comments and suggestions. I am also grateful to friends and colleagues for taking an interest in my work and providing feedback. In particular, I would like to thank Nicole Anderson, Claire Colebrook, Jac Dalziell, Rick Elmore, Amy Hickman, Mike Lundblad, Lynn Turner, Thom van Dooren and Dinesh Wadiwel for their comments, encouragement and advice at various stages in the development of the project. Special thanks are due to Francis Russell for the many, many conversations over the years about Derrida, ideas, politics and much more besides. Above all, I am grateful to Matt Chrulew for inviting me to contribute this work to his *Animalities* book series and, most significantly, for creating the conditions, in the form of the 'Reading Culture Animality Technology' reading group, in which the very thought of the animal-to-come was born.

1   Following the Animal-To-Come...

> *To follow* and *to be after* will not only be the question, and the question of what we call animal. We shall discover in the follow-through the question of the question.
>
> Jacques Derrida[1]

To all appearances, Jacques Derrida's *The Animal That Therefore I Am* offers a sustained engagement with animality as a philosophical problem. Yet Derrida indicates on more than one occasion throughout his discussion that the central, indeed, the 'only' problematic organising the reflection concerns not animality or animals, but rather 'following': 'my only question today would be, if one wanted to reduce it to a word, the question ... of the "to be followed" [*à suivre*]: what is meant by "to follow" ...?' (A 54). Of course, Derrida is well known for his rhetorical excesses, and so this seemingly unlikely declaration can easily be read as just so much hyperbole. That *The Animal That Therefore I Am* engages primarily with the subject of 'the animal', if not also with the animal as subject, is quite clearly shown in the book's title, even if the original French title – *L'animal que donc je suis* – also flags the discussion's concern with the theme of following. As Derrida remarks – and as is reiterated by his translator David Wills (A 162) – part of the investigation turns on the 'ambiguity' in the French language of 'the little homonym *suis*, which, in the first person of the indicative conjugates more than one verb – *être*, to be, and *suivre*, to follow' (A 64). The sense of the 'je suis' that features in the original title of the work – but not only in that title – thus oscillates between or splits into two possibilities in the English translation: 'I am' and 'I follow'. Wills neatly 'condenses' both senses into the one construction – 'I am (following)' – and, picking up on the French title's obvious reference to Descartes's 'formulation of consciousness and the thinking animal as human', goes on to suggest that Derrida effectively rewrites that 'priority . . . to read "the animal that therefore I follow after"' (A 162).

To what extent, however, can the chiasmatics of following be encapsulated or elaborated by this interpretation or translation – or, indeed, by any other? While the constructions 'following the animal' and 'coming after the animal' highlight the fact that, evolutionarily speaking, the human animal is late to arrive on the zoological scene, the multiple senses of 'following' disrupt any simple relation of priority. The very temporality that enables one to see in the human animal a 'later' stage of evolution, for instance, courts a teleo-logic, in which all events are ultimately drawn towards an eventual goal or end of development. Temporally or sequentially speaking, then, 'following' is pulled in two directions at once, in that someone or some event follows, occurs later, comes after a time that has passed or been left behind; or conversely it follows the lead, pursues a goal, sets out towards what is out in front and has not yet happened. As a 'being-after' and a 'being-before', so to speak, following entails or implies two opposing orders of priority. The senses of 'following' travel in a range of other directions, moreover, a disseminative quality to which Derrida frequently draws attention by weaving one such sense or another into different moments of his analysis. Thus, a structure, relation or logic of following permeates and incorporates 'hunting' and 'chasing' but also 'tracking' or 'investigating' (following a trail), and even 'deciphering' (following the clues), 'understanding' (following an argument or train of thought) and 'deduction' (as a conclusion follows from a premise). It can also entail 'compliance' and 'obedience' (following orders), and so 'training', 'discipline' and 'application' (following a model), as well as 'ritual' and 'routine' (following tradition). Indeed, the scope of 'following' extends to cover a whole range of dispositions and actions that might be performed by a body of followers – 'attention', 'observation', 'approbation', 'patronage', 'imitation', to name but a few.

As both Derrida's argument and Wills's translation make clear, moreover, 'following', in the French at least, comprehends even 'being' itself. The logic or structure of following thus displaces not only the presumed 'ontological priority' of humankind with regard to the question and the politics of animality but, further, the priority and priorities of *ontology itself* with regard to philosophical thinking and political action more generally. 'Before', Derrida writes – though such an expression of precedence is likewise rendered equivocal in or by the chiasmatics of following – 'before the question of (the) *being* as such, of *esse* and *sum*, of *ego sum*, there is the question of following, of the persecution and seduction of the other, what/that I am (following) or who is following me, who is following me while I am (following) it, him, or her' (A 65).

This declaration would hardly constitute the first time that Derrida had sought to challenge the ontological or ontologising impulse. But there remains something troubling, something significant, about the performance of that gesture in the context of an extended engagement with philosophy's non-engagement with the question of the animal. For it's one thing to critique the logocentric determination of being-as-presence by 'deconstructing' the speech-writing opposition and affirming a differential 'play' of 'meaning'. But it's another thing entirely, or so it would seem, to deploy such modes of argument in order to call into question the human-animal distinction, where the 'objects' under investigation cannot be comfortably reduced to a signifying system, a cultural technology, a literary practice or some other product of human artifice, but rather 'occur within the world' as entities that, to use Heidegger's formulation, 'produce themselves'.² Respect for that fact of autopoiesis, respect for animals as *living beings*, would appear to demand recognition of animal ontology, and a corresponding inquiry into the qualities and attributes of different kinds of animals, and into their specific ways of being in the world.

It's not at all certain, moreover, that a neo-Levinasian ethics of animal alterity suffices to challenge the privileged role of ontology in attempts to think philosophically about animals. Emmanuel Levinas's thought of alterity and his corresponding affirmation of ethics as 'first philosophy' constitute, of course, the paradigmatic challenge to the philosophical primacy of ontology.³ Accordingly, Derrida spends some time in *The Animal That Therefore I Am* focusing precisely on Levinas's discourse on the face and on his refusal to grant to an animal the status or attribute of 'face' (A 105–18). 'If I am responsible for the other, and before the other', Derrida asks, 'isn't the animal other more other still, more radically other . . . than the other in whom I recognise my brother . . . ?' (A 107). With this remark, Derrida gives expression to an enticing, if not exactly unprecedented, strategy for introducing the animal into philosophical thinking by pursuing an ethics of the animal other. His apparent affirmation of Bentham's utilitarian concern for suffering over Descartes's focus on consciousness appears in this regard to lend much support to this strategy (see Chapter 3), as does the avidity with which Derrida positions his entire speculation as a response to a bathroom encounter with his cat, 'truly' 'a real cat' (A 6), in all 'its unsubstitutable singularity' (A 9). But to the extent that any such ethics of response in the face of the animal other thereby has recourse to a certain fact of *being* – the existence of the singular animal, '*this* irreplaceable living being' (A 9) – we might have cause to believe that there is more to the question of following and its challenge to the priority of ontology than can be developed by an ethical affirmation of animal alterity.

So Derrida's apparent displacement of the ontological question in relation to the theme of animals and animality warrants further thought. To be sure, the neo-Levinasian gesture, particularly when followed through to its most challenging conclusions, has undoubtedly played, and will continue to play, its part in broaching the animal question in contemporary thought.[4] However, the disseminative quality of 'following' invites consideration of other possibilities, not least of all those possibilities that may follow (or follow from) the divided temporality of following – its non-contemporaneity, or 'out-of-joint-ness', as it were. For this problem of temporality is far from marginal to Derrida's work generally, and so it would not be impulsive to expect to see it operating (or awaiting operation) in his work on animals and animality in particular. Most notably, in a series of speculations published in the years surrounding *The Animal That Therefore I Am*'s composition, Derrida sought to thematise a certain kind of deconstruction of time and history via speculations on the possibility of a justice and a democracy 'to come'.[5] Following a trail laid by these publications, therefore, we might have cause to suspect that the logic of following not only enables but perhaps even demands an approach to the animal question in terms of the motif of 'future-to-come' (*à-venir*).

Speaking of the urgency of justice in 'Force of Law', for instance, Derrida links the essential openness and transformability of law and politics to justice's relation to the future, a 'to-come', the 'very dimension of events irreducibly to come', which he 'rigorously distinguish[es] from the future that can always reproduce the present'.[6] 'As the experience of absolute alterity', justice is thereby 'unpresentable' (FL 27), and is indeed absolutely unlike anything that could be presently imagined as justice. But it remains, for Derrida, the very 'chance of the event' and the condition of 'an unrecognizable history' (FL 27), in which 'the metaphysico-anthropocentric axiomatic that dominates, in the West, the thought of just and unjust' confronts its limit (FL 19). In *Specters of Marx*, he returns to this formulation as part of a meditation on 'a radically dis-jointed time' and on 'the very concept of democracy as a concept of a promise that can only arise in such a *diastema*'.[7] Such a relation to what Derrida therefore refers to as 'a democracy *to come*' is perhaps easily confused with the kind of asymptotic function or movement that would define the inaccessibility of a utopian or regulating ideal. However, Derrida is at pains to differentiate this thought of democracy from such forms of inaccessibility, which 'would still retain the temporal form of a future present, a future modality of the *living present*':

> Even beyond the regulating idea in its classic form, the idea, if that is still what it is, of democracy to come, its 'idea' as event of a pledged injunction that orders one to summon the very thing that will never present itself in the form of full presence, is the opening of this gap between an infinite promise . . . and the determined, necessary, but also necessarily inadequate forms of what has to be measured against this promise. To this extent, the effectivity or actuality of the democratic promise . . . will always keep within it, and it must do so, this absolutely undetermined messianic hope at its heart, this eschatological relation to the to-come of an event *and* of a singularity, of an alterity that cannot be anticipated. (SM 65)

Far from designating simply an endless deferral, in the name of perfectibility, of democracy's future arrival, democracy-to-come names the inscription of an infinite, hence excessive, aporetic promise *within* the present event, within the 'living present', within the very action or programme or decision that would otherwise hope to be a response to that pledged injunction to respond.[8] Democracy-to-come names not an ideal, therefore, but a performance, or a dimension of the performative, which necessarily introduces a gap, a possibility or play of possibilities, within (as it were) empirical or material events taking place within the world. Accordingly, the possibility of some wholly other, unanticipatable 'future' – an 'absolutely undetermined messianic hope' – can be found to be operating at the very heart of the present.

In this trace of the possibility of another future, of something otherwise than the present, Derrida suggests, we may see 'a stroke of luck for politics, for all historical progress' (FL 14). For this gap, this trace of an eschatological relation to an unanticipatable future-to-come, opens the possibility of transformation:

> justice remains, is yet, to come, *à venir*, it has an, it is *à-venir*, the very dimension of events irreducibly to come. It will always have it, this *à-venir*, and always has. Perhaps it is for this reason that justice, insofar as it is not only a juridical or political concept, opens up for *l'avenir* the transformation, the recasting or refounding of law and politics. (FL 27)[9]

As with democracy's relation to an infinite promise, this aspect of justice that makes it 'irreducible to any juridical or political concept' is also what marks the crucial difference between justice as Derrida characterises it and conventional interpretations of a utopian or regulating ideal. By the same token, what Derrida nicknames 'undeconstructible' justice (FL 15) does not therefore present itself in or as some metaphysical substance, in or as the form of natural law. 'Justice in itself, if such a thing exists' (FL 14) is not an original presence that would be inevitably compromised or curtailed by the violence of its unavoidable re-presentation in (positive, deconstructible) law. Rather, to the extent that 'there is' justice, the to-come of justice takes the form of an irreducible *excess*, a future (justice) made possible or imaginable by the very existence of law: by the law's attempts to present justice, that is, as much as by its failures or shortcomings. Justice-to-come, in that sense, might be understood as something more like a missed opportunity that wasn't an opportunity, that couldn't even have arisen as an opportunity, until 'after' it was missed – an excessive absence or a non-present excess, an irreducible anachrony that marks an essential discontinuity or untimeliness within the time and place, within the eventness or being, of the event 'itself'. And in this sense, the divided temporality of the future-to-come, as with the logic of following, can be seen to displace or undermine the priority and priorities of ontological thinking to the extent that it introduces non-presence within the present, within whatever is (seemingly) present.

It is in this potential analogy between the two motifs of following and *à-venir* that we might find some warrant for approaching the question of animality in terms of the logic of 'future-to-come'. But what might it mean to speak of the (or an) '*animal*-to-come'? With its reference to futurity, hence historicity and perhaps even progress, a logic of future-to-come would doubtless sit at odds with conventional concepts of animality, and so the structure of 'to-come' might make for a strange point of departure for approaching the question of the animal – notwithstanding the fact that it is precisely the metaphysics of animality that Derrida and many others explicitly seek to challenge when they engage with that question. More significantly, where the formulations of justice-to-come and democracy-to-come appear to derive their consequence from their critical relation specifically to juridico-political institutions – the law, parliament, the various institutions of the state – the question of the animal seems, again (always?), to require that reflection attend to such beings *qua* beings that 'produce themselves'. In the name of pursuing a nonanthropocentric mode of inquiry, that is – one which avoids prioritising the human or putting the human world at the centre of the investigation – contemporary speculation on animals and animality demands respect for the ways in which or the extent to which animals are not reducible to objects at the service of the human animal. And in this regard any focus on such institutions as law and government, at the expense of focusing on animals themselves, would fall short of this ideal of nonanthropocentrism. It could well make important contributions to existing work on 'animal rights', perhaps even providing more sophisticated readings of the institutional conditions to the possibility of 'animal justice' than might otherwise be expected. But by centring the analysis on human institutions and their capacity to accommodate or respect the animal, such an approach could equally be judged as inevitably limited, as incapable of attending to aspects of the animal world that would fundamentally challenge assumptions about the nature not only of animal existence but of human existence too.

Yet it is precisely by virtue of its potential to raise the *question* of the institution, I want to argue, that the thought of the animal-to-come may serve as a means for reflecting on and further developing not only Derrida's discussion of animality but (post)humanities engagements with the question of the animal more generally. What the thought of the animal-to-come and the question of the institution that it raises may bring to such engagements, moreover, is a means for interrogating 'the' human-animal distinction in a way that can follow Derrida's displacement, precisely via this question of institutionality, of the language and leanings of ontology. For Derrida spends some time attending to this 'human-animal' distinction, and this focus is perfectly in keeping with what was once all-too-frequently portrayed as his 'deconstructive strategy' of 'undermining' 'binary oppositions'. But in turning his gaze towards this (literally) specific division Derrida seeks not to deny something like a limit, an abyss or rupture, between the '*so-called* human' and 'what he *calls* the animal or animals', but rather to approach that rupture in terms of the more 'interesting' question of 'limitrophy':

> The discussion becomes interesting once, instead of asking whether or not there is a limit that produces a discontinuity, one attempts to think what a limit becomes once it is abyssal, once the frontier no longer forms a single indivisible line but more than one internally divided line ... Beyond the edge of the *so-called* human, beyond it but by no means on a single opposing side, rather than 'The Animal' ... there is already a heterogeneous multiplicity of the living ... a multiplicity of organizations of relations between living and dead. (A 30–1)

Derrida's depiction of this apparent discontinuity as one between the *so-called* human and what the latter *calls* the animal points to the extent to which he reads the distinction not in terms of ontology or ethics, as these are classically understood, but rather as a question or effect of *naming*. Hence Derrida's interest in Genesis and the biblical narratives in which the animals are named (A 15–18).

Of course, the focus on 'naming' here should not be interpreted as a moment of naïve linguistic determinism, in which the ongoing acceptance of a 'human-animal' distinction is taken as the simple consequence of a nominal differentiation. For it is not the names that matter but rather the practices of *naming*, where 'naming', as a structure or process homologous to what Derrida has on other occasions called 'writing', is always a matter of *institution* and *power*. To be sure, Derrida's use of the term 'writing' – along with all the terms that appear to be most immediately synonymous with it: 'inscription', 'trace', 'graphematic mark' or simply 'mark' – has often been read as designating merely the generalisation of a more complicated, less 'determinate' structure of the linguistic sign in which the signified is endlessly deferred. On this reading, Derrida's 'writing' may challenge the authority of knowledge by questioning the certainty of (human) meaning and the (human) subject's control over that meaning; but it nevertheless (or thereby) construes 'the world' purely in terms of idealist and ultimately linguistic operations of 'meaning' and 'interpretation'. Yet Derrida routinely deploys the notion of writing as a means of emphasising questions of action, force, institution, ritual, organisation and a whole array of other 'non-linguistic' practices, processes and phenomena.[10] Indeed, the 'generalisation' of writing is precisely the means by which Derrida depicts attributes or elements of force, institution, technique, convention, government – or rather differences of force, institution, and so on – as central to and constitutive of 'the entire field of what philosophy would call experience, even the experience of being'.[11] As highlighted by his reading of Genesis, these facets of writing, of power and of institution, become only more prominent in the act, convention, event or structure of naming. And it's in this sense that the 'abyssal limit' between what is named 'human' and what is named 'the animal' or 'animals' might be seen to mark not an ontological divide as such, but something perhaps better imagined as an *institutional field*: an effect of an 'inhuman' process in which a propensity for human exceptionalism gets iteratively reinscribed. Thus conditioned by operations or iterations of force, convention, technique, and so on, modes of existence – both 'human' and 'non-human' – take shape in or as a differential array of institutional inclinations and outcomes.

To characterise this abyssal limit in terms of an institutional field is not to suggest, therefore, that Derrida's thinking about animality remains confined simply to an analysis of the linguistic and institutional uses of 'the' human-animal distinction, at the expense of any consideration of animal existence ('ontology'). To understand the work of naming – the effects of writing – in that way would be to re-introduce into the problematic a conventional nature/culture distinction that gives priority to 'being' over 'technics', positing the latter as external and secondary to a pre-existent, self-present substance or essence. This priority is, of course, one of the many values or structures that Derrida calls into question in his deconstruction of the speech-writing opposition. Likewise, the institutional processes participating in the reinscription of differential modes of humanity and animality cannot in themselves be taken as simply 'human'. For the operations of naming, as operations of writing, entail another concept of 'institution' altogether, one which can, among other things, countenance the thought that animal existence might also take shape in relation to forms of conduct and modes of organisation whose very iterability speaks to the possibility, at least, of their 'conventionality'. Indeed, what's at stake here is a field of institutionality that precedes, as it were, the very distinction which has otherwise aligned notions of 'institution' with those of 'man', 'culture', 'technics', 'law'. As Derrida made clear as far back as 1988 – if not already, in 1967, with the publication of *De la grammatologie* – 'writing' and 'iterability' imply concepts of law, convention and invention that are irreducible to

> the classical opposition between nature and law, or between animals alleged not to have language, and man, author of speech acts and capable of entering into a relation to the law, be it of obedience or of transgression. It is in order to minimize this risk and to keep in reserve an entire deconstruction of onto-theological

humanism (including that of Heidegger) that I prefer always to speak of the iterability of the *mark* beyond all human speech acts. Barring any inconsistency, ineptness, or insufficiently rigorous formalization on my part, my statements on this subject should be valid beyond the marks and society called 'human'.[12]

Outside or beyond a quasi-formulaic statement about 'deconstructing' the opposition between nature and institution, exactly what is entailed by or might result from this other logic of institution is something that will undoubtedly have to be developed over the course of the discussion to come. But for now I want simply to underscore the extent to which the notion of the animal-to-come, premised as it is on several crucial aspects of Derrida's thought, foregrounds an approach to the animal question – questions of animal politics and (or as) questions of animal existence – that on the one hand avoids, as far as possible, the language of conventional ontology, but that on the other hand does not for that reason preclude consideration of animals 'themselves'. And if the logic of this approach seems unlikely, or fatally obscured by Derrida's occasional privileging of 'writing' as a name for this field of institutionality, a proxy for the principles of the position might alternatively be developed with reference to contemporary philosopher of animality Dominique Lestel. Much of Lestel's work is yet to appear in English, but the existing translations and English publications provide considerable evidence for the novelty of his philosophy as well as its relative proximity to or consistency with the arguments that Derrida elaborates in *The Animal That Therefore I Am*.[13] In particular, Lestel's way of accounting for the relationships between 'the human' and 'animality' may help us to see in this institutionality factors or dimensions that might otherwise be depicted as 'onto-evolutionary'.[14] His key argument in this regard is that 'humans constitute themselves as humans in the very *texture* of animality' (LFH 61). With this gesture, Lestel not only acknowledges the fact that *Homo sapiens* exists by virtue of an evolutionary process and a phylogeny which can be characterised as a kind of inheritance, but he also captures the extent to which the characteristics and forms of existence that we think of as 'human' have developed in conjunction with and not separately from an entire history of interaction with animals. Humans have become (and continue to become) human, that is, 'over hundreds of thousands of years through [their] arrangements with the animal (and through the arrangements of those who made up [their] line of descent)'.[15] Accordingly, as Lestel argues,

> the human is not no longer animal, but more animal ... The human is that animal who practises animality in modalities to which other animals have never had access but of which they are nevertheless the condition. The human is not the end point towards which all animality would strive, but an intersection from which animality can engage in completely new arenas.[16]

On this basis, we might therefore say that 'humanity', the human animal, remains bred within and articulated to a broader, differential field of animality. Such animality, moreover, can now be recognised as being not distinct from what I have been calling the field of institutionality in which an 'abyssal limit' between the so-called human and the so-called animal is inscribed, but rather as a *dimension* of that institutionality. While a conventional (metaphysical) concept of 'institution' seems continually to resist including 'onto-evolutionary' phenomena within its scope – even *after* that concept's deconstruction on the basis of Derrida's notion of writing – Lestel's emphasis on the *practising* of different *modalities* of animality, his depiction of the *texture* of animality and of the '*inter-texturity*' (LFH 62) of human-animal relations, provides some basis for rethinking the concept precisely to this end. And while Lestel chooses the language of 'texture' with a view to foregrounding the metabolic relation between the human and the animal,[17] the word's proximity to another term routinely associated with Derrida should bring home the point that *zoē* and *bios* do not stand apart from textuality, as though the former were substances that are *subsequently* merely marked by writing.[18] On the contrary: life, biology and the living organism are textual (textural) through and through.[19]

Ultimately, the point in speaking in terms of the 'inter-texturity' between the human and the animal is, for Lestel, to avoid 'all substantialist ontology . . . without, however, denying the unique place that the human has *culturally* acquired in the sphere of the living' (LFH 63). In that respect, Derrida's insistence on a residual, insuperable 'abyssal limit' between 'the human' and 'the animal', read now as a question of naming, hence of institution and power, not only displaces the language of ontology and its attendant insistence on the primacy or presence of being, but also helps to keep in sight a certain *privilege* that the non-'nonhuman' animal has acquired or seized for itself over the course of a complex history of human-animal interaction. Certainly, 'we' who call ourselves human – 'we' who have seized or exploited the power to name ourselves and others – are the ones who have overseen the institution of 'carnophallogocentric' regimes of zoo-bio-politics. And in *The Animal That Therefore I Am*, Derrida devotes numerous pages to acknowledging just some of the sites and characteristics of such regimes, indicating (provisionally, to be sure) lines of questioning as well as several factors that may complicate conventional analyses of those structures. Part of what gets designated by the *name* 'human', then, is this partial and provisional, if nevertheless seemingly perpetual or pervasive, monopolisation of the power to name.[20] To the extent that these naming operations have thus far issued in carnophallogocentric regimes, moreover, any hope for future 'human-animal relations' that do something other than merely reproduce those regimes would perhaps lie less in simply letting the human-animal distinction go, as some may want, than in attending precisely to the multiple and diverse sites, practices and events that continue to 'feed' the limits between human and nonhuman animals.[21]

In maintaining this scrutiny, Derrida's formulation of the question thereby helps to guard against the temptation to ground zoopolitical intervention on a form of presence – on an imagined fundamental equality of (animal) beings, say, or on evidence of the presence 'in' animals of certain dispositions or capacities that would otherwise be taken as exclusively human. It is for this reason that the thought of the animal-to-come also calls for another concept (hence another politics) of the 'animal-machine'. Descartes's notorious characterisation of animal bodies as 'machines' 'made by the hand of God', such that animal movement, reaction and behaviour can be recognised as the determined effects of a complex internal mechanical structure, is understandably one of the major targets of critical thinking about animals and animality.[22] Derrida likewise calls this formulation into question, and argues further that the re-evaluation of this mechanistic tradition entails not only 'a reinterpretation of the living creature called "animal", but also another concept of the machine, of the semiotic machine, if it can be called that, of artificial intelligence, of cybernetics and zoo- and bio-engineering, of the *genic* in general' (A 76). Elsewhere, Derrida has indeed broached this rethinking of the machine, understood as 'the calculable programming of an automatic repetition', in a reflection on the im/possibility of thinking '*both* the machine *and* the performative event together'.[23] And it is this dimension of the calculable automaticity of the programme – the calculable, programmed automaticity of animal *reaction* – that is at stake when, in *The Animal That Therefore I Am*, he explicitly challenges the Cartesian concept of the animal-machine by questioning the rigour of the supposed distinction between (animal) reaction and (human) response (A 119–40).[24]

But as Derrida's passing reference to 'zoo- and bio-engineering', to 'the *genic* in general' – hence to the engine (from the Latin *ingenium*, literally 'that which is inborn') – already suggests, the *rethinking* of the animal-machine might also take aim at the metaphysics of *interiority* that captures a significant portion of thought, even critical and speculative thought, about animals and animal behaviour. Alongside the impulse to ontologise, that is, the strategy of affirming 'animal subjectivity' as a means to counter the Cartesian view of the animal-machine is perhaps a seductive one. Read in the context of Descartes's mechanistic materialism, proclamations of animal subjectivity take the form of a strategy of sabotage: throwing spanners in the animal-mechanical works. But the potential complicity of such gestures with the Cartesian tradition they otherwise seek to challenge is evident both in the language of 'autonomous personhood' that seems inevitably to shadow them and in the apparent difficulty in attributing such 'subjectivity' to something other than a quality or substance – will or consciousness, perhaps – identifiable 'within' the individual animal. In contrast to these gestures – though not necessarily nor always in opposition to them – the thought of the animal-to-come would direct us to engage this question via a different concept of the animal-machine, one which might characterise animals in terms not of their interiority but rather of their relations to the 'outside', to the general element of exteriority.[25]

In this regard, Derrida's discussion of the political philosophy of Thomas Hobbes in the first volume of *The Beast and the Sovereign* may prove as illuminating as his critique of the supposed automaticity of animal reaction.[26] Derrida's principal aim in that volume is to investigate in the history of political philosophy the 'double and contradictory figuration of political man' as *superior* to animality but also *as* animality (BSI 26). Hobbes's *Leviathan* serves as 'the most arresting example' of this figuration (BSI 26), insofar as it depicts, on Derrida's reading, the institution of political sovereignty in the form of the state, the Commonwealth, as a kind of 'prosthetic and artificial animal' (BSI 27), a 'monstrous' product or amalgam of artifice and nature. For 'Leviathan is the state and political man himself, artificial man, the man of art and institution, man producer and product of his own art' (BSI 27), an art which can only imitate the art of God, creator of nature and the natural animal (BSI 26). 'Art is here, like the institution itself, artificiality, like the technical supplement, a sort of animal and monstrous naturality' (BSI 27). Accordingly, the absolute sovereignty that Hobbes attributes to the state – a product of artifice and institution – is, as Derrida explains (citing Hobbes), 'like an iron lung, an artificial respiration, an "Artificiall *Soul*"', and 'the state is a sort of robot, an animal monster', which 'extend[s], mime[s], imitate[s], even reproduce[s] down to the details the living creature that produces it' (BSI 28).

Here, 'animality' figures on both sides (as it were) of the supposed divide between nature and artifice, or nature and institution, a condition which mirrors, even as it appears to invert, the ambivalent status of political sovereignty as sometimes rising above the order of beasts and as sometimes being the very manifestation of animality. This bestiality operates in (and as) the state not merely analogously, but substantively too, insofar as fear or terror lies at the centre of Hobbes's depiction of politics and political subjection. Fear, fear for one's life in Hobbes's 'war of all against all', is what drives the institution of political sovereignty; and fear of punishment is what produces obedience to the instituted law. It is for this reason, then, that Derrida appropriates the terminology of *animal-machine* to characterise the apparatuses of the state:

> Leviathan is the name of an animal-machine designed to cause fear . . . a prosthetic and state *organon*, a state as prosthesis, the organ of a state prosthesis, what I nickname a *prosthstatics*, which runs on fear and reigns by fear. (BSI 39–40)

As such a 'prosthstatics', as supplementary institutional *prosthesis*, the 'political animal' which (in all senses of the word) *constitutes* Leviathan does not spring, therefore, from a natural, inherent and prior disposition towards politics – as a certain reading of Aristotle might have it – but rather consists in and as a form of exteriority, an institutional framework.[27] And it is in that sense that Hobbes gives us a model of the animal-machine that could not be further from that implied by Descartes's concept of animal as automaton or engine, according to which animal movements, behaviours and competencies are the determined, calculable outcome of the mechanistic operation of what is *inborn*. But at the same time this account of political sovereignty perhaps also points to a concept of animal action that is not premised on a concept of subjectivity grounded in a metaphysics of interiority. For on this alternative thought of the animal-machine as 'prosthstatics', sovereignty over action is to be found not 'within', but rather in distributed relations to various institutional 'outsides'. Characteristics or modes of animality might be identified, in other words, in terms of their appearance and functioning throughout the distributed, prosthetic and artificial animal called 'Leviathan'.

To be sure, the version of 'the animal-machine' that we can take from Derrida's characterisation of Hobbes's Leviathan seems at this point wholly inappropriate for speculating on animals and zoopolitics. To the extent that it appears, on the one hand, restricted to the institutions of the Commonwealth, which are themselves the products of 'Man's artifice', and, on the other, to gain its purchase through the reduction of political life, at its basis and in its mechanism, to the operations of fear, this animal-machine hardly serves as an inspiring emblem for a 'nonanthropocentric' politics. Further, the Hobbesian version of political sovereignty 'presupposes the right of man over the beasts' (BSI 29), a 'right' which understandably constitutes the primary target of most critical engagements with the question of the animal. But already in the deconstruction of institutionality and in the thought of 'to-come' we can find the conceptual resources for developing this alternative logic (and politics) of the animal-machine along paths that would take us far from the Hobbesian view of sovereign power, if not quite entirely out of its scope. These are paths that I attempt to explore across the chapters to come, but for now it is possible to begin to glimpse some of the consequences that may follow from privileging the language of 'institutionality' over that of 'ontology' in formulating a thought of 'the animal-to-come'. For such a move underscores first of all the possibility of accounting for animal 'behaviour', animal 'reaction', animal 'being', and so on, in ways that do not *begin* by abstracting 'animal being(s)' from the networks of relations, interactions and power – the animal-machines – that contextualise (animal) existence. In that sense, the language of institutionality offers an alternative to grounding zoopolitical thought and analysis on a prior identification of this or that – isolated, autonomous – individual, or on the delineation of this or that – invariable, autopoietic – species, whose abilities and inclinations are 'inborn', defined and circumscribed from the outset, by bio-genetic or onto-evolutionary factors, for example. To deploy the language of institutionality, in other words, is to attempt to resist the tendency or temptation to look simply 'inwards' when searching for signs of animal capacities or potentialities – to resist grounding discussion of animality in something like a 'theoretical biology', for example, and thereby failing to consider the extent to which such capacities may be *constituted*, or at the very least *in/effectual*, in relation to any number of factors, forces or conditions (see Chapter 3).

For this field of institutionality – this texturity of animality – that feeds the limit between *so-called* 'man' and what is *called* 'animal' is precisely what opens up 'animality itself' to the possibility of the animal-to-come. As Derrida says of the animal-machine that is Leviathan: 'if sovereignty, as artificial animal, as prosthetic monstrosity, as Leviathan, is a human artifact, if it is not natural, it is deconstructible, it is historical; and as historical, subject to infinite transformation, it is at once precarious, mortal, and perfectible' (BSI 27). And again, in *The Animal That Therefore I Am*, speaking this time explicitly of that abyssal limit between human and nonhuman animals, Derrida insists that 'the multiple and heterogeneous border of this abyssal rupture has a history' (A 31). As historical, this rupture – along with all the forms of institutionality that differentially feed into it and issue from it – is structured by the untimeliness of the trace of the future-to-come. But if we are to recall the abyssal, differential – indeed, *differantial* – nature of this rupture, then we must attend to the practices of division or distinction also as sites of intersection and interaction.[28] From the perspective of the animal-to-come, that is, human-animal 'distinctions' become imaginable also as events of human-animal *convergence* – albeit a convergence without any necessary unity or consistency. They become processes of human-animal *co-creation* – albeit a co-creation without any necessary cooperation, harmony, or equality of input. Lestel, again, gives approximate expression to this possibility when he proposes to consider 'all human/animal differences' as 'secondary compared to their mutual convergences', and argues that in these moments we find 'a difference that does not divide, but rather allows a life in common that far exceeds mere cohabitation' (LFH 62). And so the thought that 'the very phenomenon of animality might undergo a change in history' calls for an attempt to think *together* 'our phylogenetic and cultural histories' (LFH 70).

Lestel in fact goes so far as to identify several aspects of the contemporary situation as indicative of the emergence of a new animality, a 'post-animality', that radically underlines the mutability of animality at the same time that it 'substantially reshapes what it means to be human' (LFH 70). Significant advances in biotechnology and genetic manipulation present the most emphatic evidence of such changes, creating the possibility of as yet unimaginable animal hybridisations and transgenic creatures. While such transgenic creatures would in themselves qualify as unprecedented forms of animality, Lestel, speaking of bio-artist Eduardo Kac and his transgenic 'creation' of a fluorescent green rabbit, emphasises instead the 'social aspects of the living being[s] thus manipulated' and 'the community aspect of the relationships that humans' would have with them. It is the 'transgenic social subjects' emerging from such scientific and artistic 'provocations', rather than the 'genetically modified objects', that prompt Lestel to speak of 'transpecies animals' and of an 'animality to come' in the sense of 'unprecedented forms of animality' and 'novel procedures of animalization'.[29] Thus spaces such as those 'emerging in the field of Artificial Life' seek 'less to reproduce *animality-as-it-is* than to conceive an *animality-as-it-could-be*',[30] while 'animalized artifacts (such as Tamagotchi or Sony's AIBO) . . . and "talking" animals (primates like Kanzi or parrots like Alex) engage us in very unsettling and unprecedented spaces, in particular because the point of view of the animal suddenly appears to *us* as very real' (LFH 70). 'In short', Lestel writes, 'transpecies animality ejects animality from the space of zoology and introduces new rules into the evolutionary game'.[31]

To emphasise the role of modern science in developing such unheard-of 'forms' of animality is not to suggest, however, that the possibilities of the 'animal-to-come', 'animality-as-it-could-be', are limited to considerations of advanced technology. *Even less* is it to champion transgenic experimentation as the future of animality. For thinking of the animal-to-come in terms of the historicity and institutionality of a prosthstatic animal-machine amounts instead to underscoring the extent to which *the modalities and possibilities of animality* are dispersed across and constituted in relation to an array of knowledges, institutions, practices and techniques, and are shaped in the context of interspecies and intersubstantial relations, as much as they might be constituted by any genetic, evolutionary or simply 'anthropocentric' dispositions. Accordingly, while biotechnological transpecies animals may make the mutability of animality particularly visible today, the transformation of animality 'as such' is far from unprecedented, such that contemporary developments offer the chance to review a long history of 'human'-'animal' interaction for signs of any number of similar 'revolutions'. Lestel himself compares the 'spectacular' implications of biotechnology today with the 'revolutionary' transformations which saw the human species 'pass from the Paleolithic to the Neolithic era, when we began to domesticate animals and cultivate plants', placing the emphasis again on how 'the new animality substantially reshapes what it means to be human' (LFH 70). And in the millennia that separate these two 'events', other transformations might yet be found. In that sense, we might speculatively project a whole series of sites or events of human-animal convergence and co-creation which have constituted – or will have come to constitute – a history of the animal-to-come: zoos, animal husbandry, medical science and research ethics, wilderness and nature preserves, animal rights, but also cities, schooling, industrialisation and all the historical accomplishments that have had a bearing on the figure of modern 'man'. Indeed, we might go so far as to imagine or revisit humanism, humanity, even the 'evolutionary' processes of hominisation or anthropogenesis as events or achievements within the history that unfolds in the wake of the animal-to-come (see Chapter 5).

Such achievements and revolutions, such technologies and interventions, undoubtedly warrant ethical consideration, particularly in view of the histories of animal suffering so often created in the wake of such inventions. But drawing impetus from the abyssal limit between 'human' and 'animal', attending to the multiplicity of organisations of relations between living and dead, and projecting before it (or after it) a 'history' of anthropogenesis in which the figure of the human emerges from the texture of animality, the thought of the animal-to-come calls furthermore for a *hauntological* interpretation of sites, practices, organisations and modalities of animal existence, 'new' and 'old'. Used only a handful of times in *Specters of Marx*, Derrida's notion of hauntology nevertheless gathers together a string of themes central to that book – haunting, inheritance, messianicity without messianism, Marxist spirit of critique, democracy-to-come – which collectively introduce within questions of historical reflection an essential openness to the future-to-come. Driven by the need to 'introduce the concept of haunting into the very construction of a concept . . . of every concept, beginning with the concepts of being and time' (SM 161), hauntology 'would not merely be larger and more powerful than an ontology or a thinking of Being . . . It would harbor within itself, but like circumscribed places or particular effects, eschatology and teleology themselves' (SM 10). Thus bearing upon fundamental questions of being and time, hauntology could rightly be called upon to guide thinking on the animal-to-come as a question of 'political' existence even if Derrida hadn't already flagged that necessity, in *Specters of Marx*, at the very moment he speaks of a 'New International' that seeks to renew and radicalise critique of the 'monstrous' suffering 'which prevails today':

> Instead of celebrating the 'end of ideologies' and the end of the great emancipatory discourses, let us never neglect this obvious macroscopic fact, made up of innumerable singular sites of suf-

fering: no degree of progress allows one to ignore that never before, in absolute figures, never have so many men, women, and children been subjugated, starved or exterminated on earth. (And provisionally, but with regret, we must leave aside here the nevertheless indissociable question of what is becoming of so-called 'animal' life, the life and existence of 'animals' in this history. This question has always been a serious one, but it will become massively unavoidable.) (SM 85)

As a 'dimension of performative interpretation, that is, of an interpretation that transforms the very thing it interprets' (SM 51), hauntology calls for an active inheritance that opens 'the past' and 'the present' to the animal-to-come. The animal-to-come would thus name, *inter alia*, the hauntological introduction of animals and animality into the events, into the 'multiplicity of relations between living and dead', that not only have given form to particular modalities or potentialities of human and animal existence but also remain as a 'reserve' from which may be derived as yet unconsidered possibilities for future arrangements.[32] Such possibilities might be read the better to *discern* them, so as to selectively intensify those transformations that can hasten the arrival of more responsive approaches to animal welfare perhaps. But these intensifications of transformation might also seek out bolder or more radical constructions of animal agency and animal potentiality, since the animal-to-come names much more than simply an ethical response to an animal other laid low by a history of human exceptionalism. Indeed, if the promise of the 'to-come' which haunts every 'to-be' demands the production of 'events, new effective forms of action, practice, organization, and so forth' (SM 89), then the animal-to-come may well call for the production of a different animal-machine. To put it metonymically, in the terms developed by Lestel in his reading of Derrida and the latter's encounter with his cat: 'the question' of human-animal arrangements 'is no longer one of knowing *if* the cat can respond . . . but what are the ways of life that we can put in place *so that* the cat can respond to us?'[33]

As evidenced already by the proliferation of objections, both academic and public, to the fate of animals today – from campaigns against horse racing or live animal exports as forms of animal cruelty, say, through expressions of concern for the survival of innumerable animal species threatened by global industrialisation and climate change, to the increasing display via various social media of animals doing all kinds of surprising things – the question of the animal is becoming increasingly urgent, and prompts a re-evaluation of the capacity of our thought to respond adequately to this exigency. But response to that question perhaps requires following or figuring into analysis not the animal or animals as such – those living beings which 'produce themselves' – so much as the animal-*to-come*, tracing the latter's tracks through the inherited traditions and discourses that continue to shape prevailing concepts of culture and politics. What happens to political thought and practice, for example, if we take the limitrophic nature of 'the' human-animal distinction not so much as something to be demonstrated or reasserted in the face of all anthropocentrisms, whether explicit or unwitting, but rather as a *given*? What capacities or modalities of animality might be revealed or produced in a *hauntological* review of the conditions that define and delimit 'animal politics' today? What must happen to thinking about politics, power, institution, invention, culture, history, world, environment, experience, appearance and more for the *fact* and the *future* of animals and animality to be taken into account in reflection on the contemporary cultural condition? How to look beyond the *present* forms of carnophallogocentrism, in other words, if not via a thought of how animality may be *otherwise*? If it is indeed no longer possible to avoid the serious question 'of what is becoming of so-called "animal" life, the life and existence of "animals" in this history' (SM 85), a hauntological thought of the animal-to-come perhaps provides, at any rate, the means for taking that unavoidability seriously.

2   Specifically Cultural

In 1953, a group of primatologists studying a troop of Japanese macaques on Koshima Island observed a juvenile female, called Imo, take a sweet potato to the edge of a brook and wash the sand off the tuber before eating it. The behaviour demonstrated was idiosyncratic to the extent that it had not been previously observed, and no other member of the troop performed the action – at least, not at that time. Over subsequent years, though, the practice was gradually taken up by other members of the troop: first by Imo's playmates and kin, then by some of the older monkeys, although not all of them. By 1959, the custom was being passed on to newborn macaques, who were evidently habituated to the practice through exposure to their mothers' own potato-washing behaviour. Around the same time, members of the troop were observed to have adopted a variation on the technique, opting to wash the vegetables in the shallow waters of the sea when conditions suited, rather than in the fresh water of the brook, indicating a possible preference for the seasoning that the seawater provided. Other variations sprung up, such as repeatedly dipping the potatoes in the salt water after each bite, which also achieved a degree of regularity of use within the troop. Meanwhile, Imo appeared to have invented another food preparation technique in the form of separating grains of wheat from sand by throwing handfuls collected from the beach into a pool of water. This practice likewise spread throughout the troop (albeit unevenly), as did a number of other practices – wheat snatching, bathing – that seemed to develop from the uptake of these food preparation techniques.[1]

Today, the forms of behaviour exhibited by the troop – or, rather, the dissemination of those forms of behaviour both throughout the troop and on to newborns – are regularly cited as indicative of 'culture in animals'.[2] Indeed, numerous accounts of tool use, social learning, behavioural plasticity and community variation in social structure have been published over the last few decades by animal behaviourists and field researchers (primatologists, in particular), with the findings routinely being framed in terms of their potential status as evidence of cultural behaviour on the part of various animal species. From the use of sponges by bottlenose dolphins for foraging purposes, through the variation and transmission of vocalisations and dialects in New Caledonian crows, to the modification of social grooming practices on the part of Mahale chimpanzees who have migrated from one troop to another, the case for 'culture in animals' appears to be mounting.[3]

On the face of it, such findings appear to strike a decisive blow to the conceptual foundations to human exceptionalism, given the widespread presumption of culture as the very mark of hominisation. Yet the thought of the animal-to-come developed to this point calls, I suggest, for a hauntological review not only of such empirical evidence but also of the historical and philosophical conditions to its interpretation. What does it mean, for instance, to characterise such forms of animal behaviour or activity as cultural? What is at stake, both conceptually and politically, in the search for 'culture in animals'? Couched in this form and introduced in this way – immediately following a *précis*, concise to the point of seeming perfunctory, of research into animal cultural practices – these questions would seem to announce the introduction of philosophical interrogation into a field of research thereby construed as lacking theoretical grounding and critical reflexivity.

Yet reflections both on the significance and on the legitimacy of identifying specific behaviours or accomplishments as instances of animal culture abound within the literature. The implications of such findings for presumptions of human uniqueness are routinely acknowledged and are explicitly cited as evidence of the research's significance. Caution and doubt remain defining features of these assessments, however, with an overall hesitancy shown in according, without qualification (or scare quotes), the name *culture* to the observed phenomena. The accounts seem caught between needing to acknowledge indisputable practical differences between human and nonhuman animals and feeling that the drawing of a sharp line between them is hardly justified given the empirical evidence of forms of animal sociality and behaviour that are strongly analogous (at the very least) with those forms which, when enacted by human animals, warrant being called 'culture'. Hence the prevalence of a kind of agnosticism or scientific prudence: 'whether one would call it culture or not . . .'.[4]

So the field of scientific inquiry into animal culture is itself already characterised by a certain theoretical debate over the meaning of culture. And at stake in such debates is not simply which kinds of phenomena may fall under the umbrella of culture, but a more sophisticated account of the structure or features of culture itself. What perhaps drives the debate as much as the aforementioned agnosticism, in other words, is less a residual human exceptionalism than a perceived lack of clarity, rigour or consensus regarding the nature of culture as such. Thus, in an influential discussion of cultural primatology, William Clement McGrew complains that

> definitions of culture are a dime a dozen, and most are of little use. Most encapsulate an idea or set of ideas, but few are heuristic enough for pursuing the possibility of nonhuman culture. Especially exasperating are the epigrams beloved of introductory textbook writers: 'Culture is what makes us human', 'Culture is the human ecological niche', or, 'Culture is to human as water is to fish'. Of what empirical use are these?[5]

McGrew goes on to cite anthropologist Edward Burnett Tylor's famous definition of culture – 'that complex whole which includes knowledge, belief, art, morals, law, custom, and any other capabilities and habits acquired by man as a member of society' – in order to condemn its vagueness, offering the kicker that 'something that explains everything explains nothing'.[6] For McGrew, what is needed to advance studies of nonhuman culture is for cultural anthropologists to 'operationalize' the criteria for culture so that primatologists, among other animal researchers, have some sense of what to look for: the 'best strategy', he argues, is for the field of anthropology 'to set up explicit standards to be met by cultural primatologists and let the chimps fall where they may'.[7]

McGrew makes this observation notwithstanding the fact that at least some theoretical works manifestly *do* define culture in more tangible terms, even if they often disagree with each other depending on their disciplinary origin. The problem facing research into 'culture in animals', in other words, is not simply that the concept of culture which it seeks to borrow from anthropology is vague and lacking authority, but also that this vagueness can perhaps be characterised as an effect or example of the culturality (as it were) of the concept of culture itself. Most obviously, for instance, what we continue to refer to as *the* concept of culture – notwithstanding the imprecision and variability that mark its' instantiations and typifications – is generally accepted as having emerged at a particular moment in European history. Prior to the nineteenth century (to recount a well-known etymology), the term culture – from the Latin *cultura*, from *colere* – was used as a noun of process more or less equivalent to the modern sense of cultivation, hence growth and development, largely in the sense of tending to crops or animals (hence, *agriculture*) but also 'metaphorically' in the sense of cultivating minds or intellectual faculties.[8] Across the eighteenth and nineteenth centuries, and by way of an intricate 'series' of mutations, inversions and linguistic cross-pollinations, *culture* eventually came to function more widely both as a synonym for *civilisation* – itself a complicated term encompassing the senses both of a process of progressive human development and the end point of that process – and as the name of the very form of life that was most threatened by such civilisation, in the sense that progress is seen to be achieved at the expense of 'traditional culture'. At the same time, the term developed, particularly in England and France, the class-based associations – linking culture, in the sense of intellectual and spiritual cultivation, with the advantage of 'high birth' – that would eventually enable it to be used to designate primarily works and practices of 'sophisticated' artistic and intellectual activity. By the time that Tylor came to use *culture* to refer to the *entire* stock of human knowledge, art, customs, in other words, that 'word' was already able to accommodate a range of quite varied, even contradictory, uses such that any concept that could accommodate all 'its' senses had, inevitably, to be vague and unspecific.

By the same token, if Tylor was able to designate such *social* phenomena as morals, laws and customs by using a word which retained significant traces of its long-standing associations with the cultivation of the *natural* world on the one hand, and of *individual* minds on the other, this is owed to the prior occurrence of certain 'political' but also 'epistemological' upheavals. As Alec McHoul argues, 'whatever its pseudoexplanatory power', culture as a concept dates roughly from the Enlightenment, with 'certain ur-forms' of it being identifiable within 'the very beginnings of political investigations of human practices *as* specifically human practices (that is, where those practices are accounted for in terms of collective human volition rather than divine or extrahuman forces)'.[9] The idea of culture, that is, arose in response to the particular problem of designating the nature of 'man-kind' as a being who 'can choose to live in justice', as Italian Enlightenment philosopher Giambattista Vico put it in 1725.[10] Thus Hobbes, for example, sought to characterise the institution of the Commonwealth in terms of its status as a human achievement founded on a sovereign decision on the part of 'men' to 'direct their actions to the common benefit' – as the outcome, that is, of a covenant in which 'a Multitude of men do Agree' to 'Authorise all the Actions and Judgements' of a chosen representative 'as if they were his own' for the purpose of living 'peaceably amongst themselves, and be[ing] protected against other men'.[11] Vico himself, recognising the many ancestral nations as 'diverse in language and custom', declared the first truth of his 'New Science' to be the fact 'that the world of the gentile nations was certainly made by men'.[12] Vehemently opposed to Hobbes's account of the natural 'condition which is called Warre',[13] and critical of the thought that stable societies could only form on the basis of sophisticated rational deduction of their desirability, Vico sought instead to identify a 'common sense' or 'vulgar wisdom of mankind' which inclined them towards such forms of social organisation, and to this end proposed a scientific approach to 'the practices through which the humanity of a nation, as it rises, can reach this perfect state'.[14]

For Vico, this science of human practices or customs, depicted in terms of an 'ideal eternal history', inevitably posited an order of developmental difference between 'primitive' nations and 'civilised' nations ruled by rational law. By contrast, Johann Gottfried Herder, writing seventy years later, rejected Vico's notion of a universal history, and its presumption of a superior European culture:

> Is there a people upon earth that does not have some Culture [*das nicht einige Kultur habe*]? and how contracted must the scheme of Providence be, if every individual of the species were to be formed to what *we* call Culture [*Kultur*], for which refined weakness would often be the more appropriate term? Nothing can be more vague, than the term itself; nothing more apt to lead us astray than the application of it to whole nations and ages.[15]

In declaring that 'every nation is one people, having its own national form, as well as its own language',[16] Herder thus introduced further ambivalence into 'the' concept of culture – providing the term with another possible meaning, but also radically *de-specifying* (so to speak) and *pluralising*, in the same gesture, the possible forms that 'culture' might take.

On the back of this brief and ultimately insufficient genealogy of culture, we can already begin to recognise the effects of that concept's ambivalence in attempts to identify 'culture in animals'. Certainly, the researchers who first observed and reported on the macaques' sweet potato-washing were aware of the difficulties involved in using the term. Being sensitive both to the phylogenetic distance between humans and monkeys and to the strong associations of culture with 'literature, art, music, pictures, academe, religion', Masao Kawai opted to depict the potato-washing behaviour as evidence of 'preculture' in the macaques,[17] a description which is, effectively, as indebted to Vico's ideal cultural history as it is to Kawai's research interest in evolutionary anthropology. By contrast, McGrew (writing with C. E. G. Tutin) dismisses such 'near-synonymous' terminology on the grounds that its use is never justified or supported by elaboration of any 'criteria for differentiating the patterns [of animal behavior] that they discuss from human patterns subsumed by the term culture'.[18] Underpinning McGrew's own impulse to retain the language of culture is his recognition that such terms as 'preculture' continue to imply, without ever substantiating the assessment, that 'what non-human animals do is somehow intrinsically inferior to or less than human culture'.[19] In this respect, affirmations of the possibility of chimpanzee culture (for example) not only echo Herder's rejection of ethnocentrism (here, anthropocentrism) but also hinge on his pluralisation of culture as the form, language and traditions of distinct *Völker* (here, species). Yet it is this same pluralisation that (so to speak) empties the concept of culture of that content – specific 'criteria' or 'standards' – which McGrew sees as essential for any empirical investigations of animal culture to be meaningful.

By the same token, this problem of specificity is not one that arises only now that the concept of culture has made its way into the study of animal behaviours. For the history of thinking about (human) culture is littered with attempts to 'specify' culture by defining it against what it is *not*. Given what might be called the expansionist and pluralist tendencies inscribed within that concept, however, the candidates for its 'other', as McHoul puts it, 'have been so mixed and variable that, depending on preferences ... they can be either included (as "cultural") or excluded (as "other") almost at will'.[20] Thus the domain of culture has variously been *opposed* to society, to the economy, to nature, to materiality, to science, to the mundane, and much more besides, but equally has at other times been taken to *include* those domains or phenomena. The implications of this variability, moreover, are not limited to the challenges it puts to developing a workable 'definition' of the term. For one disturbing aspect of this fundamental ambivalence, McHoul notes, is that the term culture has never been used simply as an analytic or descriptive concept. Indeed, throughout Enlightenment and modern thought, 'culture', in its various conceptualisations, 'has also had a strong element of normativity about it, such that it not only appears to *account for* human practices (as it were, after the fact) but also, perhaps inevitably, is used to control and prescribe those practices'.[21] Such normativity is as apparent in Vico's ideal eternal history (with its claim that for human development to attain perfection 'there is need only for some sect of philosophers to complete and consolidate it with maxims reasoned in accordance with the idea of an eternal justice'),[22] as it is in Herder's insistence on the need to respect and value cultural difference ('let justice be done to other ways of life').[23] It is quite obviously at work in elitist conceptions of culture as designating, exclusively, works of literature, art, philosophy, and so on, as distinct from the 'mundane' practices and crafts of everyday life. And it is manifestly what is at stake in the search for animal culture and that research's associated challenge to the anthropological presumption that culture is a human prerogative. As McHoul puts it, then, 'the act of *choosing* a circumscription of the domain of culture, from the long list of available circumscriptions, always involves a political-ethical choice that has consequences for the judgment (as well as the analysis) of human practices'[24] – an observation to which we might now have cause to add, 'and animal practices, too'.

For this reason, culture is never simply a question of 'definition' or 'delimitation', a case of listing criteria or standards. And this is why McGrew's suggestion that the pursuit of a general definition of culture is irrelevant to the problem of animal culture and would be better subordinated to pragmatic considerations – 'define culture as you must to tackle the task at hand, just make it clear, fair, and most of all, productive'[25] – does not avoid the problem of cultural specificity. For there is always something at stake in designating a given set or form of phenomena as cultural. The point here is not to say that 'therefore' the use of the concept of culture in any and every context is a dishonest exercise, or a pointless one at best. Indeed, for McHoul, the key issue here is less the overt 'political' dimension to this normative gesture than the fact that,

> the concept of culture seems to want to do double duty in this field: to cover everything (the totality of facts and values 'purely' from outside those facts and values) *and* to discriminate, to value this or that as – factually – 'cultural' or 'other-than-cultural', for example, as 'economic' or 'natural'. And this would mean that if culture is to be a central concept of any investigation, it is always already duplicitous.[26]

The complications pertaining to the concept of culture relate not simply to that concept's normative implications, therefore, but also to the fact that, as much as any deployment of that concept may enable the development of new insights, it nevertheless risks obscuring certain problems whose *significance* remains, always, to be investigated and elaborated. For instance, and leaving aside the question of whether the demand for pragmatic utility does not already betray a normative impulse within a field that might otherwise self-represent as value-neutral, the principle of grounding concepts in their usefulness would surely reach its limit with any 'definition' of culture that included various natural (physical, non-sentient) processes or conditions within its scope. In the context of 'culture in animals', that is, 'nature' stands not simply as the leading candidate for *not-culture* but moreover as the unquestionable first consideration in any attempt to 'operationalise' culture as a concept appropriate to the study of animal behaviours and societies. Hence the identification of animal culture with a certain kind of intraspecific 'transmission' of forms of behaviour that cannot be attributed to genetic or ecological determination.[27] Here, the exclusion of such forms of determinacy speaks to a requirement for a certain kind or degree of arbitrariness, in the sense of an unmotivated (nondeterminate) production of novelty or difference in the expression (use or form) of behaviour or action. Such arbitrariness is in turn the condition for 'cultural difference': variability in the expression or uptake of a given behaviour within or between populations. Whatever else may be insisted upon as a criterion of (animal) culture – evidence of social learning, normative force or coordinated action, say – it is this sense of relative autonomy from 'natural' (genetic or environmental) determinants, this possibility of doing otherwise than what is predetermined or programmed, as it were, of being otherwise than a pre-programmed animal-machine, that is *necessarily* in play in any thought or demonstration of 'culture in animals'. To the extent that some forms of intraspecific transmission may be said to be caused by genetic or environmental conditions, that is, it is this structure of arbitrariness or *in*determinacy that constitutes the *sine qua non* of culture.

While culture is routinely characterised as being a form of transmission, then, the cultural forms thus 'transmitted' must necessarily be neither determined nor determining in the strong sense of those terms, which is to say, in any sense that would contradict this essential arbitrariness, hence in-principle optionality, variability, transformability. To the extent, moreover, that arbitrariness is the production, discovery or deployment of what is not determined, hence *not given*, 'culture' necessarily implies *inventiveness*, in the sense of finding or creating a difference in use or response. Today, the thought of invention is largely dominated by images of technological innovation, or perhaps narrative fabrication. However, this conceptualisation, as Derrida has noted in a long reflection on the historical and institutional conditions of invention, sits alongside an 'earlier' sense, one that interestingly enough predates (as it were) the invention of 'culture':

To invent has always signified 'come to find for the first time', but until the dawn of what we might call technoscientific and philosophical 'modernity' (let us say in the seventeenth century, as a very rough and inadequate empirical marker), it was still possible to speak of invention (but later this would no longer be true) in regard to existences or truths that, without, of course, being created by invention, were discovered or unveiled by it for the first time – were found to be there . . . [For example] the invention of the body of Saint Mark.[28]

Accordingly, invention has not always implied a kind of creation of something that did not exist prior to that act; and, indeed, even according to the modern concept, an invention is 'not created, in the strong sense of the word, [but] is only put together, starting with a stock of existing and available elements, in a given configuration'.[29] As a consequence, what characterises invention, what remains relatively consistent throughout its semantic variations and displacements, on Derrida's account, is 'the "coming", the *venire*, the event of a novelty that must surprise'.[30] An in-vention, then, on the basis of this logic that remains the kernel of its concept, is the 'incoming' of a novelty, the 'coming-about' of the difference of a *first time*, be it an unprecedented discovery or an original construction. As *in*-coming, moreover, this difference or novelty always appears or arrives as if from elsewhere, as if from 'outside'. An invention thus introduces a form of transgression with respect to existing or 'normal' states of affairs: for it to be the in-coming of a first time, 'an invention ought to produce a disordering mechanism, to open up a space of unrest or turbulence for every status assignable to it when it suddenly arrives'.[31] *Qua* transgressive and disordering, therefore, invention or inventiveness marks not only the structure or essence (as it were) of culture, but also the moment or principle of (that) culture's undoing. Indeed, as Derrida asks, 'how can we sort out and name the cultural groupings that make a given invention possible and admissible once the invention in question has in turn modified the structure of the context itself?'[32]

On this basis it is possible to hypothesise that this inventiveness of culture, or rather the complex relation of culture and invention, is what induces attempts to account for 'culture in animals' to be thrown, perhaps inevitably, into disarray. Fittingly, this effect seems most evident when attention in studies of animal culture is directed at the question of the origin of a given cultural practice. Thus, for instance, McGrew registers a residual doubt about whether frequently cited examples, like the macaque potato-washing behaviour, can be properly identified as instances of culture in nonhuman primates. The problem with these classic cases, he reports, is that,

> their origins lie in human facilitation; the monkeys were lured to the beach or into pools by artificially providing them with domesticated plant foods. This enhancement takes nothing away from what happened next, how the habits spread by horizontal or vertical transmission or continued to elaborate or became fixed. But one must always wonder: How many of these habits would have occurred without human assistance?[33]

It is in such doubts that we can begin to see the duplicitous normativity at play in investigations into 'culture in animals'. According to the concept of culture as intraspecific transmission, that is, invention – whether because it amounts to an in-coming from elsewhere, such that its origin lies 'outside' the 'culture' in question, or simply because it amounts to a first time that is *yet* to be 'transmitted' – cannot be properly understood as cultural. If there is some hesitancy in accepting the macaque practices as cultural, notwithstanding the evidence both of their indeterminacy (non-necessity) and of their transmission, therefore, this is not because the practices aren't cultural *as defined*, but because they can't be satisfactorily depicted as 'spontaneous', as 'uncontrived', which is to say – in a sense of the term very different from the one otherwise operating in concepts of animal culture – as *natural*.

The difficulties that beset the question of 'culture in animals', in other words, lay as much in a certain ambivalence in the characterisation of (animal) nature as in the vagueness of the concept of culture. In the circumscription of one ('culture' as transmission), we can see a sort of expansion and pluralisation of the other ('nature' as genetic and environmental conditions, but also as autonomous, spontaneous, non-'artificial' action). With respect to the problem of animal culture, moreover, this move allows the entry or operation of a certain normativity: the valuing, that is, of the autonomy or self-sufficiency of 'nature'. For the question of 'culture in animals' seems most regularly to be posed in such a way as to take culture's *autochthony* as given: the spontaneous (nondetermined) eruption, development or birth of cultural behaviours ('habits') from within, as it were, as though having arisen out of the land in which they are found. And only culture that conforms to this model – or so we must conclude from those reservations directed at the accomplishments of the Japanese macaques – can be properly identified as such.

The duplicity of this move can be registered in the first instance by noting the fact that in Herder's influential philosophy of culture – to which McGrew's own thought is indebted, knowingly or not – environmental features, such as climate and geography, far from being excluded as factors in the formation of culture, are positioned as its very *determinants*.[34] Speculating on the possibility of 'a *physico-geographical history of the descent and diversification of our species* according to periods and climates', Herder accounts for a whole range of differences not only in 'body' but also in 'mind' (temperament, inclination and custom) in terms of the influence of environment.[35] He reasons that 'since man is no independent substance, but is connected with all the elements of nature' he must therefore be changed by those elements,[36] and beginning from this principle attributes the development of diverse 'modes of life', even the presence or absence of technological artefacts, to different ecological conditions:

> The islanders, whom Nature feeds with vegetable productions, particularly the salubrious breadfruit, and clothes in a delightful

climate with the rind of trees, lead a tranquil happy life. Birds, we are told, sat on the shoulders of the natives of the Ladrone Islands, and sang undisturbed: with the use of the bow they were unacquainted, for no beast of prey obliged them, to have recourse to weapons of defence. They were strangers to fire, also; for the mildness of their climate rendered it unnecessary.[37]

If this view appears steeped in Romanticism, hence marked by its own forms of ethnocentrism, it should be remembered that Herder's intention was precisely to value such cultures *as* cultures, to value them for what they are, and therefore to respect their *specific* difference(s) instead of seeing them as 'inferior' moments in a broader movement towards the 'pinnacle' of culture in European civilisation. Herder's theory is not entirely devoid of all legitimacy or pragmatic utility, moreover, since 'it can be used to explain, for example, the cultural differences between the cities of Sydney and London', as Niall Lucy suggests: 'Sydney's sun and humidity attracts people to an outdoor lifestyle, getting them out into very public places, whereas London's mist and cold induces them to find pleasure and warmth at home or in the corner pub'.[38] Nevertheless, that residual ethnocentricity – taking the term in the sense not so much of evaluating 'other cultures' by the standards of 'one's own', but rather of understanding culture precisely as *being* 'one's own' or as *belonging* to 'another', as being *centred* on a given nation or people (*ethnos*), hence as being a fact or expression of such a collective's autonomy – brings to the fore precisely the normativity of that thought of culture which questions the authenticity of the macaques' potato-washing habits. Culture, once again, is marked by what is indigenous, autochthonous, to the collective that practises it.

Of course, Herder's (effectively) *environmental* theory of culture stands in stark contrast to the imperative within research into animal culture to exclude ecological factors as a possible cause of the behaviour that stands as a candidate for 'culture'. Accordingly, the presumption of autochthony, as the etymology of that term would already demonstrate, should, in principle, have no role in assessments of such research. Indeed, the possibility of autochthony would rather be the very obstacle to determining the fact of 'culture in animals'. It is perhaps for this reason, therefore, that another investigator of animal culture, Robert Sapolsky, also registers doubts about the conclusiveness of the macaque case study, but for reasons that are almost the precise opposite to those expressed by McGrew:

> One of the most famous cases of animal culture is renowned not just for its careful documentation over decades, but also because its 'inventor' was identified. In such cases, there is still the possibility that ecological or genetic factors, while not causing the spread of the behavior beyond its originators, may nonetheless facilitate its spread. As such, the gold standard for culture is one that can only occur in an experimental setting. This is when an individual(s) is removed from a group, is taught a new behavior that is genetically and ecologically arbitrary, is returned to the group, and where that novel behavior is then shown to spread.[39]

Certainly, one would think, the presence of a water source (for example) favours the invention and dissemination of a technique that hinges on the use of a water source! But what is significant about Sapolsky's reflection is not its apparently uncompromising dedication to removing all doubt over a given practice's arbitrariness, but rather the specific characteristics of its relation to the Herderian concept of culture. For Sapolsky's exclusion – in the name of attaining the 'gold standard' of scientific certainty – of the fact of invention (literally speaking) from the ambit of culture in favour of introducing a practice that is (as it were) foreign to the group presents a radical challenge to the presumption of culture's essential autochthony. And the radicalness of this challenge derives not simply from its reversal of the reasoning behind conventional doubts, reported by McGrew, concerning the cultural status of the macaques' potato-washing technique, but also from its implicit conceptualisation of culture as potentially *heterochthonous*.

In its cavalier approach to any moral claims to autonomy on the part of the hypothetical test subjects, Sapolsky's experimental scenario could easily be condemned, to be sure, as exemplary of the irresponsible, anthropocentric tendencies of experimental ethology. Nevertheless, the rationale informing his hypothesis expresses its own commitment precisely to the *autonomy* of animal cultures. This is to say that, if Sapolsky excludes the fact of invention from consideration, all the better to circumscribe solely those phenomena that evidence culture as transmission, he also excludes with that gesture the in-vention or in-coming of the prospective, heterochthonous practice that would, hypothetically, be transmitted as cultural. He thereby excludes from those moments of transmission that alone would count as (properly) cultural not just the in-vention of the practice but the 'first time' of *transmission*: from human to animal subject, via the practice or process of *instruction*. If Sapolsky diverges from McGrew's Herder-like presumption of autochthony, in other words – arguably throwing chauvinistic indifference to animal autonomy into the bargain – he nevertheless reproduces that aspect of Herder's 'ethnocentrism' that takes such autonomy as unquestionable, precisely by delimiting the field of culture to *intraspecific* transmission. A certain normativity can be seen, once again, to operate in the deployment of the concept of culture: only feats of transmission that take place within the limits of the natural (uninvented), pre-existing coherence of a population of conspecifics – a bounded, literally *specific* network of transmission – may be properly identified as culture.

Regardless of whether the origin of a given cultural practice is figured as 'internal' or 'external' to the 'culture' that would be evidenced by that practice's 'transmission', therefore, the thought of animal culture continues to be articulated in relation to a (cultural) delimitation of a more general field of phenomena to one defined in terms of a species' or a population's (presupposed) autonomy. In this way, 'culture' becomes identified with something that is internal to that species or population, as that collective's 'property'. Undoubtedly, there is a certain critical gesture implied in this move:

affirming the propriety of the animal other's 'own' culture so as both to counter the arrogance of presuming culture as a human prerogative (human exceptionalism) and to protest the actual forms of violence enacted by any number of human interventions within animal communities, ecologies, lives. But this critical move, this 'political-ethical choice', also serves as the means by which animals' actual accomplishments in terms of participating in cultural processes – whether ostensibly 'their own' or not – continue to be overlooked, diminished or doubted on the suspicion that some improper form of determination (heteronomy) or intervention (heterochthony) may be at work. And this is precisely because this 'choice', this deployment of the concept, seems always to seek 'culture *in* animals', to identify it with a (biological, phylogenetic) disposition that is imagined to be *inborn*. To the extent that culture is not equatable to transmission as such, however, and is rather structurally – hence always – *in-ventive*, its *sine qua non* necessarily lies 'without': in or as a 'first time' that, by definition, does not (yet) constitute an element of transmission. On this thought of the in-coming of culture, then, culture is irreducible to an inborn quality that can be identified within the individuals of a given species, and which would thereby constitute a trait belonging to a population, troop or community modelled on the image of such individuals. 'Culture' would rather name a form or condition of openness to the in-coming of the new, of the otherwise, from the 'outside'.

This is perhaps as much as to suggest, as Dominique Lestel does – albeit via a very different route to the one laid out here – that culture be understood not as a property of given living beings but rather as a tendency fashioning 'the living' as such. Noting that the predominant conceptions of animal culture 'content themselves with suggesting that the border' between 'nature' and 'culture' must be merely 'moved', Lestel argues by contrast that it is a matter of 'contesting [that border's] existence altogether':

> We could consider that one of the fundamental tendencies of the living, and this since its beginnings, is to gain spaces of liberty

in relation to internal (physiological) and external (ecological) constraints to which the organism is subjected – and that cultural behaviors constitute one of the most interesting occurrences of these tendencies . . . The essential question that the notion of culture poses is to know in what measure a given animal is capable of establishing a distance in relation to necessities it is subjected to, and in what measure it can give sense to this. The notion of 'subject' thus becomes essential for understanding the evolution of culture, not as subject who must interiorize norms but rather as subject who is capable of establishing them – *and of distancing itself from them*. Nature and culture are interdependent rather than antagonistic.[40]

Lestel's references here to liberty, constraints and capability will need to be put in quotation marks, so as to register the need for their qualification in view of a thought of zoopower still to be elaborated (see Chapter 3). For now, though, we may note that, on Lestel's account, if 'culture is intrinsic to the living', this interiority or inwardness marks not the pregiven autonomy of a subject but rather the in-coming of a difference that divides a so-called subject: a form of *self-distance* through which an 'individual' achieves the possibility of 'behaving', 'living' or 'being' *otherwise*.[41] Such would be the inscription, as it were, of a double movement of institutionalisation and equivocation. Thus the formation of habit, for example, sees the in-vention of a certain 'freedom' or scope to expend otherwise a surplus of energy and attention acquired through an economy of action.[42] And in that sense, 'culture' would arrive not as the *expression* of 'autonomy' but rather as its very *attainment* – or better, its *infliction*: the endurance of a certain degree or moment of discretion or decision by way of the exteriorisation, institutionalisation, of modes of behaviour, forms of life, ways of being.

Which organisms may have achieved or may hope to attain such moments or degrees of autonomy, and what may be the possible forms and effects of such autonomy, in which contexts and under what conditions – these are questions that, no doubt, can only be adequately investigated in an empirical manner. Pursuing them in such a manner would quite obviously drive the development of a science of animal culture aimed at generating not only detailed knowledge of the taxonomic distribution of various propensities for culture – identifying the relative differences in reliance on social-learning strategies and public-information use among different species of sticklebacks, say – but also insight into the phylogenetic basis for such differences, perhaps culminating in the development of an evolutionary theory of culture and cognition.[43] In being thus oriented towards evolutionary conditions, however, such research would perhaps be focused on different objectives – and, indeed, oriented by a different temporality – than those that animate a *cultural theory* of animals and animality. Where a science of animal culture, that is, might 'look back' (as it were) to an evolutionary past and to the phylogeny of a biological substrate for knowledge of literally *specific* forms and possibilities of culture, the thought of the animal-to-come would approach animal culture as a very different problem. Here the concern would be not with establishing the existence and explaining the origins of 'culture in animals', but rather with speculating on the possibilities that are opened by the fact, and by recognition of the fact, that the (future) existence of any given animal, and of animals generally, is owed in part to a certain institutionality (as habituality or conventionality, for example), which is to say, to something other than simply a phylogeny and an ecology, as these are conventionally understood.

What cultural and political implications or possibilities may derive, that is, from the fact that animals may (yet) 'be' more or otherwise than what (or how) they have previously been taken to 'be'? We can already see, at least, that the principle of (biological) *specificity* need not always be granted authority when considering the possible relations between animals and culture. After all, there is no in-principle reason why forms of self-distance should always derive from networks of sociality constituted solely by conspecifics, a point already evidenced by the interspecific human-animal interactions that are felt by some to compromise the autonomy of (con)specific forms of animal culture. Moreover, to the extent that a mode of behaviour or form of life is exteriorised, habitualised, institutionalised, and thereby distanced from a given organism (or 'subject') rather than proper to it, that mode or form is, from the beginning, necessarily *appropriable* – by that organism, to be sure, but also, in principle, by some other. Indeed, it is the exploitation of such appropriability – otherwise known as copying – that defines what is most regularly presented as the basis of (animal) cultural transmission: 'social learning' amongst conspecifics. Given that networks of sociality may be inter- or even multi-specific, then, forms or modes of animality remain, in principle, iterable beyond the species or population to which they would otherwise be confined.

And that is how a squirrel, for example, may come to act the part of a cat. There has been more than one anecdotal report, in fact, of a postpartum feline fostering an orphaned squirrel, nursing it alongside her own kittens, with the unrelated neonate engaging in kitten-like forms of behaviour, including purring.[44] If the anecdotal nature of these reports ostensibly undermines their scientific validity (though, see Chapter 4), more credible evidence of cross-fostering is available in peer-reviewed journals, including one reported case of intergenus adoption 'in the wild'. In the latter case, a marmoset was integrated into a group of capuchin monkeys and nurtured by 'two successive adoptive "mothers"'.[45] While formal studies and informal reports alike often focus on the so-called nurturing instincts evidenced by these instances – the former publications deploying the language of evolutionary mechanisms, and the latter a discourse of sentimentality – the significant detail for our purpose lies rather in the adoptees' respective adoption of forms of behaviour and sociality practised by their guardians. Thus, the study of the capuchin-raised marmoset found that the juvenile 'was clearly socially integrated into the group': 'it traveled and fed with the group, [and] responded to alarm vocalizations given by members of the group . . . including participating in mobbing a snake'.[46] It engaged in 'social play with [capuchin] juveniles',[47] and scavenged leftovers in a way that 'fully resemble[d] the common capuchin pattern of scrounging infants and tolerant adults'.[48] It even 'behaved like an infant for a longer period than is the pattern in [its] species'.[49] What might otherwise be described as specifically capuchin 'culture', in other words, has been shown to be appropriable and practicable by non-capuchin individuals.

To the extent that animal culture continues to be most readily and regularly identified, both empirically and theoretically, with conspecific transmission, what is perhaps evidenced both by the phenomenon of cross-species adoption and by the human 'enhancement' of nonhuman primate innovation is the in-principle 'porosity', as Lestel puts it, of (animal) 'cultures' (DN 93, 101–5).[50] Accordingly, and as Lestel also suggests, where studies of animal culture tend to focus on (con)specific populations, perhaps the greatest insights into animal culture may be derived from those moments or contexts in which such populations are most open to an 'outside', to the in-coming of difference: 'it is perhaps precisely in situations of instability and mixture that the [cultural] nature of the animal is best revealed' (DN 100). Rather than being a cause for *doubt* over the cultural status of macaque potato-washing, therefore, the potential 'heterochthony' of that practice's development would, in terms of this idea of porosity, be the very *confirmation* of the operations of culture.[51] And it is perhaps for this reason that Lestel insists on the need 'to think the question of animal cultures *in* human cultures' (DN 101).

Lestel speaks to two distinct but related scenarios to illustrate this last point. The first concerns the very prevalence of situations in which humans and animals, both as individuals and as populations, come into contact every day, such that the empirical and theoretical isolation of the one from all relations to the other seems increasingly implausible. In the case of human societies, this is shown in the fact that 'not one ethnologist has ever described a human society' that had not 'developed *privileged* relations (that is to say that they are not purely instrumental) with *at least* one ... natural species which is found to be part of the society considered *ipso facto*' (DN 94). In this sense, it is a mistake to think of human societies as simply or purely human, since such societies seem always to include nonhuman agents – pets, sacred animals, local wildlife – and to be characterised by relations with such agents as much as by human-to-human relations. So-called human culture, in other words, has never taken the form of a culture of conspecifics. By the same token, such nonhuman individuals and populations themselves come into existence increasingly within an environment already structured by human societies and human activities. To that extent, one can no longer take for granted the 'noncultural' status of the environmental factors (for example) that are imagined to 'determine' certain forms of animal behaviour, nor can one ignore the potential for those nonhuman animals to become to a degree acculturated to their non-nonhuman neighbours. In Lestel's view, and as already evidenced above with reference to McGrew, many ethologists remain committed to the ideal of the 'pure' animal, one uncontaminated by human contact, such that they studiously ignore, or actively devise methodologies aimed at minimising, the 'capacity that many species have to be "contaminated" by the cultural behaviors of humans' (DN 102). Yet for Lestel, one of the most interesting observations to be made of 'animal culture' is that,

> a certain number of evolved animals, among them many species of primates and birds, are capable of 'humanizing' in contact with humans, which is to say that they adopt behaviors and postures that are directly understandable for humans and that augment their effectiveness at living in the same spaces as *Homo sapiens*. (DN 102)

Perhaps more significantly, such 'humanisation' is not limited to changes in the relations between animals and humans. For 'the presence of humans', Lestel argues, 'also modifies the behavior of animals between themselves' (DN 102). Lestel cites the case of chimpanzee research subject Lucy, who adopted a cat as a 'pet', but, once again, numerous informal reports could be cited as indicative of the claim.[52] In view of such phenomena, anecdotal or not, one would surely be forgiven for wondering at the point, if not the validity, of any search for 'culture in animals' that denied or excluded *from the start* such a potential for acculturation, precisely by striving to minimise all scope for 'contamination'.

At any rate, Lestel's second scenario, concerning the rehabilitation of endangered species, points to the implications – potentially disastrous for the nonhuman animals concerned – of continuing to ignore the reality of such 'humanisation'. Many such rehabilitation efforts proceed by way of captive breeding programmes and the reintroduction of individuals into their 'natural' environments. In their simplest forms, however, such programmes must presume not only the noncultural status of a given animal's interactions with its so-called natural *habitat*, but also that ongoing *habituation* to the rhythms, environments and agents (human and nonhuman; animal, vegetable and mineral) of the breeding programme has no lasting impact on that animal's living *habits*. As Lestel argues, however, anthropoid apes raised by human carers, for example,

> have been humanized. The forest is not their natural element. It is perhaps that of their species, but it is not theirs. Releasing them in the forest supposes that they would be trained for it. They must learn to survive in an environment that is *a priori* hostile to them. A wild orangutan knows how to collect the hundreds of species of fruits and vegetable matter that it consumes. A rehabilitated orangutan does not know this. This situation of rehabilitation is exemplary from a cultural point of view. It concerns, in effect, teaching an intelligent animal to become wild (to become rather than to re-become, since the majority of them never were). It is a matter of *dis-acculturizing* them! The question posed, expressed concisely, is in effect to make them lose the cultural habits acquired with humans – irrefutable proof of their capacities to adopt cultural behaviors. (DN 103–4)[53]

Contrary to the idea that 'culture in animals' can be found only in their complete isolation from human 'contaminants', therefore, the most convincing evidence of a given animal's 'culturality' would lie in its capacity to be subject to processes of acculturation. Indeed, if culture constitutes something that comes to an individual from without, as it were – a condition or characteristic irreducible to the biology of given species; a condition or quality which constitutes a habit or practice from the outset as appropriable from and by others – recognition of that fact perhaps demands concern not for 'culture in animals' so much as for *animals in culture*, with the *crucial* qualification that 'culture' here can no longer be understood as specifically human. In view of the various complications that have revealed themselves in the investigation of that concept, moreover, it can perhaps be recognised that culture here names less a set of behaviours and practices, habits and dispositions, devices and technologies, nor even their transmission, than the form or degree of arbitrariness that is attributable to such behaviours, practices and so on. Culture, that is, would be the potential for such practices and the like to be *otherwise*: to be adopted or transformed via processes both of acculturation and invention.

Such a 'definition' of culture no doubt risks generalising or de-specifying the concept to the point that it loses all utilitarian value in attempts to identify which species 'have' culture, and to differentiate within a given population those behaviours which are 'genuinely' cultural from those which are genetically or environmentally 'determined'. But the concept would not, for all that, be entirely devoid of significance, for at least two consequences – one perhaps less palatable than the other – follow from the move to thinking in terms of animals in culture. The first is that 'human exceptionalism', to the extent that it constitutes a *cultural* practice, may have to be rethought not simply as an ideological conceit held by an arrogant creature which calls itself 'human', but moreover as a practice or modality of *animality*, understood in Lestel's sense of the texture of animality (as discussed in Chapter 1). Various animals – human and nonhuman, as individuals and as populations – participate, in other words, in the cultural practice, in different cultural practices, of 'exceptionalising' the human animal and the situations and artefacts which that animal creates.[54] Through the normalisation of certain forms or degrees of exposure to humans, various types of 'wildlife' (birds, for example) living in contemporary urban environments adopt dispositions and practices of familiarity and security that would, in other environmental contexts or historical moments, greatly increase their chances of being killed. Likewise, certain other types of 'urban-adaptable' animals (particular species of rats and cockroaches, say) thrive in the globalisation of such environments, participating, alongside human-driven environmental engineering, in the extinction of local species.[55] Or again, in a very different vein, Lestel notes that it is not uncommon for chimpanzees raised in captivity to 'become depressed' on being introduced into the wild 'because they find themselves in a natural environment' (DN 104) – and if that is the case, what happens to the question of animal *interests* in the critique of practices of human exceptionalism? At the very least, such scenarios might force one to consider the possibility that human exceptionalism operates via cultural practices – which is to say, practices that are habitual and transmissible, but also variable and transformable – that are *more than* human in locus and in character.

If it seems that by this stage I have begun to confuse environmental conditions with artificially produced circumstances, biological behaviour with cultural practice, this outcome is, if not exactly the point, then perhaps an ineradicable consequence of the duplicity of 'the' concept of culture. To the extent that this confusion derives from an engagement with the *question* of (animal) culture, moreover, we might see in it one example of what follows from a hauntological pursuit not of the animal but of the *animal-to-come* through the historical and intellectual conditions of contemporary 'culture'. The potentiality exhibited in and by such a confusion of culture and ecology is one to which we will have to return (see Chapter 5). But for now we may simply note a second consequence of reversing the conventional order of things. For the question of animal culture, formulated rather as a matter of 'animals in culture', not only foregrounds the cultural, hence institutional, nature of the so-called human-animal distinction, but also *thereby* underscores the fact that 'the animal-to-come' does not simply name a future animal or form of animality. It speaks, rather, to an alternative model of the animal-machine, in which animal behaviours and practices take shape in and as a form of exteriority (see Chapter 1). Underscoring such distributed and differential, prosthetic institutionality, the animal-to-come articulates, therefore, *both* the potentiality and transformability that already inhabits (as it were) contemporary engagements with animals and animality, *and* the possibility of animal invention, which is to say, among other things, the possibility of the in-vention of the (animal) other(s).

When Derrida reflects on the status of invention, he notes that its apparent transgressiveness remains defined by a 'feature of very great stability': 'never, it seems to me, has anyone assumed the authority to speak of invention without implying in the term the technical initiative of the being called man'.[56] If the very search for 'culture in animals' seems to imply that at least some commentators now feel authorised to speak of animal inventions, the recurring expressions of scientific doubt serve to call that authority into question, underscoring the 'techno-epistemo-anthropocentric dimension' to the convention or law which continues to assign a status to invention.[57] For Derrida, this stability suggests the need for a 'reinvention of invention', which would be pursued 'through questions and deconstructive performances bearing upon this traditional and dominant value of invention, upon its very status, and upon the enigmatic history that links, within a system of conventions, a metaphysics to technoscience and to humanism'.[58] For him, it is through such questions and performances that one might begin to prepare for the invention of the other, in or as the future-to-come – 'allowing for the adventure of the event of the entirely other to come'.[59] Applied retrospectively, such an objective or endeavour may help to explain why the thought of the animal-to-come has led us through a hauntology of ideas about culture, not towards the circumscription of an autonomous population of cultured animals, nor, of course, towards the reproduction of a conventional humanism, but rather towards the sites or events of human-animal intersection that may complicate both of these normative impulses. Enfolding not only 'the human' and 'the animal' but also 'the theoretical' and 'the empirical', such occasions of intersection or convergence would appear to register a moment of undecidability between that transformability which 'already' inhabits contemporary thought on the one hand, and the observable practices, behaviours and achievements of various animal beings on the other – suggesting in turn that the forms of cultural practice that might best prepare for the arrival of the animal-to-come are beyond the capacity or *power* of any given species. It is for this reason, then, that the next chapter turns in the first instance not to further instantiations of animal culture, but to the contemporary theorisation of power, with a view to assessing precisely the latter's potential to allow for the invention of the (animal) other.

3   Zoopower

Of the many moves that Derrida makes in *The Animal That Therefore I Am*, one of the most productive and frequently cited is his displacement, after Jeremy Bentham, of reason in favour of suffering as the key question in thinking about animals. For Bentham, Derrida writes, 'the question is not to know whether the animal can think, reason, or speak ... The *first* and *decisive* question would rather be to know whether animals can suffer.'[1] The ethical aura of this gambit is, of course, undeniable, particularly when read alongside the book's extended engagement with Levinas, and the corresponding articulation of the question of the animal as a broadening of the concept of alterity. Understandably then, Derrida's turn to the phenomenon of suffering – and, by extension, questions of violence and vulnerability – has been taken up and assessed within areas of scholarship and activism that are oriented towards the goal of fostering critical concern for the interests and welfare of animals.

The most sophisticated engagements with Derrida in these studies have given to this ethical focus an ostensibly political veneer, by reading the situation and status of animals through the frame of biopolitics. Thus Cary Wolfe, for example, reads Derrida as capping off a series of advances in the theorisation of biopolitics made by Michel Foucault, Giorgio Agamben and Roberto Esposito.[2]

Through work by these figures and others, the forms and fortunes of biopolitical theory have multiplied and diversified over the last two decades or so (particularly in the wake of the English translation of Agamben's *Homo Sacer*), such that it resists characterisation in general terms. Not the least troublesome in this regard is the virtually contradictory inflections that Foucault and Agamben respectively give to the term 'biopolitics', notwithstanding Agamben's own claims to be merely 'completing' the 'Foucauldian thesis'.[3] At the core of most recent biopolitical thought, though, lies the fundamental insight that the scope of politics extends beyond the institution of legal rights and freedoms to encompass the broader operations of state power over life as such. For Agamben, in particular, the key point is that the conventional space of politics, and its attendant focus on securing the livelihood of people and preserving their freedom, is itself instituted on the basis of a sovereign (and potentially violent) decision regarding which lives and which *ways* of life can legitimately claim the right to inclusion within the sphere of political life. In the classical context, such a decision sees the lives and the life of 'mere' subsistence – natural or biological, reproductive life – excluded from political life, denying such lives the 'right to have rights', to use Hannah Arendt's phrase, but also (crucially) situating them beyond the interest, hence beyond the scope and *authority*, of political processes.[4] In the transition to the modern context, governmental processes – as forms of what Foucault calls biopower – make this once excluded life the very target of political calculation and regulation, seizing hold of life in order to optimise and protect the health, wealth and happiness of a population. And in view of this transformation, the institutions of liberal democracy, which ideally provide individuals with the power to exercise freedom of speech, action and choice, can be seen to be conditioned by a sacrificial logic. Deploying a power *over* life, contemporary biopolitical governance not only reduces the 'dignity' of political life to the maximisation of 'mere life', but also reserves that sovereign power to exclude given lives (or forms of life) from the political community at any time. Thus abandoned, such lives become 'bare life', left vulnerable to violence and death and without recourse to legal protection or recompense.

While Agamben and many others tend to deploy their biopolitical readings in the service of revealing the increasing reduction of human existence to the status of 'bare life', Wolfe finds in biopolitics a useful framework for thinking through the political status – and stakes – of animal life in modern societies. The obvious point of interest here is in the potential to recognise in the category of 'bare life' the fate of all nonhuman animals, which – by seeming not to possess the attributes that distinguish the rational, responsible, ensouled human individual from animal existence – do not warrant the rights and protections granted by the state to properly autonomous human beings. The concerns of a conventional politics of human freedom thus remain underpinned by the decidedly illiberal treatment of animals as merely so much 'property'. As Derrida puts it: 'politics presupposes livestock', the 'power to command beasts, to order the becoming-livestock of the beast' (A 96).[5] For Wolfe, however, the virtue of the biopolitical frame is not only that it can attend to the inevitable exclusion or sacrifice of (animal) life on the altar of (human) political freedom, but that it also demonstrates the essential contingency and inadequacy of the very rights-based model that underpins conventional philosophies of politics. In this way, biopolitical thought reveals the fact that 'to live under biopolitics is to live in a situation in which we are all always already (potential) "animals" before the law – not just nonhuman animals according to zoological classification, but any group of living beings that is so framed' (BL 10). Thus campaigns to grant protection to animals (for example) by legislating for animal rights remain inadequate, from the biopolitical perspective, and ultimately compromised, to the extent that they amount simply to a partial and problematic redrawing of the line between forms of life that 'count' and those which retain the status of bare (killable) life.[6] The point is powerfully illustrated by Wolfe's discussion of a decision made in 2008 by the Environmental Committee of the Spanish Parliament to grant basic rights to great apes, which he juxtaposes to statistics provided by the US Department of Agriculture that evidence the staggering number of factory farm animals – nine billion! – killed for food in the US in 2007 alone (BL 11–12).

What Derrida 'adds' to this biopolitical approach, on Wolfe's account, is not only a diagnosis of the sacrificial regimes of what Derrida calls 'carnophallogocentrism', but also 'the direct address he gives, alone in this group [of biopolitical thinkers], to . . . nonhuman animals as potential subjects of justice' (BL 102–3). To be sure, Derrida arguably pays far more attention than Agamben, Foucault and others to the existence and conditions of nonhuman animals. But, on Wolfe's account, the key contribution that Derrida makes with regard to biopolitical thought is his articulation of an 'ethical responsibility to animals' (BL 16) that is not premised on a juridical model of reciprocal rights and responsibilities. Rather, the thought of what we might call 'biopolitical justice' would, on Wolfe's reading, be grounded in a 'shared vulnerability and finitude . . . that forms the foundation of our compassion and impulse toward justice for animals' (BL 17). It's on the basis of this insight, then, that we would be able to question, for example, 'the extent to which certain animals, employed in factory farming or experimentation, may be seen in terms of the concept of bare or naked, unprotected life',[7] without thereby committing ourselves to the inescapably humanist, hence anthropocentric, language of legal rights.

This take on Derrida's rendering of suffering as foregrounding a compassionate ethics in the face of a vulnerable (animal) other finds considerable support not only in Derrida's text but in many commentaries on that work.[8] There is some cause, however, to wonder whether the ethical reading of Derrida's reference to Bentham – hence also the biopolitical position that reproduces that ethics – adequately accounts for what might be described as Derrida's subsequent questioning of the question. For Derrida follows his appeal to Bentham with a series of reflections that attend less to the fact or phenomenon of suffering as such than to the form of the question itself:

'Can they suffer?' asks Bentham, simply yet so profoundly.

Once its protocol is established, the form of this question changes everything ... The question is disturbed by a certain *passivity*. It bears witness, manifesting already, as question, the response that testifies to a sufferance, a passion, a not-being-able. The word *can* [*pouvoir*] changes sense and sign here once one asks, 'Can they suffer?' Henceforth it wavers. What counts at the origin of such a question is not only the idea of what transitivity or activity (being able to speak, to reason) refer to; what counts is rather what impels it toward this self-contradiction ... 'Can they suffer?' amounts to asking 'Can they *not be able*?' And what of this inability [*impouvoir*]? What of the vulnerability felt on the basis of this inability? What is this nonpower at the heart of power? What is its quality or modality? How should one take it into account? What right should be accorded to it? To what extent does it concern us? (A 27–8)

Having displaced reason for suffering, then, Derrida appears to displace in turn the phenomenon of suffering for a certain condition or structure of passivity: a nonpower at the heart of power. To be sure, Derrida's own use of the term 'vulnerability' would appear to confirm the ethical (and biopolitical) register of his argument, testifying to a double, asymmetrical passivity that functions as the locus of an obligation in the face of the suffering of others, the feeling of 'being bound' (*ob-ligare*) to an other 'laid low', an other affected by the operations of power or by the unaccountable event of a disaster.[9] But the questions that immediately follow this reference gesture at the possibility of reading the modality of the concept otherwise. For, '*once its protocol is established*', the form of the question '*changes everything*'. What might come, therefore, of reading this 'nonpower at the heart of power' *vis-à-vis* animals but beyond the biopolitical characterisation of nonpower as 'vulnerability'?

In view of this question, it is worth recalling that Derrida had already thematised a certain sense of passivity well before the original publications not only of Agamben's *Homo Sacer* (in 1995) but also Foucault's *The History of Sexuality* (in 1976).[10] Reading Saussure's account of the 'faculty of constructing a language' in *Of Grammatology*, for instance, Derrida sought to demonstrate the originary passivity of speech on the basis (as it were) of the thought of the trace and of differance, of 'the being-imprinted of the imprint'.[11] At stake in this reading is the 'subtle but absolutely decisive heterogeneity' between the sound of the spoken word and the sound-image, the 'being-heard' of the sound – the 'psychic imprint' or impression of the sound as received by or impressed upon an auditor – which alone constitutes the 'signifier' within the structure of the sign. This 'being-imprinted', for Derrida, testifies to the essential passivity of speech:

> The idea of the 'psychic imprint' ... relates essentially to the idea of articulation. Without the difference between the sensory appearing [*apparaissant*] and its lived appearing [*apparaitre*] ('mental imprint'), the temporalizing synthesis, which permits differences to appear in a chain of significations, could not operate. That the 'imprint' is irreducible means also that speech is originarily passive, but in a sense of passivity that all intramundane metaphors would only betray. This passivity is also the relationship to a past, to an always-already-there that no reactivation of the origin could fully master and awaken to presence.[12]

Thus the so-called power of speech is owed to 'the irreducibility of the always-already-there and the fundamental passivity that is called time'.[13] Here, a certain nonpower at the heart of power functions as the *play* of writing, which, Derrida writes, 'effac[es] the limit starting from which one had thought to regulate the circulation of signs' – an 'overwhelming [that] supervenes at the moment when the extension of the concept of language effaces all its limits'.[14]

In a piece written a few years later, Derrida goes on to characterise this play and passivity precisely as a fundamental 'powerlessness'. Reflecting on the relations between writing and power implied by the questions 'Who can write? What can writing do?'

Derrida immediately rejects the idea that writing simply *befalls* power, that it serves or complements power, a formula which 'excludes in advance the identification of writing *as* power or the recognition of power from the onset of writing'.[15] It is with the latter possibility, of course, that one might seek to challenge the logocentrism that always situates writing as a simple technique exterior to a more originary capacity for language. But Derrida goes further than noting this possibility, to register, with passing reference to the points from *Of Grammatology* just recounted, something even more surprising: 'what is astonishing', he says, 'is not writing as power but what comes, as if from within a structure, to limit it by a powerlessness or an effacement'.[16]

What is 'astonishing', in other words, is a certain nonpower at the heart of power – and at the moment in which Derrida here remarks on it, there is not an animal or vulnerable body in sight.

From this thought of power and powerlessness Derrida proceeds to affirm – not for the last time – a concept of power, as it were, that refuses the singular abstraction:

> There is not *one* power, *the* power of *the* mark. This singular would still lead to some mystification: fostering the belief that one can do otherwise than to oppose powers to powers and writings to other writings, or again that the unity of *power* (and of *knowledge*) is always itself, the same, wherever it is and whatever force it represents.
>
> But there are *powers, knowledges*, in every instance interlinked and linked to marking forces in a general agonistics.[17]

Here, the nod to Foucault, to his 'micro-physics of power' and earlier analyses of 'power/knowledge', seems obvious even if the reference remains unacknowledged.[18] But this nonsubstantialist account of a general agonistics of powers is already derivable, in any case, from Derrida's earlier thinking of difference. 'Force itself', Derrida writes in that now famous essay, 'is never present; it is only a play of differences and quantities. There would be no force in general without the difference between forces.'[19] A number of years later, moreover, Derrida elaborated on this point, expressing at the same time a 'sense of uneasiness' about using the terms 'power' and 'force'. This time, the reference to Foucault is explicitly made, and here it is worth citing Derrida at length:

> Even if, as Foucault seems to suggest, one no longer speaks of Power with a capital P, but of a scattered multiplicity of micropowers, the question remains of knowing what the unity of signification is that still permits us to call these decentralized and heterogenous microphenomena 'powers'. For my part, without being able to go much further here, I do not believe that one should agree to speak of 'force' or of 'power' except under three conditions, at least:
>
> A. That one takes account of the fact that there is never any thing called power or force, but only differences of power and of force, and that these differences are as qualitative as they are quantitative. In short, it seems to me that one must start, as Nietzsche doubtless did, from difference in order to accede to force and not vice versa.
> B. That, starting from this qualitatively differential thought, one opens oneself, in attempting to account for it, to this apparently perverse or paradoxical possibility: the ostensibly greater forces can also be the 'lesser' (or the 'strongest' force is not 'strongest' but 'weakest', which supposes the essential possibility of an inversion of meaning, that is to say, a mutation of meaning not limited to the semantics of discourse or the dictionary but which also 'produces' itself as history).
> C. That one takes into account, consequently, all the paradoxes and ruses of force, of power, of mastery, as traps in which these ruses cannot avoid being caught up.[20]

On the surface, these three conditions go a long way towards articulating in other terms the 'principles for analyzing power' that Foucault outlines in *The History of Sexuality*.[21] But Derrida's references to 'the unity of signification' and to a 'mutation' and an 'inversion' of the meaning of power, force, and so on, without necessarily registering or enacting a 'critique' of Foucault's 'theory', nevertheless signal a complication that has direct bearing on the problem of reading Derrida's 'nonpower at the heart of power'.[22] Far from constituting a simple 'reduction of discursive practices to textual traces' or a privileging of 'relations of meaning' over 'relations of power' as another Foucault might have retorted,[23] Derrida's remark points to the problem of identifying the very 'object' at stake, and therefore of accounting for the very thing one had set out to analyse. Circumscribing a heterogeneity of microphenomena as so many forms or instances or relations *of* power presumes a certain unity of signification – however open or nebulous it may be – by which such phenomena may be characterised *as* power(s). But this unity of signification itself constitutes an element of force, hence an element in the relations of force being brought under the power of the analytical or theoretical gaze, and so the theorisation already compromises, by exercising 'its own' force over or within, what it theorises. The paradoxical reversibility and mutability of which Derrida speaks, therefore, refer not just to reversals of power relations and the inevitability of resistance, but moreover to a reversibility of the 'meaning' of power, such that (for instance) deployments of given concepts of power – however heterogeneous and differential such concepts conceive power to be – always run the risk of falling into the trap of power (of mastery, for example) by overlooking something *other than* power, or something other than what one may currently or historically identify by the term 'power'.

Investing in these caveats not just a cautionary but also a 'productive' significance, it becomes possible to suggest – as an initial, provisional hypothesis – that the passivity, the 'nonpower at the heart of power', that Derrida speaks of in *The Animal That Therefore I Am*, might thus be understood to name not the vulnerability of the animal (whether 'human' or 'nonhuman'), or at least not merely such a vulnerability. Instead – or in addition – 'nonpower' might, on the basis of the preceding hauntology, be read as Derrida's name for the differantial condition in which power is originarily divided and delayed, referred and relayed, such that power is always owed to an absolute, irrecoverable 'past', and always haunted by something extraneous both to the semantics and to the history of power. From this perspective, if 'one can write' (to return to the example used by Derrida in his earlier discussion of writing and power), this power can be understood not as one's own, not as a capacity possessed by anyone or anything, but rather as manifesting as the effect of a set of conflictual and divergent conditions – institutional, economic, technological, but also psycho-bio-graphical, anthropological and even evolutionary – that 'produce' this possibility. Accordingly, the 'not-being-able', the 'inability' (or *impouvoir*), named 'nonpower' would be attributable neither to a simple fact of an oppression – a 'power-over' – exerted by one (individual, class, species) over another, nor even strictly speaking to an essential 'lack' of capacity – or, at least, not a lack that would constitute an innate trait of a *specific* form of life. Rather, this nonpower would be attributable to – would in fact 'constitute' or 'channel' – this anterior dispersion of power, or the dispersion from which a force differential may produce something like a capacity, a competence or a possibility. As this example of writing as a capacity or competence already indicates, then, the power(s) at stake in Derrida's various deployments of that 'concept' have, from the beginning as it were, always included those relating not just to forms of 'repressive' power but also (and already) those relating to forms, operations or events of 'productive' power, encompassing even those moments of pulsion that might otherwise be referred to as 'agency'. Indeed, understood in the terms just elaborated, Derrida's 'nonpower' might be taken as 'animating' the very phenomenon of *ipseity*, marking the very structure of every form of 'I can'. It would be for *this* reason, therefore, and not simply for the purpose of avoiding 'human exceptionalism', that Derrida insists in *The Animal That Therefore I Am* that the question of the animal 'is *not just* a matter of asking whether one has the right to refuse the animal such and such a power . . . It *also* means asking whether what calls itself human has the right rigorously to attribute to man, which means therefore to attribute to himself, what he refuses the animal' (A 135).

The problem of ipseity, of the power or possibility announced by the form 'I can', thus constitutes the thread by which a point of connection may be established between Derrida's early work on writing and not only his first extended speculation on the question of the animal but also his later engagement with the 'political' problem of sovereignty, as developed in *Rogues* and in the two volumes of *The Beast and the Sovereign*. For early on in *Rogues*, Derrida links the problem of sovereignty precisely to the question of ipseity:

> By *ipseity* I ... wish to suggest some 'I can', or at the very least the power that *gives itself* its own law, its force of law, its self-representation, the sovereign and reappropriating gathering of self in the simultaneity of an assemblage or assembly, being together, or 'living together', as we say ... Each time I say *ipse*, *metipse*, or *ipseity* ... I thus wish to suggest the oneself [*soi-même*], the 'self-same [*même*]' of the 'self [*soi*]' ... as well as the power, potency, sovereignty, or possibility implied in every 'I can.'[24]

Pursuing the implications of what can now be recognised as the 'nonpower at the heart' of *ipseity*, a series of conceptual developments, mutations to the meaning of 'power', may present themselves for elaboration or intensification. First, notwithstanding Derrida's frequent recourse to the language of 'sovereignty', the 'power' at stake in any 'I can' becomes irreducible to a simple expression of *freedom* or *authority* – 'I can' in the sense of 'I am free, I have the authority' – but would remain divided and relayed by the apparent presence or absence of a capacity, competence or potentiality – 'I am capable' – even to the point of expressing a contingency, the possibility of a possibility: 'I can' in the form of 'it is possible, it may be possible'.

Second, a process or analysis, which a few decades ago might have been called the 'deconstruction' or 'dismantling' of the sovereign (human) subject – via Foucauldian archaeologies of the human sciences and genealogies of disciplinary power, say – comes to be applicable to forms of life more generally. If ipseity can name 'the sovereign and reappropriating gathering of self in the simultaneity of an assemblage or assembly', that is, the possible referents of 'I can', the deictic 'I' or *'autos'* itself, can therefore be understood as exceeding the members of the human species, to include perhaps every form of agency imaginable under the form of 'it can'. At its limit, such a conception of ipseity would extend far beyond even 'animal ipseity', perhaps excluding only that which could be subsumed unequivocally under the form of 'it cannot not'.[25] To the extent that ipseity remains owed to the fundamental passivity and differential relay of forces called 'nonpower', moreover, the *extension* of the concept of ipseity to nonhuman organisms would constitute at the same time a *questioning* of the 'self-sameness' of those forms of life. As Derrida remarks, when challenging the apparent distinction between (free) response and (programmed) reaction: 'it suffices as a minimal requisite to take into account the divisibility, multiplicity, or difference of forces in a living being, whatever it be, in order to admit that there is no finite living being (a-human or human) which is not structured by the force-differential between which a tension, if not a contradiction, is bound to localize – or localize itself within – different agencies, of which some resist others, oppress or suppress others'.[26] On this account, the apparently given capacities, competencies or potentialities of animals, for example, whether taken as a particular species or as individuals, would be understood as manifesting as such by virtue of a certain force-differential that is owed to a passivity or nonpower at the heart of power.

Thirdly, and consequently, these forms of 'ipseity' would not be the property of the living organism in question – the simple expression of an innate, 'inborn' faculty – but would be dispersed or distributed across – would be owed to – so many 'outsides', such that the powers and possibilities of a 'living being' owe their effectuality (or ineffectuality, for that matter) to any number of factors, conditions, environments. Here it is not a case of simple reaction or determination, of course – of behaviours and actions being the calculable effect of external but uniform forces or conditions – but rather one of a less determinate 'indissociability' of what is otherwise imagined as 'inside' and 'outside'. Hence Derrida's specification, in the second volume of *The Beast and the Sovereign*, when he reflects briefly on the structure of auto-affection and self-determination *vis-à-vis* the relations between historical, technoscientific and economic conditions of invention:

> Beyond ... relations of causality or induction, I am thinking, rather, of a structural configuration, both historical and genetic, in which ... everything that can happen to the *autos* is indissociable from what happens *in the world* through the prostheticization of an ipseity which at once divides that ipseity, dislocates it, and inscribes it outside itself *in the world*, the world being precisely what cannot be reduced here, any more than one can reduce *tekhnē* or reduce it to a pure *physis*.[27]

Such a structural configuration of ipseity, in which 'there is no ipseity without this prostheticity in the world',[28] in which the 'can happen' of the '*autos*' is indissociable from what happens in the world – this structural configuration speaks of the possibility of examining the prosthetic operations of power with respect to their role not only in bringing about animal suffering or vulnerability, but also in producing forms of animal behaviour, capacity, response, action and even invention. On this basis it becomes possible to recognise that what an animal (nonhuman or otherwise) 'can' do, whether or not an animal 'can' *respond*, for instance, remains contingent upon an array of external factors, conditions and forces that are irreducible to the operations of a faculty that is imagined to be 'inborn'. And 'external' here means environmental *and* institutional (and perhaps more besides), given the extent to which animal existence today remains shaped by the social and economic inventions of anthropos – farming practices, scientific research, veterinary medicine, pollution, hunting, housing, animal welfare legislation, and so much more. But, as I argued in Chapter 1, while the political effects of such socio-historical accomplishments are undoubtedly significant, the institutional conditions underpinning forms of animal existence need not in themselves be taken as simply 'human'. For the thought of power at stake here is one articulated to a deconstructive concept of 'institution', one which 'disturbs' 'the opposition of nature and institution, of *physis* and *nomos*', and which observes 'the iterability of the *mark* beyond all human speech acts'.[29] In that sense, the 'institutionality' of animal ipseity, as explored in Chapter 2, might be seen in the economy of habit and in the iterability and appropriability, hence conventionality, of forms of animal conduct, modes of organisation and interanimal (or interagential) relationships. What we have taken to thinking of as 'institutional power', that is, might now, on the basis of Derrida's 'nonpower' and the consequent deconstruction of ipseity, be understood as a 'qualitatively differential', 'paradoxical' and reversible form or moment of *zoopower*. And what is otherwise thought of as 'vulnerability' would, in turn, be understood as the very condition of action, response, invention. Indeed, vulnerability – taken in the sense, perhaps, of susceptibility, hence of receptiveness and sustainability – would be the condition for being able to do anything at all: for, as Derrida has put it, 'there is no affect without life . . . that *power to be affected* called life'.[30]

In view of such an account of zoopower, it becomes possible to return to the ethical reading of Derrida's 'nonpower' with which we began and to identify in it the operation of something like a *ruse* of power – the *lure* or the *allure*, that is, of the language of 'vulnerability'. Multifaceted, the ruse pulls and pushes, attacks and attracts. It exerts or enacts, *on the one hand*, a double reduction, *confining* (by defining) the significance of 'nonpower' or 'passivity' to a given organism's condition of vulnerability, potentially reducing the latter in turn to pure incapacitation, a state of absolute jeopardy: a self-same body whose autonomy remains ceaselessly exposed to what is nevertheless characterised as the *gratuitous* operation of violence. But as a hauntological tracing of Derrida's remarks on (zoo)power suggests, in such references to compassion and suffering may lie the jaws of a trap. That's not to say that there isn't more than a little textual warrant in *The Animal That Therefore I Am* for reading Derrida's remarks on nonpower as a matter of vulnerability: the ethical aura of his argument is sustained not only by his direct references to vulnerability (A 28, 107), but also his remarks on compassion, anguish and pity (A 28–9), as well as his subsequent reading of Levinas and the ethics of response (A 105–18). And so association of Derrida's nonpower with vulnerability cannot be construed as a simple misreading, as an interpretation lacking in sufficient attention to Derrida's text. Indeed, those recent accounts, such as Wolfe's, that draw out from Derrida's work an ethics of compassion and a sense of the heteronomic force of justice, sit alongside some of the finest and sharpest, not to mention most inspiring, commentaries on deconstruction. That the language of vulnerability nevertheless asserts itself – even in the careful reading of a philosophy that is in turn so attuned to the violence and variability of meaning – testifies, *on the other hand*, to that language's *seductiveness*, to its exceedingly attractive force. It testifies, that is, to the enthralling power of a certain discourse of power 'itself' – a power which can be seen to affect the assessment of biopolitics more broadly, as is perhaps evidenced by the conclusion to Wolfe's powerful reflection on humans and animals in a biopolitical frame:

> What is useful about biopolitical thought is that it puts us in a position to articulate the disjunctive and uneven quality of our own political moment, constituted as it is by new forces and new actors not very legible by the political vocabulary of sovereignty we have inherited, enabling us to see not just the dramatic, affirmative shift announced by the Spanish Parliament's decision [in 2008 to grant basic rights to Great Apes], but also . . . [to see] that that decision is shadowed, indeed haunted, by the mechanized killing of billions of animals each year . . . [in] a 'war' on our fellow creatures. The biopolitical point is no longer 'human' vs.

'animal'; the biopolitical point is a newly expanded community of the living and the concern we should all have with where violence and immunitary protection fall within it. (BL 104–5)

What is noteworthy about this conclusion to *Before the Law* is not that Wolfe doesn't recognise the extent to which specific forms of animal behaviour or response are conditioned by a multiplicity of force differentials, which remain irreducible both to the imagined automaticity of Descartes's 'animal-machine' and to the pure incapacitation so regularly implied by the language of vulnerability. On the contrary, he affirms an account of animal behaviour and capacity that is consistent with the deconstructive concept of institutionality implied by the thought of zoopower. His account of various conceptions of biopolitical power highlights, moreover, the idea – albeit attributed to 'Foucault's reorientation of the problem' of power (BL 34), rather than Derrida's – that 'a potentially creative, aleatory element . . . inheres in the very gambit of biopower' (BL 32). As a consequence Wolfe underscores the fact 'that "resistance" and "freedom" are not to be thought of as constitutively on the order of "persons" or agents in the traditional sense . . . but rather of forces and bodies that only partially coincide with what we used to call the "subject"' (BL 33–4). And, in this way, he is far from incognisant of the 'rhetorical glare of terms like "freedom" and "power"' (BL 37). But if biopolitical thought thus enables the identification of forms of force or agency that exceed the political vocabulary of sovereignty, if that thought thereby gives rise to 'a new, more nuanced reconceptualization of political effectivity' (BL 34), the biopolitical point – 'what is *useful* about biopolitical thought' – nevertheless seems always to come back to the possibility of a biopolitical justice that is imaginable only in terms of *protection*.

Here the problem centres on the extent to which the language of vulnerability ties analyses premised on the principle or promise of biopolitical justice to what Derrida calls, with reference to Carl Schmitt, a pessimistic anthropology. For Schmitt, as Derrida remarks, 'the only theories of politics worthy of the name are based on ... a vision of man as bad, corrupt, dangerous, fearful, or violent'.[31] Hence Schmitt's identification of the friend-enemy distinction as the basis of all politics. Hence too his strong approbation of the political philosophy of Hobbes – 'truly a powerful and systematic thinker' – whose *protego ergo obligo* and *bellum omnium contra omnes* capture, in Schmitt's view, the reality of the friend-enemy distinction.[32] It is a fear of the enemy, and the fear of being made the enemy, on this account, that makes the citizen obey the state. The very guarantee of protection harbours within it the threat of violence, in other words, since as Schmitt notes, it is the protector who 'decides who the enemy is by virtue of the eternal relation of protection and obedience'.[33] It is for this reason, moreover, that Derrida imagines 'a conceptual genealogy of terrorism' that would include 'all the political theories that have made fear or panic (and so terror or terrorism as knowing-how to make fear reign) an essential and structural mainspring of ... submission or political subjection'.[34] After all, it is only too possible for the protector to exercise violence on the protected precisely in the name of protection – which is, of course, exactly the kind of scenario that Wolfe has in mind when he remarks that 'to live under biopolitics is to live in a situation in which we are all always already (potential) "animals" before the law' (BL 10).[35]

By the same token, and as already suggested, even when sovereign power – in the form of the juridico-political state – isn't exercising such violence in this manifest way, the language or discourse of vulnerability and protection from violence may be seen to carry out its own form of violence: in the reduction, that is, of the referent of that language to the status of perpetual victim. On Antonio Negri's account, this is particularly true of Agamben's theory of the sovereign exception and the inclusion-through-its-exclusion of 'bare life'. In Negri's view, 'the nature of power' for Agamben is such that, 'in the final instance, power reduces each and every human being to such a state of powerlessness'. But 'to conceive of the relation between power and life in such a way actually ends up bolstering and reinforcing ideology ... Isn't this the story about power that power itself would like us to believe in and reiterate?'[36] What's more, the language of (sovereign) power evoked here – a language which awaits the discourse and politics of (animal) protection like a trap – lays out a stark image of power as something that only human animals (or some human animals) wield and which nonhuman animals can, at best, only ever resist. To that extent, it's unclear how far critical, political, even biopolitical accounts of animal existence are able to go towards evading inscription, alongside all the other political theories premised on a pessimistic anthropology, within Derrida's proposed genealogy of terrorism.

Clearly it would be disingenuous in the extreme to deny the massive suffering, torment and extermination inflicted on animals by present practices of carnophallogocentrism, and so equally disingenuous to deny the force of the call for biopolitical justice inscribed within the vulnerability of the animal other. And if the question of power *vis-à-vis* animals seems invariably posed in terms of the exercise of human (sovereign) power over (vulnerable) animals, this is surely owed in considerable part to the indisputable fact of the near complete monopolisation of power over nonhuman animals acquired by *non*-nonhuman animals through a long and ongoing history of human exceptionalism and through the corresponding institution of carnophallogocentric regimes. But if the politics aimed at reducing animal suffering can be seen as acceding to the ideological effects (to use Negri's terminology) of the language of vulnerability, and in that sense as participating in the production of (animal) powerlessness, then the attempt to think through the question of animals and power confronts something of a challenge. For today, as David Farrell Krell has remarked, the 'pessimistic view of humankind *rules*, and that is its attraction: it has power; it is *in* power . . . [It] dominates so much of our public and private lives, whether we look left or right, that we do not know where we might go to find an *optimistic* anthropology, one that could undergird a democracy to come.'[37] There is, of course, no question here of rejecting the pessimistic disposition in favour of an unbridled optimism that would accordingly find no need to support, for example, the institution of measures to protect animals from unaccountable cruelty and violence. But if, as Krell suggests, 'one wants to resist the identification of political life ... at every level ... with fear and aggression',[38] then the principle of biopolitical justice and protection would have to form only one basis to a political thought that hopes to attend to the question of the animal.

At different times in his engagement with Derrida's discussions of animals and animality, Wolfe is quite explicit about the extent to which Derrida's nonpower refers to a more radical conception of passivity than that usually implied by the term vulnerability. In these moments he is careful to distinguish between two senses of passivity and vulnerability in Derrida's thought: the first being the frequently acknowledged 'ethical' sense; the second referring to 'our subjection to a radically ahuman technicity or mechanicity of language'.[39] And so if, on Wolfe's account, 'what Derrida adds' to the biopolitical approach is his analysis of carnophallogocentrism and affirmation of animals as subjects of justice, and not his more radical rethinking of (non)power as such, the curtailed nature of this contribution speaks less to the inadequacies either of Derrida's philosophy or of Wolfe's reading of that philosophy than to the force of the biopolitical frame itself. It speaks to the delimiting effects, that is, of that frame's predominant focus on the question of violence and immunitary protection, hence its presumption that, in the last instance, the only power that counts, (bio)politically speaking, is power 'over' life. As Wolfe remarks early in *Before the Law*: 'framing decides what we recognize and what we don't, what counts and what doesn't' (BL 6). And while he speaks at this point of a biopolitical frame understood (after Heidegger) in a quasi-ontological sense, his observation holds as well for biopolitics understood as an analytical or theoretical apparatus. What's at stake here, then, is a variability in the frame of reference, and the possibility of looking beyond biopolitics, or of underscoring other developments within biopolitics, in order to begin to imagine another form of analysis, a zoopolitics, perhaps, that seeks (after Krell) to avoid identifying the politics of animality 'with fear and aggression' 'at every level'.[40]

In this regard, the thought of zoopower as the dispersal of ipseity – as the prostheticisation of the capacity or the *possibility* otherwise expressed in the form 'I can' or 'it can' – may present itself as another, supplementary point of focus within (or beyond) such a framework. Thus where a familiar model of domestication, for instance, might depict a situation in which the lives of animals are subjected to the human animal's will and sovereign power – in which animals are deprived of a natural existence and made to submit to the organisation and imperatives of factory farming, say – the thought of zoopower could attend to a longer and certainly a more differential history in which human-animal interactions can be read for moments of mutual transformation, of convergence and co-creation, of resistance and reversal, of habituation and invention, as much as of obedience and exploitation.[41] The very form of the question would subsequently change or multiply. The analytical task would no longer be confined to assessing and responding to the biopolitical injustice that a history and an economy of domestication has had on the lives of animals. Beyond this focus – though certainly not simply in opposition to it – the question of the animal, the thought of the animal-to-come, might seek after the ways in which the accomplishments – the evolutionary and social accomplishments – of different animal collectives have enabled (for example) the domestication of the human animal. Indeed, how have they enabled quite *divergent* modes and scenes of domestication to emerge? For there is much that distinguishes the domesticity of the city household from that of the rural farm, and both of these from that of the nomadic flock.

In the first instance, then, such an approach to scenes of domestication might begin to differentiate and elaborate the operations of power by attending to the sort of minute eruptions and relations of force that Foucault sought to thematise in *Discipline and Punish* with his proposed micro-physics of power. Here, power is conceived as 'a network of relations, constantly in tension, in activity, rather than a privilege that one might possess', such that its 'effects of domination are attributed not to "appropriation", but to dispositions, manoeuvres, tactics, techniques, functionings'.[42] Rather than being simply 'repressive', power is understood to 'invest', differentially, those through which and on which it operates, and to do so via 'innumerable points of confrontation, focuses of instability, each of which has its own risks of conflict, of struggles and of an at least temporary inversion of the power relations'.[43] Understood in these terms, domestication would present not as a straightforward relation of domination or exploitation – a simple 'power-over' – but as something more like a *strategy* deployed in contrasting ways and to varying effects in different contexts.

In their manifestation as strategy, moreover, forces of domestication would inevitably encounter forms of resistance and entail processes of negotiation. In this regard, Jocelyne Porcher's sociologies of commercial dairy farming stand out as exemplary for their attention to such complexities.[44] Porcher's main interest lies in what it might mean to think of the cows' participation in the activities of dairy farming as *work*. While operations such as commercial farming might, from one perspective, be taken as the paradigmatic scene of animal exploitation, for Porcher the question of animal work 'obliges one to consider animals as other than victims or natural and cultural idiots that need to be liberated despite themselves'[45] – and this because, at the very least, 'cows *do* things: they take decisions and initiatives; they facilitate or complicate the farmer's work'.[46] Indeed, by observing the movements and behaviours of cows both in routine and unusual situations on a commercial dairy farm, Porcher manages to identify not only the tactics and stratagems employed by individual cows in response to the directions or expectations (the 'rules') of the farmer – sometimes anticipating expectations, sometimes resisting them, at other times observing and learning new protocols – but also those deployed in relation to other cows with a view to maintaining social peace, observing or subverting hierarchy, confirming relations of friendship or enmity, and more. And in this way Porcher is able to make *visible* the otherwise invisible work that livestock performs. As Vinciane Despret puts it in her discussion of Porcher's studies:

> When everything runs well, one doesn't see the work ... Everything has the look of something that functions or of a simple *mechanical* obedience ... It is only during conflicts where the order is disrupted ... that one begins to see, or rather to translate differently, these situations where everything functions. Everything functions because [the cows] have done everything so that everything functions. Periods without conflict, then, are no longer natural, obvious, or mechanical, for they in fact require from the cows a total activity of pacification where they make compromises, groom one another, and offer polite gestures to one another.[47]

What appears on the surface to be a scene of simple domination or exploitation, in other words, is revealed as a site of 'innumerable points of confrontation', to use Foucault's terms – not a simple act of appropriation but a more complicated play of moments of zoopower: 'dispositions, manoeuvres, tactics, techniques, functionings'. And the scene plays out in this way notwithstanding the fact that the nonhuman animals live in a 'totally human-made' world, such that 'the living conditions of animals and their behaviors clearly appear to be embedded in a working relationship'.[48] Crucially, moreover, what's in evidence here is a zoopower that manifests not simply in or as a capacity for resistance, but also in and as certain forms of action or initiative, belying the Cartesian view of the animal-machine as well as any hypothesis of absolute submission to heteronomy.[49] Undoubtedly, these capacities to resist, to act and to create are owed in part to certain operations of disciplinary power – or perhaps a governmental 'conduct of conducts', to use another of Foucault's fertile formulations[50] – underscoring again the fact that the prosthetic form of animal ipseity is inscribed within institutional as much as evolutionary conditions. But they speak also to the extent to which processes of domestication not only depend upon a degree of cooperation on the part of animal agents, but also enable and entail inventiveness and ingenuity on the part of those same agents.

It is this possibility or sense of inventiveness that Donna Haraway is keen to highlight in her provocative account of the relations of domestication enacted or produced through her partnership with Australian shepherd Cayenne and their participation in the sport of agility. Her autoethnographic reading of the agility performances she and her canine partner engage in is significant in the first instance for its attention to her partner's *investment* in the sport.[51] The apparently hierarchical nature of the handler-dog relationship is thus transformed into a more complex, less one-sided interplay of expectations, interests and recognition. *Qua* competitive team sport, agility events demand investment of different, highly refined forms of authority on the part of each participant, as well as a high degree of trust in each other's capacity to play their part and to demonstrate the appropriate behaviour. These behaviours are the product of a long and involved training programme, to be sure. But where others might see in agility drills a 'human training "of" another critter' (WSM 222), Haraway sees in her workouts with Cayenne a 'training together', a perspective which allows her to attend to the subtleties of the relations between power and behaviour (WSM 207). Indeed, the very techniques developed to facilitate such training – in particular, positive reinforcement: the delivery of 'an appropriate reward to the behaving organism with a timing that will make a difference' (WSM 211) – are themselves indicative of and responsive to the intricacies of conduct and responsiveness as such. Drawing insight from the effectivity of such positive training methods, Haraway thus arrives at an account of behaviour that is attentive to its conventional, institutional – or, in her terms, 'natural-technical' – status:

> A behavior is not something just out there in the world waiting for discovery; a behavior is an inventive construction, a generative fact-fiction, put together by an intra-acting crowd of players that include people, organisms, and apparatuses all coming together in the history of animal psychology. From the flow of bodies moving in time, bits are carved out and solicited to

become more or less frequent as part of building other patterns of motion through time. (WSM 211)

The passive form of this last construction ('bits are carved out and solicited') perhaps speaks to the nonpower at the heart of behaviour formation, signalling the extent to which training is irreducible to the application of a formal set of procedures aimed at cultivating specific aptitudes, but can be read further as a constitutive dimension of the most basic forms of experience, interaction and development. But this radical passivity would therefore also signal the play of differences and qualities that inevitably characterise the site or process of disciplinary power. In the case of agility training, for example, the liver cookies that serve as rewards in early stages of training are made to function as tricks or distractions in later moments, and are eventually made redundant altogether, such that – as Haraway observes in respect of Cayenne – the agility run itself becomes the 'chief positive reinforcement' (WSM 220). This end result is, of course, the very objective and *fruition* of training as a strategic regimen, and thus the most visible sign of the efficacy of disciplinary power. But it is also a mark of the *essential* mutability of interest, desire, satisfaction, pleasure, disposition, behaviour and, ultimately, capability. And if a history of human exceptionalism can be said to have exploited or animated that mutability in particular, narrowly defined ways – via projects and practices of 'domestication' (of nonhuman animals), on the one hand, and of 'civilisation' (of human animals), on the other – then challenges to that form of anthropocentrism might begin as much from the pursuit of qualitatively different forms of engagement with the productivity of zoopower as from critical reassessment of the biopolitical sites of immunitary protection.

It is in this sense, then, that Haraway's account of what we might call (in all senses of the term) the *adventitious* nature of 'training-with' draws out some of the implications of thinking the animal-to-come, understood now as a differential engagement of or with the potentials of zoopower:

> The coming into being of something unexpected, something new and free, something outside the rules of function and calculation, something not ruled by the logic of the reproduction of the same, *is* what training with each other is about. That, I believe, is one of the meanings of *natural* that the trained people and dogs I know practise. Training requires calculation, method, discipline, science, but training is for opening up what is not known to be possible, but might be, for all the intra-acting partners. Training is, or can be, about differences not tamed by taxonomy. (WSM 223)

It is hard to imagine an account of the nature of training that could be further from a conventional view of the operations of disciplinary 'power-over' in the 'training-of' directed at a vulnerable, docile body. Against the thought of training as the production of a determined outcome, Haraway here attends to the divided nature of its effects, to the point that discipline in the sense of regimen and strict reproduction serves as a basis for generating unexpected difference. And where disciplinary power is, even after Foucault, all too frequently understood to issue from a power-*full* centre, to be exercised over or on a submissive or (at best) resistant other, Haraway's account of training attends to its dimensions of interactivity, collaboration and exchange, such that the powers of training effect a mutual transformation. Training, in these senses, occurs in and as the very antithesis of training.

Recalling Derrida's caveats concerning the analysis of power, we might say that Haraway reveals the perverse or paradoxical possibilities of disciplinary power, the inversion or mutation of the very meanings of domestication, training and taming. To the extent that such inversions would exceed 'the semantics of discourse or the dictionary',[52] we should not be surprised if it turns out that the traces of this mutability are not limited to the particular scenarios of agility training that serve as Haraway's primary context of investigation, but rather can be seen in the broader 'production' of those traces in and as history. The historical dynamics of domestication can thus be understood not only to have given form to particular modes of human and animal existence but also to remain as a 'reserve' from which may be derived as yet unconsidered possibilities for future arrangements. Indeed, as Peter Sloterdijk has remarked:

> historians of culture have made it clear that with domesticity the relationship between men and animals changed. With the taming of men by their houses the age of pets began as well. Their attachment to houses is not only a question of civilizing, but also a matter of direction and upbringing.[53]

Sloterdijk's focus is on the role of humanism in the 'taming' of men and the 'breeding' of good citizens – as part of an ongoing battle against forces of 'bestialisation' – but his passing reference to the 'civilising' influence of pets offers an intriguing image of domestication as a form of mutual, if nevertheless uneven, transformation. Such cohabitation speaks, in other words, to a co-creation of the very figures of 'the (domesticated) human' and 'the (domesticated) animal', foregrounding the possibility that it is not just 'our relation' to animals that is subject to historical transformation, but along with it the very forms and potentialities of (animal) existence 'as such'.[54] Thus where Sloterdijk, following Heidegger, concerns himself only with the domestication of humanity – and, ultimately, the 'bestialisation' of 'man' – we might also see in this history, not the 'civilisation' of animals, to be sure, but rather a somewhat less programmatic adaptation or acculturation of diverse *animalities*.

While the seemingly epochal character of this event perhaps invites research into 'the adventure of humanization'[55] – if not also into instances of convergent evolution[56] – the multidimensional and constitutive nature of domestication can be illustrated on smaller timescales and with reference to more recent endeavours. One particularly illuminating example can be drawn from Dominique Lestel's unique reading of experimental research into the linguistic capacities of nonhuman hominids. As Lestel notes, there have been numerous expressions of scientific scepticism about research results that appear to demonstrate impressive communicative abilities on the part of bonobos (such as the famous Kanzi) and chimpanzees. As might be anticipated following the discussion of animal culture in Chapter 2, at issue in these calls for doubt is whether results obtained have been compromised by the very presence of humans in the experimental situation, and whether the communicative acts performed by the apes can be acceptably likened to human language use. In contrast to such injunctions to institute the apparatus of scientific objectivity, Lestel proposes an anthropological approach which focuses not on the extent to which 'the "language" of the primate can be similar to that of the human' but on

> knowing how particular cultural and institutional organizations allow human beings to modify profoundly the animal's cognitive competencies. The talking ape is first of all an 'acculturated' ape who has been integrated into particular communities: hybrid communities of humans and animals in their division of meanings, interests and affects.[57]

For Lestel, in other words, arguments that the research proves nothing about hominids' 'natural' capacities for communication overlook the rather remarkable achievements evidenced and produced by the experimental situation itself. That situation is one in which 'human beings domesticate the chimpanzee by means of an institutional and physical apparatus', while the 'chimpanzee, by contrast, domesticates human beings by putting them to its service' (HCD 13). Undoubtedly the power to domesticate in this scenario is asymmetrical, and access to domesticatory opportunities is unevenly distributed. But the exercise of power can hardly be said to operate simply in one direction, if only because the human carer, 'for reasons which are specifically human – those of scientific research – is nearly always predisposed to grant the chimpanzee a great deal of satisfaction' (HCD 14). As a consequence, the chimpanzee 'gains access to services that it would never aspire to without its interactions with the human beings, who, for their part, depend professionally on these primates' (HCD 13). And out of this transactional, biopolitical hybrid community something else arises: a kind of 'cognitive innovation' (HCD 13) that consists less in the *demonstration* of 'natural' 'inborn' competencies, than in the *acquisition*, rather, of new ones.

In such cognitive innovations we can catch another glimpse of the distributed prostheticisation of ipseity, of the divided externality of the capacity or the possibility otherwise expressed in the form 'I can' or 'it can'. What the chimpanzees 'can' do, what they 'can' experience, is 'indissociable from what happens *in the world*' – a predominantly human-made world, to be sure – 'through the prostheticization of an ipseity which at once divides that ipseity, dislocates it, and inscribes it outside itself'.[58] Their capacities, competencies, potentialities, in other words, do not take shape as an expression of an inner nature, so much as await activation, organisation and development via specific relations to the differential element of exteriority in general. As Lestel explains:

> The chimpanzee is unable to provoke and direct this innovation itself. A human being takes charge of this operation. The chimpanzee is thus exploiting in conjunction human representations, human actions and the human ability to trigger cognitive change in the chimpanzee.
>
> Chimpanzees turn the cognitive capacities of human beings to their advantage; they profit from human representations, actions and language. In other words, they use human cognitive competencies to transform their own. The human being becomes a form of cognitive prosthesis. (HCD 13)

Thus dispersed and prosthetic, the ipseity of the animals in question here operates via the external circuits of a textural-institutional, natural-technical animal-machine. Capacities, behaviours, sovereignty over action – all appear as such in their division, dislocation and inscription within the configurations and operations of different cultural and institutional spaces.

The same holds, moreover, for the human members of this hybrid community, and indeed for the various actors in other situations. Human agents, their own ipseity inscribed within external relations, exercise at most an imperfect monopolisation of control over the processes of domestication in such spaces, and so the possibility of exception, resistance, innovation and transformation remains ineradicable. Between highly regulated contexts and those more oriented towards enabling forms of initiative and interaction the degrees and forms of autonomy and action on the part of (animal) agents undoubtedly vary significantly. Understood as sites or scenes of zoopower and re-read as moments within a hauntology of the animal-to-come, however, such processes and practices of domestication may give to thought the chance to imagine and to cultivate another sense of the politics of animality, one premised less on protection from the power of anthropocentric authority than on the nonpower at the heart of all power. To the extent that it would not only allow for forms of 'nonpower' understood as vulnerability, but also recognise – perhaps even *enable* – forms of animal action, hence accomplishment, creativity and inventiveness, the thought of zoopower would work towards developing new ways both of understanding and of establishing 'a multiplicity of organizations of the relations between living and dead' (A 31). It would work towards the hauntological production of 'new forms of action, practice, organization'[59] that may invest in (animal) life the potential to surprise, to invent and thereby to challenge existing ways of thinking about and engaging with animals, nonhuman or otherwise. Such a thought of zoopower, in other words, would work towards a transformation of the *animal-machine* in which the existential possibilities of animalities of varying kinds take shape.

In pursuing that task, the analysis of zoopower will, no doubt, find cause to appeal to traditions of political thought that diverge from the pessimistic anthropology that underpins Schmitt, Hobbes and Agamben, finding novel uses for forms of thought that perhaps avoid even the language and the institutions of political sovereignty, be it a sovereignty of the state over its population or a sovereignty of 'man's dominion' over animals. Whether such a focus could still amount to a politics undoubtedly depends a great deal on what we understand the term 'politics' to designate. Faced with the indisputable fact of animal suffering on an industrial scale, this alternative zoopolitics is perhaps unlikely to bring home the ethical challenge presented by that situation with all the force demonstrated by Wolfe's biopolitical account, for example. And so it should go without saying that it would not be a case of deciding between the two perspectives, or of convincing ourselves that the phenomena taken as indicative of animal action, response or inventiveness are not already implicated in complicated sacrificial regimes. It could not be a question, that is, of believing that in the signs of 'zoopower-from-below', so to speak, are not already the makings of a trap or a ruse of power.

We might expect, nevertheless, that a form of analysis premised on a concept of zoopower would countenance a disseminative reinterpretation of the animating terms of biopolitics – the concepts of vulnerability, welfare, protection, sacrifice, say – and a reinterpretation of their influence, in turn, on the reception of attempts to establish radically different protocols for engaging with the *question* of power – as a question, for instance, of 'nonpower'. But further, or concomitantly, such analysis might enable a reinterpretation of the spheres in which animal lives are understood to be at stake, seeking to reveal in such spheres the forms and conditions of animal action in and on the so-called human world, phenomena that otherwise remain concealed by an anthropocentric account of history and politics, but also potentially by a biopolitics centred on vulnerability, violence and the redistribution of immunitary protection. Perhaps such a zoopolitics would pursue a reinterpretation even of the concept of life, configured, after Derrida, as a 'sur-vivance', but one owed less to pessimistic forces of protection than to 'creative' forces of in-vention, of the in-coming, hence of the future as always to-come.[60] Perhaps it would be via such a reinterpretation, then, that we might begin to think and to welcome the possibility of the arrival – the arrival *as* possibility – of something like the animal-to-come.

4   Political Animals

What must happen to thinking about politics for the fact and the future of animals and animality to be taken into account? Given the philosophical, social and environmental developments over the last few decades, it hardly seems any longer necessary to summon a long history of political philosophy in order to evidence – with a view to condemning, no doubt – its fundamental 'anthropocentrism'. If common sense weren't on its own sufficient to accept that contemporary concepts and practices of politics presuppose that the latter constitutes a thoroughly human activity, then already countless critiques of classical and modern thought could be called upon to prove the point. But if, in view of the most sophisticated engagements with the animal question, we take the limitrophic nature of 'the' human-animal distinction as a *given*, then the philosophical challenge perhaps lies less in diagnosing yet again the anthropocentric tendencies that pervade, wittingly or not, our intellectual traditions than in speculating on, if not also intensifying, the scope for politics, both theoretically and practically speaking, to respond to the possibilities of the animal-to-come. In that regard, it's worth underscoring the fact that the questions raised in the previous chapter with respect to the pessimistic anthropology underpinning the biopolitical language of protection and vulnerability stem less from that underpinning's anthropologism than from its fundamental pessimism. Indeed, to the extent that the biopolitical frame analysed by Cary Wolfe designates not merely a theoretical perspective but moreover a set of very real and often violent institutions and practices, the biopolitical point is that the 'anthropological' border so often imagined to separate humans from (other) animals is always able to be redrawn, and routinely has been so, in response (and sometimes in opposition) to the politically powerful demands of the status quo. As Wolfe insists, 'the history of slavery, colonialism, and imperialism' demonstrate only too well the fact that 'the distinction "human/animal" . . . is a discursive resource, not a zoological designation'.[1]

This insight in turn raises the question of the *ways* in which that 'distinction' or 'border', its limitrophic edges, might be redrawn – iteratively, differentially – within the very conceptualisation, operation and interpretation of the otherwise exclusively human sphere of politics. To raise the question in this form ('the otherwise exclusively human sphere') is not to reject all the evidence suggesting that any number of different 'animal societies' feature complicated distributions of authority, freedom and social function, and other kinds of social phenomena that we would be inclined in respect of 'human' societies to call 'political'. As Derrida remarks, however, 'it will not suffice to take into account these scarcely contestable facts to conclude from them that there is *politics* . . . in communities of non-human living beings'.[2] For it is not a question here either of attributing to animals or of denying them some capacity or inclination for 'political activity', but rather one of determining the extent to which inherited concepts of politics can be made to accommodate the *question* of the animal. Accordingly, it is a matter of tracing the extent to which that question can be inscribed within such concepts, and therefore of speculating on how the meaning (hence possibilities) of politics inevitably changes in the wake of such reinscription. How, in other words, might animals be said to appear within the scope of politics? In what sense can animals other than 'man' appear as political animals?

Or, more simply, how can an animal appear? Put in that form, outside any contextualising remarks, this question itself has the appearance of being oblivious to the obvious, or perhaps of engaging in abstraction to the point of irrelevance. In view of my elaboration, in the previous chapter, of Derrida's concept of 'nonpower' and the deconstruction of ipseity, however, the capacity or possibility expressible in the form of 'it can' (ergo, 'it can appear') takes on a specifically political significance at least insofar as that capacity or possibility takes shape as an effect of the plays of *power*, understood as a distributed and differential zoopower. In that sense, the fact or eventuality of appearance is always owed to the presence or absence of particular, conflictual and divergent conditions, the institutionality of which accounts for the contingency or non-necessity of zoopower's specific effects. But the possibility of appearance also takes on political significance in a more restricted sense, given the fact that the question of appearance can be and has been read as integral to the activity of politics understood as a dimension of exclusively human affairs. Indeed, for Hannah Arendt, appearance, understood in a quite specific sense, is the very condition of politics as such.[3] Most conventional versions of contemporary politics, moreover, seek to account for this condition through the principles and mechanisms of representative democracy. Understood in terms of such mechanisms, animals appear on the political scene as members of one or more constituencies or interests represented by activists or politicians who campaign for the institution of legal protections for animals, whether those protections be granted on the basis of a traditional (liberalist and humanist) model of rights or in view of a more diffuse, less anthropocentric concern with addressing vulnerable others as potential subjects of justice. But if, as argued in the previous chapter, such thinking remains grounded in the identification of (political) life with fear and aggression, then it is perhaps this very model of political representation that also needs interrogation. To investigate the possibilities of a zoopolitics beyond this model thus means asking the question of the conditions under which animals may *appear otherwise* within the space of politics, alongside the question of what might otherwise come to define the *space of politics* once animals and animality can be engaged as political figures in their own right.

Notwithstanding the focus expressed by its title, therefore, Arendt's *The Human Condition* remains relevant to a hauntological investigation of the animal-to-come precisely for its phenomenological recovery of 'the original Greek understanding of politics' (HC 23) in terms of the three *vita activa* (labour, work and action) and the public space of appearance. Arendt's work has, of course, already been brought into proximity with the question of the animal – or, at least, of the animality and 'animalisation' of humankind – through Agamben's account of the politicisation of 'bare life' and the biopolitical 'transformation of the political-philosophical categories of classical thought'.[4] As announced in his *Homo Sacer*, Agamben's account of the 'sovereign decision' owes much to Arendt's recollection of 'the classical distinction between *zoē* and *bios*, between private life and political existence, between man as a simple living being at home in the house and man's political existence in the city'.[5] In developing the study of biopolitics, moreover, Agamben makes considered use of Arendt's work on totalitarianism, sovereignty and the idea of human rights. But where his reference to *The Human Condition* is limited largely to its 'critical' 'restoration', as he puts it, of the *zoē/bios* distinction, the phenomenological focus of Arendt's investigation depicts 'political life' as tied to certain worldly conditions that perhaps exceed those explicitly analysed in *Homo Sacer*'s inquiry into 'the hidden point of intersection between the juridico-institutional and the biopolitical models of power'.[6] And it is perhaps by way of investigating these and other phenomena which might otherwise fall outside the scope of political philosophy that the question of that (marginalised) form of life called 'animal' might begin to be addressed.

Certainly, this distinction between the *polis* and the household is, on Arendt's account, 'a division upon which all ancient political thought rested as self-evident and axiomatic' (HC 28). On this understanding, political life begins when the citizen (literally) leaves the household and enters the *polis* to engage in activities related to 'the realm of human affairs ... from which everything merely necessary or useful is strictly excluded' (HC 25). Here, a double exclusion of 'mere' biological (hence animal) life is entailed. In the first place, the citizen's ability to engage in a life devoted to political matters presupposed his being the master of a household, hence having mastery over the necessities of life, being free from the need to concern oneself with earning a living, so to speak. 'To be free meant to be free from the inequality present in rulership' – as was the case with the master-slave relationship in the household (*oikos*), for instance – 'and to move in a sphere where neither rule nor being ruled existed' as was the situation of the *polis* (HC 33). Second, this political life itself was, on Arendt's account, concerned only with 'excellence' in the production of 'beautiful deeds' (HC 13), and not with the wealth or welfare either of the free citizenry or of the population of the city at large. What characterised specifically political life, then, was not simply freedom as mastery over biological necessity – political life's fundamental separation from 'mere' living – but further its devotion to *action* performed in view of 'a freely chosen form of political organization' (HC 13). For the Athenian situation offered other 'ways of life (*bioi*) which men might choose in freedom' (HC 12), including a life devoted to bodily pleasure (*bios apolaustikos*) and a 'quiet' life devoted to contemplation (*bios theoretikos*). Moreover, political life excluded not simply any activity devoted to meeting life's necessities (labour), but also any instrumental activity (work), including both the fabrication of what would today be registered as great works of art and architecture (HC 156–7), as well as – crucially – the work of legislating, the crafting of laws:

> Before men began to act, a definite space had to be secured and a structure built where all subsequent actions could take place, the space being the public realm of the *polis* and its structure the law; legislator and architect belonged in the same category. (HC 194–5)

Fabrication's incongruity with political activity stemmed, according to Arendt, from its teleological nature, and the way in which it thereby established 'usefulness and utility as the ultimate standards for life and the world of men' (HC 157). For 'during the work process, everything is judged in terms of suitability and usefulness for the desired end, and for nothing else' (HC 153). Thus determined or constrained from the outset by their orientation towards a specific end, work and fabrication stood at odds with the freedom presupposed by life in the *polis*.

Ruled by necessity in the one case and by utility in the other, therefore, neither labour nor work (including the work of legislating), on Arendt's account, was considered by the Greeks to possess the dignity of political action. Action – great words and great deeds – was granted this higher significance by virtue of the Greek cosmology, in which 'men' appeared as 'the only mortal things in existence': 'against the background of nature's ever-recurring life and the gods' deathless and ageless lives stood mortal men, the only mortals in an immortal ... universe' (HC 18). The fundamental frailty of human existence, this inevitability that one's life would pass into nothingness, drove the desire to attain a kind of immortality via a lasting remembrance of the excellence of one's words and deeds. For speech and action are the modes by which human beings stand apart from the natural world, allowing them to appear to each other in their 'unique distinctness' (HC 176). Such distinctness in turn speaks to the human condition of plurality, which is 'specifically *the* condition ... of all political life' (HC 7), because, 'if men were not distinct, each human being distinguished from any other who is, was, or will ever be, they would need neither speech nor action to make themselves understood' (HC 175–6).

But if it appears that the political significance of action thus lies in its revelation of 'who one is', Arendt's reconstruction of the Greek experience nevertheless complicates that account by attributing action's significance to *natality* – or, rather, to its *reinstantiation* of the natality evidenced by one's own birth: 'with word and deed we insert ourselves into the human world, and this insertion is like a second birth' (HC 176). Consequently, Arendt argues, action amounts always to an act of beginning, setting something underway:

> To act, in its most general sense, means to take an initiative, to begin (as the Greek word *archien*, 'to begin', to lead', and eventually 'to rule', indicates), to set something in motion (which is the original meaning of the Latin *agere*). Because they are *initium*, newcomers and beginners by virtue of birth, men take initiative, are prompted into action. (HC 177)

As a marker of *distinction*, moreover, action is always the beginning or initiation of something *unexpected*, something which stands out from the mundane world of everyday affairs and predictable occurrences. For 'it is in the nature of beginning that something new is started which cannot be expected from whatever may have happened before', and 'this character of startling unexpectedness is inherent in all beginnings and in all origins' (HC 177–8). Further, to the extent that it cannot be ruled by the teleological principle of utility, action is defined as much by the unpredictability of its outcome or significance as by the spontaneity and unexpectedness of its occurrence. Indeed, for Arendt, an action's 'full meaning can reveal itself only when it has ended':

> In contradistinction to fabrication, where the light by which to judge the finished product is provided by the image or model perceived beforehand by the craftsman's eye, the light that illuminates processes of action, and therefore all historical processes, appears only at their end, frequently when all the participants are dead. Action reveals itself fully only to the storyteller, that is, to the backward glance of the historian. (HC 192)

Arendt's 'restoration' of the classical distinction between *zoē* and *bios*, therefore, does more than oppose a classical politics of freedom to the modern state's biopolitical rule over life. For what defines the political *act* on this account is not merely its autonomy but the startling unexpectedness of its origin and the inherent indeterminacy of its end. Political activity consists less in the exercise of sovereignty, in other words, than in the initiation, via words and deeds, of a process which introduces a difference, a mark of distinction, in the form of the wholly unexpected departure for an ultimately unanticipatable destination.

On Arendt's account of the *vita activa*, moreover, only action qualifies as an essentially *political* activity, understood in the literal sense of an activity undertaken within the *polis*, that is, within 'the constant presence of others' (HC 23). While both labour and work 'are conditioned by the fact that men live together . . . it is only action that cannot even be imagined outside the society of men' (HC 22). For action 'can never occur in isolation': 'all action is action "in concert", as Burke liked to say; "it is impossible to act without friends and reliable comrades" (Plato); impossible, that is, in the sense of the Greek verb *prattein*, to carry out and complete'.[7] In this sense, the *polis* was 'the original, prephilosophic Greek remedy' for the frailty of action (HC 196), for 'only the foundation of the city-state enabled men to spend their whole lives in the political realm, in action and speech' (HC 25). Serving both 'to multiply the occasions to win "immortal fame"', and to increase 'the chances that a deed deserving of fame would not be forgotten, that it actually would become "immortal"' (HC 197), the *polis* thus created 'the conditions for remembrance, that is, for history' (HC 9), assuring 'the mortal actor that his passing existence and fleeting greatness [would] never lack the reality that comes from being seen, being heard, and, generally, appearing before an audience of fellow men' (HC 198). And so we might say that the more fundamental significance of the *polis* perhaps lay in the part it played in enabling 'men' not simply to appear as political actors, but rather to be a political actor by *appearing* as such. On Arendt's account, that is, 'the political realm arises directly out of acting together' (HC 198), and so the *polis*,

> properly speaking, is not the city-state in its physical location . . . It is the space of appearance in the widest sense of the word,

namely, the space where I appear to others as others appear to me, where men exist not merely like other living or inanimate things but make their appearance explicitly.

This space does not always exist, and although all men are capable of deed and word, most of them – like the slave, the foreigner, and the barbarian in antiquity, like the laborer or craftsman prior to the modern age, the jobholder or businessman in our world – do not live in it. No man, moreover, can live in it all the time. To be deprived of it means to be deprived of reality, which, humanly and politically speaking, is the same as appearance. (HC 198–9)

Notwithstanding the overt anthropocentrism characterising both this particular passage and the overall argument, it is by virtue of this emphasis precisely on action and appearance that Arendt's phenomenological reconstruction of classical Greek thought may be said to enable an alternative approach to the animal-to-come as a political question. To be sure, derivation of such an approach from Arendt's work remains risky, contestable, perhaps even treacherous, to the extent that it runs counter to everything Arendt *explicitly* says about animal life (and much more besides), and further *betrays* (in all senses of the term) her recollection of the classical Greek cosmology. The specific confinement of politics to the 'realm of human affairs', the impetus granted to the desire to win 'immortal fame', the significance attached to word and deed – none of these details speaks directly to the problem of animal existence in any way, while the apparent repetition of the Greek assessment of animal beings as undifferentiated moments in 'the circular movement of biological life' (HC 19) seems the epitome of what Derrida calls the 'asinanity' of 'depriving the animal of every power of manifestation'.[8] Moreover, her insistence on action as a 'faculty' that 'distinguishes us so radically from all animal species'[9] makes the 'species chauvinism' imbuing her political philosophy plain for all to see. In these moments one would find little that could inspire or promote an interrogation of such human exceptionalism in view of the animal-to-come. Indeed, every moment in which Arendt's phenomenological *recollection* of the Athenian experience functions rather to promote *instauration* of that experience – in the insistence, then, not only on the exceptionality of 'mortal man', but also on the original separation of *polis* and *oikos*, of public and private, and also (more significantly, if also more ambivalently) on 'the even more fundamental Greek distinction between things that are by themselves whatever they are and things which owe their existence to man, between things that are *physei* and things that are *nomō*' (HC 15)[10] – all this could be called upon rightly to object to her inscription (her conscription, rather) within the thinking of zoopolitics we are pursuing here.

By the same token, the specific sense of public political action 'recovered' by Arendt in *The Human Condition* is one that – understandably, given its basis in Hellenic society – operates outside any reference to the legislative, judicial and executive institutions of the modern state. Read for their *genealogical* force, moreover, for their tracing of the differential 'origins' of what today can be imagined under the name 'politics', her insights into the 'original' Greek experience bespeak a significance that cannot be reduced or confined to the function of supporting or elaborating a given metaphysics or view of politics. Such insights remain open, in other words, to hauntological revision in view of the animal-to-come. In this way, Arendt's dissociation of the politics of action from representative government enables a first step towards an alternative conception of zoopolitics to the extent at least that it eschews both the (humanist) logic of rights and the (pessimistic) logic of protection. Indeed, on Arendt's account, 'the space of appearance', the very condition of politics, 'precedes all formal constitution of the public realm and the various forms of government' (HC 199), and in that sense depicts a space of political possibility that exceeds the machinations of the sovereign state. Undoubtedly, in view of the chiasmatic logic of following (discussed in Chapter 1), this image of the *priority* of appearance to formal institutions will have to be returned to, as will the characterisation of action via the language of 'faculty', which invites reconsideration in view of the nonpower at the heart of zoopower (elaborated in Chapter 3). But for now we might find in Arendt's analysis the chance for another politics of animality, one released from the need to reference specifically governmental processes or judicial concepts, and oriented instead towards the recognition and recollection of forms or moments of natality that irrupt within the context of action.

In this regard, Arendt's occasional appeals to the miraculous are notable for characterising natality in terms that deviate markedly from her frequent attribution of action to the human agent:

> Whenever something new occurs, it bursts into the context of predictable processes as something unexpected, unpredictable, and ultimately causally inexplicable – just like a miracle. In other words, every new beginning is by nature a miracle when seen and experienced from the standpoint of the processes it necessarily interrupts.[11]

To the extent that such qualities as novelty, unexpectedness and unpredictability appertain not to the initiators of action but to acts or events of natality themselves, action – as the performance of great deeds, as the beginning of something new – cannot be confined, strictly speaking, to what is otherwise thought to be the *exclusively* human sphere of politics. Indeed, the natality of action may be said to present itself *wherever* the spontaneity of action 'happens against the overwhelming odds of statistical laws and probability, which for all practical, everyday purposes amounts to certainty' (HC 178). Such natality may be found, that is, *wherever* action counters the 'various rules' that 'tend to "normalize"' the members of a polity so as 'to make them behave', rules which would thereby serve 'to exclude spontaneous action or outstanding achievement' (HC 40). And so the effects of natality may be felt wherever action *breeches* the 'conformism, behaviorism, and automatism' that reduce distinctness and plurality 'to the level of a conditioned and behaving animal' (HC 45), which is to say, to 'the species character of animal life' (HC 8, n. 1).

It is in this sense, moreover, that the name 'action' might be said to apply – *pace* Arendt – to remarkable deeds performed not only by human agents but by nonhuman 'actors' too. Thus the efforts of 'Clever Hans', the horse who could provide answers to arithmetic problems by tapping his hoof, would appear to serve as an exemplary case of the startlingly unexpected happening (to use Arendt's terms) 'against the overwhelming odds of statistical laws and probability' (HC 178). Certainly, Hans's extraordinary performances, in which he would give frequently correct answers to multiplication and division problems among other tests of intelligence, appear not only to have set him apart, to have marked his *distinction*, from his conspecific contemporaries, but also to have won him a kind of immortal fame (in the behavioural sciences, at least) with the lasting remembrance of the 'Clever Hans effect'. Moreover, while his seemingly miraculous feats were attributed in the end to a capacity not for mathematical reasoning but for reading involuntary cues – 'natural expressive movements' – on the part of his questioners, this fact does little to negate the startling novelty of his acts.[12] Indeed, with a backward glance we might justifiably claim that his was a performance which ultimately produced the occasion for others to act in concert in order to carry out a process thus set underway. For, as Vinciane Despret tells it – albeit without reference to the Arendtian framework we have established here – Hans's actions not only prompted a series of innovations in the study of influence, but today remain significant for their potential to force radical changes to the theoretical and practical distribution of agency, authority and interest in human-animal interactions.[13]

Central to Despret's interpretation is not solely the fact that in 1907 the German board of education established a panel of thirteen 'gentlemen belonging to different spheres of social life' in order to investigate the authenticity of the claims that Hans genuinely possessed such intellectual capacities.[14] Nor is it simply that psychologist Oskar Pfungst subsequently undertook extended experimental study both of human subjects and of the horse's responses to questioning under different conditions, and was thereby able to conclude that Hans was reading cues that his questioners weren't aware they were making. In addition to these factors, which already speak to the beginning of something unexpected and a subsequent acting-in-concert, Despret highlights within Hans's actions (and the case more generally) a degree of unpredictability or incalculability that has continued to haunt his legacy to this day. For the story of Hans is routinely retold as a tale of the 'menace' of experimental bias, whereby results from psychological and behavioural research are 'influenced' by experimenter expectancy. On this version of events, the actions of Hans and his human counterparts can be held up as directly responsible for the establishment and enduring authority of a cautionary research principle. But on Despret's recounting of the story, this lasting remembrance has forgotten the most interesting and significant – the 'greatest', to use Arendt's Athenian schema[15] – features of the horse's acts. While it has long been recognised, for example, that well-trained horses are excellent muscle readers, and this fact could thus be acknowledged in accounting for Hans's performances, Pfungst's report understates what perhaps set Hans apart even from these adroit conspecifics. Hans's reading of his interrogators' muscle movements, that is, was not kinaesthetic in nature. As Despret puts it: 'talented horses generally read [the gestures and movements of their riders] through their skin and muscles; Hans could read all these signs visually. Hans was truly talented.'[16]

Further, the data acquired through Pfungst's own observations suggest that the communicative exchange, hence the flow of influence, between the horse and his interrogators was not all one way. As Despret notes in her close reading of the psychologist's report, 'the form of the signals that indicate "zero" and "no" was taught to the humans by the horse, without their realizing it'.[17] When Pfungst asks his human subjects

> to think about the answer 'null' or 'zero', he notes that the minimal gesture is not the same as when they are in the horse's presence. When they concentrate on the thought 'null' or 'zero',

for Pfungst, the minimal gesture is a slight ellipse with the head; when they ask the horse, it is a shaking of the head that is observed, which is exactly the movement used by the horse to answer. How could it happen that humans replace their own spontaneous movements with that of the horse, unless we assume that Hans taught them the gestures he needed? Hans has made them move otherwise, he changed the habits of their bodies and made them talk another language.[18]

Where Hans's performances are largely remembered for having initiated the development of procedures geared towards eliminating influence, therefore, Despret's reading of the case uncovers the more complicated relations of influence that the celebrated story has failed to account for. The result for Despret is that Hans's 'testimony is always called upon to impoverish the range of explanations'.[19] And so we might say that this legacy of Hans is one which fails to remember precisely his outstanding achievement. For it is a story in which his distinctness is reduced to a 'conformism, behaviorism, and automatism' that is taken to name (in Arendt's terms) 'the *species* character of animal life'.

Such is the unpredictability of action: the story begun by Hans's performances sets in motion a particular transformation to the practices of experimental research, practices that are in turn being transformed by another version of Hans's story. For Despret is one of a handful of thinkers whose work is now being championed for pursuing a new kind of ethology notable for its reflexive approach to ethological practice and its attentiveness to the differential conditions and nuances of animal behaviour. As is the case with Dominique Lestel's (see Chapter 1), much of Despret's work on animals, presented in a string of books published over the last two decades, awaits translation into English. That work which is available, however, routinely challenges the logics of species and of behaviour that characterise conventional ethology (as well as the forms of modern social life that Arendt sees as being antithetical to political action). An exemplary practitioner of what has for this reason come to be called 'philosophical ethology',[20] Despret 'does philosophy' by way of an ethology of ethology rather than through study of mainstream philosophical traditions.[21] Her novel approach to the analysis of 'animal action' is hinted at by the provocative title of her recently translated abecedary, *What Would Animals Say If We Asked the Right Questions?* Here the term 'question' functions as Despret's shorthand, in the first instance, both for the mode of address or stance directed towards animals in ethological studies, and for the nature of the specific experimental protocol or device used in these studies. Such devices include the often limited and unimaginative hypotheses that inform these studies, which, for her, are all too frequently indifferent to the question of whether the studies provide the animals with anything much of interest to respond to. In formulating research questions 'about' animals to be tested by field or laboratory research, in other words, ethology effectively puts questions *to* animals, such that unsophisticated, closed and repetitive questions produce simple or indifferent responses. On Despret's account, then, the possibility of response, of the capacity to respond and of the power to 'speak', is contingent upon the formulation of 'the right questions', ones that both 'interest' the animal subjects being studied and give them 'a choice in whether to respond to [the researchers'] expectations'.[22]

By way of its generally unreflexive – and frequently violent – questioning, ethology all too regularly induces, in other words, the forms of 'species behaviour' it sets out to find. Thus scientific findings that rats engage in practices of infanticide emerge from experimental research designed to determine the conditions – absence of food, presence of hostile environments – under which this behaviour emerges. As Despret remarks, with an appropriate degree of incredulity:

> The conditions that are said to 'reveal' infanticide appear as, above all, conditions that are actively created by the researchers. Who had the idea to starve the rats? . . . How did the environment become stressful or hostile? One cannot ignore that these are

extreme conditions of captivity, that is, conditions of experimental captivity manipulated so as to induce stress, hunger, hostility, fear and so on. In short these are pathological conditions, carried to the extreme, that clearly have the goal to force the behavior; the researchers will repeat and vary the test until the desired behavior appears. We are dealing with a tautological operation. (WW 107)

In this tautological operation we can see perhaps the clearest demonstration of the flows of zoopower that limit and enable what an animal – a rat, for example – is capable (or incapable) of doing. To the extent that so-called 'species behaviour' is thus 'confirmed' by such experimental procedures, moreover, that behaviour can be recognised as being all too frequently the product of research practices that explicitly set out to suppress the appearance or any evidence of initiative on the part of its animal subjects.[23] Such practices can be understood to deny from the outset, in other words, the distinctness and plurality that would otherwise breech what Arendt calls the 'conformism, behaviorism, and automatism' of what is *thereby* engendered as 'a conditioned and behaving animal' (HC 45, 8, n. 1). For the research not only presupposes such automatism, in the form of conformity to invariant biological programmes, but also aspires to reach it via the repetition and standardisation of experimental and observational scenarios.

To this way of 'doing science' Despret opposes 'another practice', one that is inherited 'from anthropology's ways of thinking and doing' (WW 114). Suspending the imperative to standardise and generalise, this alternative practice 'seeks to explore, by focusing on their flexibility, the singular and concrete situations encountered by animals', and in doing so approaches 'every event as a particular problem that animals are experiencing and attempting to handle' (WW 114). Attuned to the variability of the contexts in which animals respond and in which their 'behaviour' manifests, it gives only provisional and limited explanatory value to the logic of species, and grants significance to the appearance of plurality and distinction, hence *invention* (see Chapter 2). Thus, for Despret, variance of response on the part of animal subjects in particular experimental situations – even the occurrence of 'failure' alongside 'success' – can be prized as an 'achievement'. In the case of research aimed at identifying self-recognition on the part of elephants and magpies, then,

> the failures of the non-self-recognizing animals not only signal the need to refrain from making generalizations: the experiment teaches us that magpies (some magpies, more specifically, magpies raised by hand) and some Asian elephants (roughly thirty years old and raised in a zoo) can, in some very specific and exceptional circumstances for magpies and elephants . . . develop a new competency. But these non-self-recognizing magpies and elephants at the same time reveal the magnitude of this type of experiment. They are experiments of invention. The dispositive does not determine the behavior that is acquired; rather, it creates the occasion for it. (WW 101)

Certain forms of animal 'behaviour' can be understood to appear, therefore, in *response* to particular institutional conditions, including those put in place by the experimental work of ethology itself. And for this very reason the *significance* of animal action – its appearance or visibility *as* action – can be recognised as defined not simply by the 'spontaneity' of that action but also by certain discursive resources. The intellectual work of ethology itself, in other words, defines a space of appearance, a space in which animal action may (or may not) appear as such, a space that is structured by the discursive techniques, experimental devices and enabling concepts – not least of all the concept of 'species' – that the discipline puts to use.

The consequences of such animal action would understandably seem restricted, for the most part, to the space in which such action can appear, which means that we might expect its unpredictable effects to be identified in the first instance within the bounds of the science of ethology itself. In this regard, Despret's re-reading of the story of Clever Hans may well stand as exemplary, insofar as it recounts the establishment and ongoing revision of a principle of influence that this talented horse helped to initiate. But the apparently specialist nature of this site of knowledge and authority begs the question of the extent to which the moments of such action may be called 'political' with regard also to the criterion of being performed in public. As distinguished as the 'Clever Hans effect' happens to be within the behavioural sciences, that is, can it be said that Hans's deeds are as well known outside those intellectual fields, even in other academic disciplines, let alone by a broader global public? Do these restricted, intellectual spaces provide much scope for occasions of animal action to attain, in Arendt's terms, 'the reality that comes from being seen, being heard, and, generally, appearing before an audience' (HC 198)?

Perhaps pertinent in this regard is the fact that, having performed in numerous exhibitions of his talents across Germany, Clever Hans garnered considerable interest among the public at the time, with his feats being reported even as far abroad as New York. Also significant here is the tendency for reports of 'great deeds' on the part of various animals – animal 'heroics', as well as scientific 'discoveries' of unexpected capabilities – to make their way into national and, increasingly, global news coverage. Thus, when honeybees are shown to be capable of counting (or capable of being trained to count), and even of recognising a null set as less than one, it is not unusual to find such stories being reported in mainstream daily newspapers and broadcast media.[24] The border between a narrow space of appearance structured by specialist behavioural sciences and a broader public sphere appears itself therefore to be far from impermeable, such that the conditions for remembrance exceed those that define the site of action itself.

It is in view of such permeability, moreover, if not also in respect of the chiasmatic logic of following, that Arendt's account of the ontological priority of the space of appearance to the formal constitution of the public realm warrants reassessment. For the possibilities of appearance, and the very experience of appearance, have changed considerably over the course of the centuries separating the early Greek situation and today's technologised and globalised world. Not only the 'formal constitution of the public realm and the various forms of government', that is, but also the large-scale intensification and expansion of communications media, have come to define and reinvent the public space over the last three centuries at least. Not the least significant transformation in this regard is the practical severance of the event of appearance in public from the seemingly requisite condition of co-presence with that public's members. Whereas once appearance in the public realm of the *polis* required physical co-location with one's peers, the rise of the periodical press gave birth to a new kind of public sphere, one in which 'great words' could make their appearance as much via the printed page as via oratory.[25] Since then, moreover, the development of audio-visual recording and broadcast, online publication, digital archiving, internet access, and more has exponentially magnified the potential for such appearance-at-a-distance, transforming the public space of political appearance still further and making the mediatisation of politics central to the functioning of democratic government. As Derrida has remarked, in conversation with Bernard Stiegler, 'the political arena is to a large extent marked and, often, determined ... by what is being said on the radio or shown on television', with the consequence that the public sphere today is made or fashioned, hence 'constantly transformed, in its structure and its content, by the teletechnology of what is so confusedly called information or communication'.[26]

'Teletechnology' here names for Derrida not simply the entire apparatus of the media and communications industries, but moreover the very processes by which time and space, hence appearance, are constituted.[27] For the advent of teletechnologies of communication radically changes our sense of the possibilities of appearance: 'as soon as we know, "believe we know", or quite simply *believe* that the alleged "live" or "direct" [broadcast] is possible, and that voices and images can be transmitted from one side of the globe to the other, the field of perception and of experience in general is profoundly transformed'.[28] Viewed hauntologically, then – as distinct, in a sense, from phenomenologically – the (public) space of (political) appearance is always constituted, if variably so, on the basis of certain teletechnological conditions. It is always constituted in and mediated by various teletechnological processes, such that, for Derrida, actual (political) appearance is always 'artifactual', is always *made*. 'Actuality', he writes,

> is not given but actively produced, sifted, invested, performatively interpreted by numerous apparatuses which are *factitious* or *artificial*, hierarchizing and selective, always in the service of forces and interests to which 'subjects' and agents (producers and consumers of actuality – sometimes they are 'philosophers' and always interpreters, too) are never sensitive enough.[29]

Derrida speaks here of *actualité*, which is translated in *Echographies* as 'actuality', but which, as translator Jennifer Bajorek notes, is 'strictly untranslatable' for the purposes of that text.[30] The meanings of the term range from a general sense of topicality, hence what is currently relevant, to a more concrete sense of what is actually and currently happening, while, 'in the plural, *les actualités* means something like "current events", or even, quite simply, "the news"'.[31] The term thus registers a certain ambivalence of reference, an ambivalence which in turn signals a more fundamental undecidability at the basis of what Derrida calls artifactuality: the producedness of actuality.[32] What we can see in Derrida's 'artifactuality', then, is a structural coupling of politics, or perhaps a more general trait of politicality, with the publicity that is owed to the event of appearance.

Thus linking politicality with publicity, Derrida's artifactuality recalls Arendt's phenomenological reconstitution of the public space of appearance, but with the key difference that for Derrida this space is teletechnological and artifactual through and through. Arendt, that is, would in all likelihood decry the socialisation of 'the' public sphere via media technologies – society being an aspect of the *oikos* whose emergence as an object of governance 'blurred the old borderline between private and political' (HC 38) and technology being defined by 'the means-end category, whose chief characteristic, if applied to human affairs, has always been that the end is in danger of being overwhelmed by the means which it justifies and which are needed to reach it'.[33] But in Derrida's view the teletechnological nature of contemporary public space does not stand diametrically opposed to a public space that corresponds to an earlier, ostensibly unmediated and nontechnological form of appearance. For the contemporary technical or empirical possibility of severing appearance from presence speaks to a structural or *in-principle* possibility, one which pertains *necessarily*, therefore, even if the empirical or material conditions for appearance-at-a-distance are missing from a given scenario. Indeed, insofar as appearance – as Despret's reflection on ethological devices well shows – remains conditioned, which is to say 'actively produced, sifted, invested, performatively interpreted', by a certain discursivity, by iterable and disseminable *techniques* of information extraction and exchange, teletechnologies cannot be said to be absent even from situations in which no contemporary media technologies are in play. As such, teletechnologies 'have always been there, they are always there, even when we wrote by hand, even during so-called live conversation'.[34] And the imagined *ontological* priority of the space of appearance *vis-à-vis* the technologies and institutions of the public realm may therefore be called into question, that space's 'originality' being, rather, derivative, already implicated within a process of teletechnological reproduction. For the same reason, moreover, the *historical* originality, 'hence' authenticity, which Arendt often seems to attribute to the Greek *polis*, can be recognised as fatally compromised – its status as radically other than or discontinuous with the structures defining contemporary politics and public appearance being already marked or haunted by that moment's artifactuality, by its ever-possible *invocation* in the service of present-day speculations on politics. The 'pre-formal', 'nontechnological' nature of the Hellenic scene appears as such, that is, on the basis of what from today, from a technologised, globalised present, appears as the obvious *lack* of various telemedia of appearance.

At stake here is the possibility of hauntologically identifying and activating within Arendt's account of the 'original' meaning of politics a 'reserve' from which may be derived as yet unconsidered possibilities for future arrangements. To stress the teletechnological and artifactual nature of the Greek experience invoked by Arendt is not, therefore, to deny the fact that present-day political public spaces remain structured by specific forms of teletechnology – technologies of telecommunication, to be sure, but also of representative government – hence by specific forms of interaction and specific possibilities of appearance-at-a-distance that were unavailable in such forms during the Hellenic period. Nor is it to overlook the unevenness of the distribution of these possibilities across the contemporary public political arena. Such a disparity is not only owed to the absence of electoral representivity, whether formal or substantive, in the many non-democratic or one-party states across the globe. It also derives from the manifold forms of political disenfranchisement (be they sanctioned legally or engendered culturally and economically) that persist within so-called Western democracies, as well as from the practical and constitutional constraints that grant the vast majority of 'free citizens' in today's psephocracies significantly limited scope to contribute directly to the operation of political processes. Owing precisely to the transformations wrought by the political and technological innovations of the last three centuries, in other words, the potential to appear publicly and to act politically, in the 'original' Hellenic sense that Arendt reconstitutes, has become severely restricted, even as the proportion of 'free citizens' within a given society has increased significantly in the name of egalitarianism. Yet the potential to *appear* in a public space, to appear in the 'presence' of others whose number far outstrips that of the Athenian citizenry, has at the same time been radically enhanced and redistributed by the advent not only of print and broadcast media but also of networked digital communications technologies. Thinking the forms and possibilities of animal appearance *today*, therefore, means registering, in order to bring into play, precisely these new media developments.

Despret goes some way towards accounting for this new mediatic situation when she reflects on the increasing use of social media to publish and share videos featuring animals and human-animal interactions. Her primary interest in this phenomenon revolves around the extent to which it speaks to the site of 'a new ethological practice', understood etymologically, that is, as knowledge of shared manners, customs and habits. 'Might it be the case', she asks, 'that the proliferation of these videos attests not only to new habits but to the creation of a new interspecific *ethos*, of new relational modalities, that at the same time construct knowledge?' (WW 196).[35] Taking wildlife documentaries as a historical precursor, and considering the role they have played in 'raising awareness for endangered animals', Despret highlights the potential for the new ethological habits – what we might rename here 'new ethomedia practices' – 'to transform the beings involved and the knowledge that unites them' (WW 197). Thus wildlife documentaries helped introduce into scientific practices dominated by the logic of species and the study of populations a concern with individual animals and 'personal' histories, a shift in focus which proved effective in promoting the cause of animal protection. With the rise of social media sharing, with the slew of recordings showing animals, both domestic and wild, performing startlingly unexpected feats – cats opening fridges; octopuses escaping jars; dogs flying planes; monkeys stealing artefacts and holding their owners to ransom; elephants painting precise, if stylised, pictures of elephants! – the customs may be said to have changed again:

> Other modes of knowledge are cultivated; amateurs have ... taken over, and this time with unrivaled means of distribution. The animals are part of the cast, even more so than in the documentaries. They are talented beings, remarkable for their heroism, sociality, cognitive and relational intelligence, humor,

unpredictability, and inventiveness, and they are now part of everyday life. Of course, these documents do not strictly speaking fall within the domain of evidence; hardly anyone is fooled, as the comments [beneath the publicly shared videos] attest; nothing is known about how these images were taken, and one can always suspect deception or the possibility that staging has occurred, with or without the complicity of the animals involved. But nearly all of them speak to the evidence of the image: 'someone saw it, and the images are proof'. (WW 198)

Central to these developments, then, is a transformation of the forms and possibilities of public appearance – not only the emergence of 'new ways of making animals visible', as Despret notes (WW 196), but also a shift in the significance of such appearances. Where the aesthetic and scientific naturalism of earlier wildlife documentaries perhaps lent itself to a logic of protecting endangered animals through a focus on growing species populations and minimising human interference, the new etho-media space enables a different kind of response. For what characterises many of these amateur videos is not their depiction of animals as victims – be it from the threat of extinction, or in the performance of comic mishap – but rather their display of individual creatures 'doing surprising things, things that are not expected of them ... This is what makes the clips interesting and arouses enthusiasm: animals teach us about what they are capable of and what we have ignored' (WW 200).

Despret values these clips primarily for their potential to supplement and connect with scientific practice, and to interest nonspecialists in turn in 'the scientific adventure that mobilizes' ethological research (WW 201). In view of Arendt's reconstitution of the principle of action, though, it seems fair to say that this new ethological development is not without political significance, too. If the 'beginnings' enacted by those events of animal natality which appear in today's etho-media spaces can be said to fall well short of the 'greatness' that earned the Hellenic heroes their 'immortal fame', it is worth noting that when it comes to specifying examples of action Arendt herself is circumspect almost to the point of silence. And this is perhaps due to the fact that the only examples that *could* be cited are precisely those that have indeed earned their initiators immortal fame. But to take as the measure of action the great deeds recounted in the Homeric epics, for example, or in the historians' accounts of the French and American revolutions, is perhaps to cede to action such a rarity that it could not rightly be counted among the *fundamental* (human) activities that Arendt collects under the name *vita activa*. To *define* action with reference only to those truly enduring tales, in other words, is perhaps to understate what is, for Arendt, one of its defining qualities: its *frailty*. Such frailty extends, no doubt, to those new etho-media audiences before whom contemporary events of animal natality would appear, audiences whose constitution, as it were, is far from comprehensive or lasting. For the fragmented, dispersed and volatile nature of the public space(s) of appearance circumscribed by teletechnological etho-media engenders, in turn, irregular, heterogeneous and transitory publics. But if such inconstancy appears to hinder the establishment of the permanence that, on Arendt's account, is the meaning of politics,[36] the distributive – sometimes virally so – and often emulative nature of social media production and dissemination is indicative of the reality of a 'commonly shared world' (HC 68) nevertheless, replete with the 'simultaneous presence of innumerable perspectives' that, for Arendt, gives expression to the condition of plurality (HC 57).

Such mimeticism testifies, moreover, to the role that new-mediatic animal action plays in organising, even transforming, the 'society of men', understood in the sense of living and acting together. As Despret suggests:

> because many of the experiences that are shared on the Web are due to the common work between a human and an animal, from the mutual learning that has developed, from a productive complicity, from a game that has been patiently introduced . . . we learn what *we* are capable of with them. (WW 200)

Beyond instigating campaigns for animal protection, that is, the public appearances exemplified in the online videos that Despret discusses speak to other ways of relating to nonhuman animals, other forms of interaction, hence another kind of collective, even transformative action. They prepare for the in-vention of other modes or moments of living together, of acting together, and in this way inaugurate other spaces of politics, rival or competing spaces that thereby *divide* 'the' space of politics 'itself'. In this sense, the very volatility, agonism and heterogeneity that define today's etho-media spaces might be understood less as undermining their political significance than as constituting that significance. Such public appearances may even be said, therefore, to contribute to the cultivation and constitution of the conditions for a new concept and practice of *democracy* – following the thought of a democracy-to-come, perhaps – precisely as a thought and experience of living together that far exceeds the constitution or form of juridico-institutional *government* ordinarily designated by that name.

Consequently, if the effectuality of this animal action would seem limited in terms of its scope to transform either the processes or the rationales that define contemporary democratic governance, such acting-in-concert nevertheless speaks to the initiation and realisation of something (as it were) new: a new place for animals and animality within the otherwise exclusively human sphere of politics. Indeed, the pertinence of the Arendtian recovery of the 'original' meaning of politics can be said to lie less in its reconstitution of a normative framework that would guide transformation of contemporary juridico-political structures than in its accentuation of the *irreducibility* of politics to the processes and institutions that define contemporary governance, democratic or otherwise. For politics, understood in the sense of the *frailty* of action, is precisely that form of activity which *could not* be submitted to a normative framework or some model of 'best practice', since politics would be essentially a matter simply of *what happens* in the public realm of (so-called) human affairs. In this regard, the new ethological practice identified by Despret – the public *appearance* of animal action and initiative, and the collective 'carrying-out' of that natality – points to the emergence of a form of (zoo)political action beyond the spaces of representative government.

Such a situation would seem to stand at some remove from a critical (bio)politics that is grounded in and responsive to a sense of suffering or passivity which 'we' share with animal others, a politics in which the real or potential vulnerability of animals lays claim to 'our' sense of justice.[37] For the form or sense of 'animal action' that is in play here is irreducible to any demand for compassion or retribution. In that sense, its genre (as it were) would diverge both from the cry of protest and from the work of testimony, coming closer rather to the event of inauguration, the act of institution.[38] By the same token, such zoopolitical action could not be said to constitute a moment or expression of any agency or power that stands apart from the differential plays of zoopower, as though such agency were unmarked by the nonpower at the heart of power. Certainly, in the context of a contemporary public sphere structured by the teletechnology of globally networked news media, 'citizens' appear more frequently as passive recipients of media address than as initiators of political action. But such passivity would not for that reason be unique to the contemporary situation, for even on Arendt's account of the 'original' sense of politics such passivity functions as a constitutive moment in the story of politics:

> The story that an act starts is composed of its consequent deeds and sufferings. These consequences are boundless, because action, though it may proceed from nowhere, so to speak, acts into a medium where every reaction becomes a chain reaction and where every process is the cause of new processes. Since action acts upon beings who are capable of their own actions, reaction, apart from being a response, is always a new action that strikes out on its own and affects others. Thus action and reaction among men never move in a closed circle and can never be reliably confined to two partners. (HC 190)

Understood not pessimistically but as the condition for 'reactivity' or 'response', hence as a way of preparing for the invention of the other (see Chapter 2), passivity would constitute the possibility of political action more generally. Both animal agent and media observer 'act', and are capable of acting, in other words, by virtue only of the passivity that structures the power of appearance as such. And the freedom and plurality which might otherwise be prized by political philosophy appear, therefore, not unconditionally, nor simply as an effect of a sovereign decision between *zoē* and *bios*, but rather by way of their inscription within those formal institutions, certain teletechnological conditions, that characterise any given public space of appearance.

In arriving at this account of 'the' space of politics and of the scope for animals to appear otherwise in such a space, we can begin to recognise, then, the extent to which the *question* of the animal can force an unexpected challenge to conventional accounts of the operations of politics – beyond, that is, the extension of a sense of justice or obligation to animal beings. For the reading of online ethological activity initiated by Despret presents a stark contrast to routine dismissals of popular new media use as failing to embrace the internet's potential to enable a truly *deliberative* democracy to emerge. Where such a politics, premised on a dialogic model of the public sphere, would perhaps despair at the widespread use of the internet for the 'frivolous' purpose of circulating cat videos (for example), the question of the animal, of the animal-to-come, perhaps finds in such activity cause to rethink the fundamentally limited nature of that model of politics, predisposed as it is to privilege *speech*, or action in the form of speech, over other modes of political appearance and activity, and to identify *governance* as the very substance of politics.[39] If the fact and the future of animals and animality is to be taken into account, in other words, political thought may have to give serious consideration to its tendency to reduce to 'mere' everyday life all that activity which appears not to take the form of explicitly political judgement, action or speech. Indeed, such thought may need to rethink the very form and potential of *zoon politikon*, that 'political animal' whose actions and affairs the history of philosophy has taken as the source of political life as such. For what the hauntology of the public space of appearance underscores is the extent to which the phenomena of natality and action – but also, for the same reasons, of reproductive life and 'species behaviour' – can appear as such only on the basis of their relation to specific teletechnological conditions (formal institutions of government, teletechnologies of communication, artifactual spaces of appearance). From the perspective of the animal-to-come, therefore, *zoon politikon* names not the specific difference of the human animal, but rather a distributed and differential, technoprosthetic animal-machine, a field of institutionality within which creatures of all kinds come to appear and to act in never entirely predictable fashions.

5   Responding (After Anthropos)

> What is it 'to respond'? To respond to? To be responsible for? To respond for? To respond, be responsible, before?
>
> Jacques Derrida[1]

In the various investigations undertaken up to this point the thought of the animal-to-come has never strayed far from that animal which calls itself 'human'. From the question of animals in culture, through the strategies of domestication, to the politics of animal appearance within the public realm of 'human affairs', the fact and the future of animality has been explored throughout with an eye on its dependence, in a very real and calculable sense, upon political decisions, practices and processes that are, in the last instance, engaged by animals other than nonhuman animals. This continued complicity of zoopolitical thinking with the sites and endeavours of human interest undoubtedly speaks to a conceptual (hence existential) problem that requires further investigation. For such 'anthropocentrism' continues to be identified as the very rationale of that carnophallogocentric violence which is responsible for the everyday denial of animal potentiality and integrity – not to mention the immeasurable suffering and untimely deaths felt by individual animals, along with the human-induced extinction of thousands of animal species. Indeed, we are witnessing, today, in what has been dubbed as the age of the Anthropocene, an irreversible anthropogenic climate change that threatens a profound transformation of the environmental conditions of present-day forms of organic life, such that carnophallogocentric violence appears now to be enacted not only through the continued (human) destruction of specific animal habitats but also by (nonhuman) global climate processes that have themselves been profoundly disrupted by human activity.

Yet there is already something 'odd', as Claire Colebrook and Jami Weinstein put it, about the fact that 'the epic gesture of the present' – naming the irreversible changes to the Earth systems that support life as we know it – 'deploys the figure of "anthropos"', *notwithstanding* the numerous theoretical challenges to the authority and identity of the ideals of 'man' and 'humanity' laid down over the last half a century or more.[2] In the figure of the Anthropocene, that is, the name of 'man' is writ large, rendering visible, so a story goes, the effects of humankind's domination of the natural world. Moreover, such domination is itself regularly traced today to the unquestioned presumption of the human's exceptionalism *vis-à-vis* other animals generally by virtue of that creature's unique capacity to respond, to separate itself from the rest of the natural world, to reflect on its condition, and to act accordingly. Following Donna Haraway, Colebrook and Weinstein suggest that this reference to 'anthropos' might therefore be understood as 'out of sync with an intellectual milieu that theorises the death of the subject and the eclipse of the human'[3] – out of sync, that is, with the various challenges, wrought by twentieth-century critical thought from Heidegger onwards, to the humanist presumption of human sovereignty. And so we could say that *the* critical move of the day is haunted by a strange kind of anachrony that recalls on the one hand the temporal out-of-jointness that forms a basis for Derrida's thought of hauntology and the future-to-come, yet announces on the other not a radically pluralist image of a 'democracy-to-come' but a monotonous reinscription of the same in the form of humankind's oppressive sway over the fate of the world. The effects of this peculiar temporality are not confined to critical reflections on the Anthropocene, moreover, but are perhaps felt wherever the posthumanist critique of human exceptionalism is played out, to the extent that every diagnosis of such anthropo*centrism* seems thereby to confirm the power of the human animal to command thought and praxis – even critical thought and praxis – to serve its ends. How to follow the human, then, in view of this *problem* of anthropocentrism? How is the human animal to be accounted for in the thought of the animal-to-come, given that it is precisely such presumptions of human sovereignty – over the nonhuman world, for example – that any critical interrogation of anthropos would want to hold in check? What kind of a *response* to the turmoil of the age can these interrogations and problematisations enable, and to what extent can such a response be taken up as a question of zoopolitics?

A first step towards addressing these questions might be made by turning again to the contemporary trend towards incorporating the biological conditions of human existence into reflections on the nature of politics, but this time with an eye focused on its explicit characterisations of the *so-called* 'human'. Here the specific contribution of Italian philosopher Paolo Virno may prove instructive for its focus on what he calls 'the extremely tight entanglement between "always already" (human nature) and "just now" (the biolinguistic capitalism which has followed Fordism and Taylorism)'[4] in terms precisely of the problem of *anthropogenesis*. For where conventional approaches to anthropogenesis would turn to the science of palaeoanthropology to consider the birth of the species *Homo sapiens*, thereby relegating the significance of the biological condition to a distant, prehistoric origin, Virno concerns himself with an 'eternal' 'biological invariable' (NH 94) as it relates to that slice of 'natural history' which corresponds to conventional histories of human civilisation through to the present day. Accordingly, he speaks of 'species-specific prerogatives' – 'the ensemble of innate dispositions that guarantee the very possibility of perceiving phenomena', of being 'emotionally involved', of 'act[ing] and discours[ing]' (NH 94) – which, for him, amount to a 'phylogenetic meta-history' (NH 95). And the task he sets himself is not to chart the 'prehistoric' birth of a cultural, technical and sovereign being from such phylogenetic conditions but rather to consider 'the question of the different socio-political expression that could be given, here and now, to [these] biological prerogatives of *Homo sapiens*' (NH 93).

While such figures of the 'eternal' and the 'invariable' may recall conventional Enlightenment appeals to 'human nature' (and, indeed, Virno uses the latter phrase almost interchangeably with those already cited), this sketch of the species-specific prerogatives takes on less the onto-theological tones of conventional metaphysics than the materialist hues of the biological and ecological sciences.[5] He thus names as features of this biological invariant 'the language faculty', understood as 'the ensemble of biological and physiological requirements which make it possible' to 'emit articulate sounds' and to 'produce a statement' (NH 96); 'instinctual non-specialization', that is, 'the instinctual poverty of the human animal' (NH 96); 'neoteny' or 'congenital incompleteness', which is the 'phylogenetic basis of non-specialization' (NH 96); and – crucially – 'the lack of a circumscribed and well-ordered environment in which to insert oneself with innate expertise once and for all' (NH 97). Contrary to routine characterisations of human nature as directing the human animal towards certain practical or socio-political ends, therefore, Virno develops with this biologically inflected account an image of anthropos as characterised not by a fundamental sovereignty or capacity for transcendence but rather by a certain 'untimeliness, a deficit of presence' (NH 95). For this instinctual non-specialisation and lack of innate expertise mean that its 'power' or '*dynamis*' is, in fact, a potentiality to do *nothing in particular*. Specified (if not also speciated) by its *non*-specialisation or genericness, in other words, its ostensible powers or capacities have the status rather of incapacities – nonpowers, as it were – to the extent that they constitute an 'expertise' not fit for anything at all. Able to 'adopt behaviours that have not been preset' (NH 96), the human animal is nevertheless (or thereby) defined by the absence of any specific end, purpose or destiny, which is to say, by its status as specifically *unfit* for the life that it leads and *un*fit for the earth it lives on. For 'it goes without saying', Virno writes, that 'a non-specialized organism is also an *out-of-place [disambientato]* organism' (NH 97) – that is to say, one which lacks an environment specifically appropriate to it.

For this reason, Virno's particular take on (bio)politics does not seek, as conventional political thought is wont, to deploy the 'nature of man', hence the presumption of human sovereignty in the form of an 'essential freedom', as the (transcendental, ahistorical) foundation to a socio-political ideal modelled on that invariant. Instead, he proposes a relatively novel 'natural history' that would catalogue the ways and moments in which 'the "eternal" exposes itself' or manifests contingently in empirical phenomena. He calls the latter 'natural-historical diagrams' or 'maps', and – unlike, say, Hegel's account of 'the History of the World', where socio-political states of affairs appear in and as the necessary unfolding and realisation of *Geist* – these diagrams are not motivated per se by the biological invariant but *just so happen* to make that metahistorical constant particularly visible. Pursuing neither an evolutionary history that attends to the birth of the species in a prehistoric past, nor a critical socio-political history which seeks to reveal the human nature driving history towards the realisation of a complete and final human society (seeking at the same time to admonish those self-interested forces that divert human history from its proper path), Virno's natural history thus 'concerns itself with all the circumstances, rather different over the course of time, in which *anthropos*, working and speaking, retraces the salient stages of anthropogenesis' (NH 95). And in this way it responds to a set of questions premised on a very different relationship between the eternal (phylogenetic metahistory) and the empirical: 'in what socio-political situations', Virno asks, does the biological non-specialisation of *Homo sapiens* 'come to the fore' (NH 97)? Or again:

> When and how does the generic language faculty, as distinct from historical languages, take on a leading role within a particular

mode of production? What are the *diagrams* of neoteny? Which are the maps or graphs that will adequately portray the absence of a univocal environment? (NH 97)

It is in the answers to such questions that Virno's natural history reveals its specifically political content. For in 'traditional' (pre-modern, pre-industrial) societies, he argues, these phylogenetic constants remain obscured by the stability of those societies' organisation, political praxis, communicative habits, and so on, which collectively constitute a 'pseudo-environment' that compensates for the human animal's fundamental lack of fitness, its lack of a defined and determinate ecological niche. Such forms of 'culture' thereby function to 'stabiliz[e] the "indefinite animal", to blunt or veil its disorientation [*disambientamento*], to reduce the *dynamis* that characterizes it to a certain set of possible actions' (NH 98). Accordingly, it is only in times of crisis or social upheaval that human (im)potentiality 'takes on the visibility of an empirical state of affairs' (NH 97–8). In such moments, the obviousness or naturalness of a given form of (social) life is practically, existentially, called into question: 'no longer selectively filtered by a complex of cultural habits, the world shows itself to be an amorphous and enigmatic context' (NH 99). The potentiality of anthropos then reveals itself in the 'institution of new cultural niches', which restore stability and once again conceal the biological invariant. But in the transition from traditional to (post-)industrial capitalist societies, the relation between phylogeny and historical praxis has changed radically: 'the dearth of specialized instincts and the lack of a definite environment, which have been the same from Cro-Magnons onwards, today appear as noteworthy economic resources' (NH 100). Far from *concealing* the human animal's phylogeny, that is, the prevailing socio-economic system, premised on vocational flexibility (non-specialisation), ongoing skill acquisition (neoteny), precarity of employment and residence (lack of a fixed environment), brings the potential animal's biological 'prerogatives' to the fore. And, in this way, contemporary capitalism amounts, as Jason Read puts it, to 'the direct exploitation of anthropogenesis. It puts to work the very capacity to learn new habits, to adopt new characteristics, which is the paradoxical artifice of human nature.'[6]

Given the significance accorded by Virno's account to the role of political and existential *crisis* in bringing to the fore the human animal's 'phylogenetic metahistory', it is perhaps understandable that the phenomenon of anthropogenic climate change (to return to where we began this chapter) has likewise directed critical attention towards the *biological* character of human existence. Thus, in Dipesh Chakrabarty's influential 'The Climate of History', the challenge presented by the Anthropocene is, in the first instance, one of determining how to reconcile the 'historical sensibility' that narrates the story of human civilisation with the geological timescales that measure the processes of climate change and the evolution of *life*. For the story of climate change, on Chakrabarty's account, presents us with a 'knowledge that defies historical understanding', leaving conventional approaches to history inadequate for 'dealing with the crisis of global warming'.[7] On the one hand, the sciences of climatology and geology (grounded in a very different discipline of 'natural history' to the one proposed by Virno) have accredited human beings with a capacity to affect the earth's geochemical processes and atmospheric patterns – a geological influence that far exceeds the forms of agency accorded to 'man' by Enlightenment philosophies of the historical process. But the consequences of climate change 'make sense', on the other hand,

> only if we think of humans as a form of life and look on human history as part of the history of life on this planet. For, ultimately, what the warming of the planet threatens is not the geological planet itself but the very conditions, both biological and geological, on which the survival of human life as developed in the Holocene period depends.[8]

Without this longer or 'deeper' history of life on earth – a history of 'the way different life-forms connect to one another, and the way the mass extinction of one species could spell danger for another' – the 'crisis of climate change has no human "meaning"'.[9] It's with one eye focusing on a deeper history, in which humans emerge as a force of nature, and the other peering towards a future made radically unknown by the effects of such geological agency, then, that Chakrabarty submits *species* as 'the name of a placeholder for an emergent, new universal history of humans that flashes up in the moment of the danger that is climate change'.[10] Read in terms of this new universal history, moreover, the contemporary geological and existential situation thus appears to present humans with a new biopolitical exigency: *freedom*, once characterised by Enlightenment thought as the *telos* driving human history, would have to give way instead to the goal of species *survival*.

To the extent that Chakrabarty's argument may be taken as an exemplar, the resurrection of anthropos within critical reflection on the Anthropocene thus appears to announce something other than a return to humanism and its metaphysics of human exceptionalism, for it sets out to displace the imagined sovereignty and autonomy of 'humanity', understood in its idealised, civilised form, by reinscribing that figure within conditions of existence that are fundamentally bio-evolutionary. And in this respect, Virno's particular reading of anthropogenesis and biopolitics, notwithstanding its focus on 'bio-linguistic capitalism' and lack of any reference to global warming, can be understood as emerging in relation to, and bearing all the hallmarks of, the same problematic that Chakrabarty addresses. In both cases, that is, the naming of anthropos recasts humankind as a (species) being which owes its existence to processes of *evolution*, derives its future or potential from its (specific) *biology*, and pursues its interests and objectives in (or as) its negotiation with an *environment*. And it is in this attention to, this affirmation of, a broader sphere of life that the authority and value of humanism's 'man' come to be dispersed. Certainly, by characterising humans as a species that demonstrates a geological agency, Chakrabarty situates humans (and human existence) as but one force or interest among others within a much longer history of life. But further, the humanist image of 'man' can only founder on the characterisation of the human not just as an *animal* but as one whose animality, in the form of a demonstrably voracious 'animal appetite' for so-called *modern* 'creature comforts', both pervades and threatens its very existence. In this regard, Virno's depiction of bio-linguistic capitalism as not only enabling but actually manifesting *Homo sapiens'* organismic nature ultimately serves to confirm the naked animality of modern life. By virtue of this biological condition, moreover, the significance and achievements of humankind can be understood as never quite transcending the human animal's species character, hence as never entirely extricable from the biological and ecological conditions or forces to which that species' existence is owed. Underscoring humanity's ultimate lack of transcendence or superiority over life – a lack of sovereignty over its own life as much as any other's, hence over life understood at a planetary scale – both the naming of the Anthropocene and the analysis of present-day anthropogenesis thereby lay the foundations for a critique of anthropocentrism. Working to clear the path to a space of thought and action that can leave the arrogance of human exceptionalism behind, this critical revaluation of life and of the biological conditions to socio-political existence accordingly appears to pave the way towards a veritably *post*-human thought.

Such affirmations of the human animal's biological condition might therefore be said to be *after* anthropos, and in more than one sense. In setting out for a time or place *beyond* humanism, that is, such responses to the problem of anthropocentrism charge themselves with the imperative to *track down*, so as to quarantine, the lingering (if unwitting) humanism, hence species chauvinism, of the human animal. Recalling the chiasmatic logic of following broached in Chapter 1, however, we might wonder at what may yet come of this imperative to overcome anthropocentrism, to succeed a form of life that *itself* is thought to arrive only after, or on the basis of, a more general and generative history or condition of life. For example, it is perhaps unsurprising, given this constitutive suspicion of humanism, that numerous misgivings have been put to the characterisation of contemporary climate change as unproblematically *anthropo*genic. Not limited to the sophistry of quasi-denialists who purport to believe that recent climate change is the simple expression of 'natural climate variability', such objections have also come from more progressive positions. Thus Slavoj Žižek argues that it is 'Capital', and not the species per se, that threatens the stability of the geological parameters of life, while in a similar vein Jason Moore (among others) has proposed 'the Capitalocene' as the more appropriate name for the current geological era.[11] These objections have in turn sparked numerous counter-objections, with Timothy Morton responding that such indictments of Capital 'miss the mark' to the extent that they shirk the basic fact that 'humans created the Anthropocene . . . not bacteria, not lemons': 'humans devised modes of agriculture . . . that now cover most of Earth and are responsible for an alarming amount of global warming emissions all by themselves, let alone the carbon emitting industry that agricultural mode necessitated'.[12] While the various 'modes of Anthropocene denial' ostensibly emerge out of a wariness for any logic that 'unfairly lumps together the whole human race', Morton argues that 'the human considered as a species' is rather 'a hyperobject, a massively distributed physical entity of which I am and am not a member, simultaneously'.[13] 'Stripped of its metaphysical, easy-to-identify, soothingly teleological content', in other words, anthropos is an 'open, porous, flickering' concept; it is a deconstructive, *de*-ontological category, as it were, one which breaks with the 'absurd teleological and metaphysical' notions that have given expression to anthropocentric thought.[14]

Yet Morton's insistence, after Chakrabarty, on the name 'species' as against 'Capital' (or any other candidate for the geological force in question) serves to bring home the potential for such discussions to be reduced to a form of deontology, understood in a much more conventional sense. Critical and philosophical arguments over the naming of the current geological era, that is, often end up focusing on the question of causal responsibility, reducing history, in both its socio-political and geological forms, to an exercise in moral judgement. At this level, the *politics* of the 'Anthropocene' seems imaginable only in terms of specific distributions of the burden of culpability – a politics confirmed already in Chakrabarty's initial attempts to anticipate objections to his summonsing of anthropos: 'Why should one include the poor of the world – whose carbon footprint is small anyway – by use of such all-inclusive terms as *species* or *mankind* when the blame for the current crisis should be squarely laid at the door of the rich nations in the first place and the richer classes in the poorer ones?'[15] And while Chakrabarty emphasises the unwitting nature of the species' effects on earth systems processes[16] – a concession which implicitly challenges the image of a rational actor in sovereign command of its actions – the very language of 'unintentionality' holds out the promise of improved self-awareness and coordinated response. Thus, when it comes to the politics not of blame but of action, this species-without-identity is confronted with the chance to transform itself into a fully-fledged, wholly global political agent:

> Climate change poses for us a question of a *human collectivity*, an us, pointing to a figure of the universal that escapes our capacity to experience the world. It is more like a universal that arises from a shared sense of catastrophe. It calls for a *global approach* to politics without the myth of global identity.[17]

In Chakrabarty's production of this Anthropocenic drama, therefore, the central geological actor makes a last-minute costume change before stepping onto the global stage and playing the role of master of its destiny. And in this way the name 'species', at least in Chakrabarty's narration of the tale, ultimately calls forth a mode of thinking and feeling that turns out to be all too human(ist).

To note this recuperation of humanism and its presumption of the human animal's sovereignty over the (nonhuman) world is perhaps to repeat – with a difference, no doubt – a critical gesture enacted by Derrida half a century ago, when he sought to underscore the 'eschato-teleological situation' in which 'the name of man has always been inscribed'.[18] Speaking to the philosophical style that was dominating France in the 1960s, Derrida firstly noted the ways in which various critiques of 'anthropologism' would *reduce* to such an anthropologism forms of thought – Hegelian, Husserlian, Heideggerian – that could just as readily be understood as already delimiting metaphysical humanism and its conceptual resources. 'The anthropologistic reading of Hegel, Husserl, and Heidegger', he remarked, 'was a mistake in one entire respect, perhaps the most serious one'.[19] But if these philosophies could so easily be 'misread' in this way, that fact itself would be indicative of the extent to which the critique or delimitation of humanism can find itself within the orbit of the figure of man.[20] For Derrida, then, the attention given in post-Sartrean 'French thought' to questions of system and structure, as opposed to 'human-reality' and hermeneutic priority, likewise fails to provide any secure means for 'overcoming' metaphysics, hence for displacing anthropocentrism once and for all. To be sure, the reduction of 'human experience' to the operations of an 'impersonal' or 'inhuman' structure hold out the promise of 'a kind of break with a thinking of Being which has all the characteristics of a *relève* (*Aufhebung*) of humanism'.[21] But in 'determining the possibility of *meaning* on the basis of a "formal" organization which in itself has no meaning', such a strategy must thereby submit itself to that *play* of meaning, exposing itself, therefore, to the *risk* of 'ceaselessly confirming' what it 'allegedly deconstructs', or 'ceaselessly reinstat[ing] the new terrain on the oldest ground'.[22] Thus so many 'transgressions' would be transformed into 'false exits' by the 'force and efficiency of the system' of metaphysical humanism.[23]

In the first instance, it is by virtue of this sense in which the risk of failure is ineradicable from the conception and formation – indeed, from the very *necessity* – of a strategy that contemporary critical engagement with the Anthropocene perhaps retains a strange intimacy with 'man'. Indeed, such modes of thinking and feeling could well be characterised as loopy – and not only in the sense captured in Morton's characterisation of ecological awareness as 'twisting', 'looping'. For Morton, it's via such 'weirdness', where 'appearance is always strange', that the 'dark pathway between causality and the aesthetic dimension, between doing and appearing' might be unblocked.[24] But where Morton names a strange loop as 'one in which two levels that appear utterly separate', such as geology and humanity, 'flip into one another',[25] the loopiness of Chakrabarty's argument turns on its recuperation of the very mode of thought which Morton hopes the 'post-anthropocentric' naming of the species might leave behind. A looping return to eschato-teleological thinking sees two distinct levels, a whole series of distinct levels in fact, *appear* as though they could ever be one: causal responsibility and formal responsibility; species behaviour and global action; aggregated activity and coordinated response; environmental outcome ('us') and political agent ('we'). Yet how else to deal with the crisis of global warming, except through an endeavour to bring forth a human collectivity and a global approach to politics? And if such attempts ultimately fall prey to the anthropocentric fancies of human exceptionalism that brought us to the situation in which 'we' find ourselves, what's a thus-named *species* to do?

Charged as it is with the imperative to usher in a posthumanist or post-anthropocentric age, the contemporary invocation of anthropos within critical thought is, again, rarely intended to reassert the status and sovereignty of 'man'. Indeed, the affirmation of the human animal's empirically, biologically defined existence as a species subject to, hence delimited by, broader conditions of life would rather serve as the vehicle for dispelling such metaphysical delusions. Yet what Chakrabarty's concluding appeal to species as a 'figure of the universal' already indicates is that 'man', even when reduced to his biological existence and stripped of his ecological hubris, all too often *survives* such critiques, and perhaps does so precisely because the very survival imagined, yearned for – in calls for global action on climate change, say – is the *continuation* of what Colebrook, following Foucault, identifies as 'a normative logic of life'.[26] This very conception of (human) species survival, that is, may be said to derive its meaning and its value from what Foucault diagnoses as 'the metaphysic of a life that converges on man even if it does not stop with him'.[27] On Foucault's well-known account, this metaphysic of life is one characteristic or tendency (alongside that of labour and language) evinced by that 'strange empirico-transcendental doublet' called 'man' which emerged two centuries ago as the condition and limit to modern thought.[28] But where Foucault's archaeological rendering of the modern episteme is all too easily reduced to a simple 'epistemological critique' of humanism, Colebrook finds in his analysis a more profound significance:

> It was the genius of Foucault to take the modern logic of life and show its direct consequences for human *disciplines*. It is the turn to *life* – the idea that social historical man can be explained by a more general process of species being (or man as a laboring political animal) – that enables social sciences. These disciplines are *reactive* because they no longer present norms as direct imperatives but as following on from the needs of life; there can only be biopolitical management of populations if there are human sciences that enable an ethics of knowledge, an organization of the human species according to broader requirements of existence. (DP 169)

For Colebrook, then, those reflections on contemporary existence that are oriented towards the survival of the human species inevitably derive their critical valence and political impetus from a normative image of the furthering of life – that is, of a long history of life in relation to which *Homo sapiens* would sit as a kind of *telos* or (as Foucault puts it) 'extremity'.[29] Indeed, by continuing to explain 'historical man' in terms of 'his' species being, the various references to biological life made in any number of versions of (bio)politics thereby grant to 'anthropos' the power once again to direct its collective existence by way of choosing the form of life most appropriate to its condition, whether the latter be that being's ontological standing as 'political animal', its self-interested character as *Homo economicus*, or its ostensible (not to mention, ironic) fate as 'endangered species'. Accordingly, the value of continued life, of species survival – achieved via a political commitment to sustainability, for example – ultimately serves as an alibi for the continued reinscription of 'man' as the normative ground of life. As Colebrook argues, 'sustainability assumes the value of continuity: if one changes it is only insofar as is required in order for life to continue, an implication that . . . accept[s] that humanity exists as something that has the right to continue' (DP 54). In this way, she adds, 'climate change is conceived as a problem of disturbance, precluding us from continuing life in the same manner; and it is only for that reason that changes need to be made' (DP 55).

What remains unthinkable, on Colebrook's account, is the potential for existence to be subject to a radical contingency and an 'explosive power or potentiality *to differ*' (DP 217) that perforce leaves open the question of 'whether the future would be one of life' (DP 57). Such a question – in seeming to welcome only a pessimistic embrace of inevitable extinction and thereby quelling every impulse to pursue global action – no doubt risks being charged as defeatist and counterproductive. But it is for Colebrook precisely the imprudence (if not also impudence) of this challenge to climate change politics which may have the most to contribute to any critique of anthropocentrism:

> At its simplest, climate change 'policy' would [in view of this questioning of the continuity of life] have to shift from being *political* – the coming together of bodies in common via a common language of sustaining and adapting – to become *impolitic*. What ways of speaking would fragment, disturb and destroy the logics of self-maintenance that have always sustained humanity as an animal that cannot question its existence? (DP 58)

If such an 'impolitic' response thereby disturbs the otherwise unquestionable presumption of humankind's right to survive, the untimely and injudicious effects of that response only intensify in the context of the thought of the animal-to-come. For Virno's account of the potential animal can be understood at one level as enabling the kind of fragmentation and destruction of the logics of self-maintenance that Colebrook asks after. The fundamental untimeliness of *Homo sapiens*, that species' lack of access to an ecological niche, the essential contingency of its varied pseudo-environments – all of these conditions point to the *incapacity* of the human animal to maintain its sovereignty or to secure its continuity. Yet what contemporary climate change and other forms of anthropogenic habitat disruption may testify to, besides the human animal's seeming ignorance of or indifference to its effects on the planet and its inhabitants, is the extent to which the 'lack of a circumscribed and well-ordered environment', which Virno counts as a 'prerogative' of the human animal, is at the very least a *prospect* that faces many nonhuman species as well. Organisms other than the human animal, that is, can find themselves 'out of place', within an environment that is *not their own*, such that 'the world shows itself to be an amorphous and enigmatic context', provoking 'by way of reaction' (to use Virno's language) 'halting behaviours, obsessive tics' (NH 102).[30] To be sure, Virno's specification of the *Homo sapiens* biological invariant is grounded in that invariant's point of difference from the phylogeny of nonhuman species: if it is a *prerogative* of the 'indefinite animal' to lack 'its own environment' and therefore to 'wrestle with a vital context that is always partially undetermined', the implication is that other organisms live in sync with their environments, existing within 'stream[s] of perceptual stimuli' that are immediately and seamlessly – which is to say, mechanistically – 'translate[d] into an effective operational code' (NH 98). Sophisticated reconstitutions of Derrida's argument on the limitrophic nature of 'the' human-animal distinction are hardly necessary here in order to complicate this point of differentiation and to affirm, instead – for at least some species of nonhuman animals – a phenomenological account of (animal) environments as fields of 'intentional' relations, grounded in 'practical, unreflective familiarity'.[31] A certain gesture of human exceptionalism might thus be defeated by the recognition that not only human but also nonhuman animals inhabit *worlds*: coherent relations of significance, that is, within which individual animals move and act not reactively but responsively, in meaningful, intentional ways.[32] Such worlds would thereby testify to each animal's proper place – not to its position within a seamless 'stream of perceptual stimuli', *qua* being whose 'effectiveness' and 'operationality' derive from the mechanicity of physico-chemical processes, but rather to its capacity to *respond* as a purposeful being related organically to, and interacting intentionally with, an environment experienced as a world of living significance.

But if such affirmations of intentionality, of the living meaning which defines the organism and its relation to its environment, appear to challenge the Cartesian and anthropocentric images of the animal-machine and of nonhuman animals as incapable of responding, they do so only by continuing to affirm a metaphysics of life that Foucault has diagnosed as specifically modern.[33] And in this way, as Colebrook explains, attempts to affirm the living meaning of animal worlds ultimately draw on a normative logic of life derived from the modern image of 'man':

> Humanism posits an elevated or exceptional 'man' to grant sense to existence, then when 'man' is negated or removed what is left is the human all too human tendency to see the world as one giant anthropomorphic self-organizing living body . . . 'Man' is effected as that animal who would be especially poised to read the logic of life, and this because of his capacities for speech and sociality; it is the creation of man that enables a certain concept of life. When man is destroyed to yield a posthuman world it is the same world *minus humans*, a world of meaning, sociality and readability yet without any sense of the disjunction, gap or limits of the human. Like nihilism, the logic is metaleptic: the figure of man is originally posited in order to yield a sense of the meaning of life, and yet when man is done away with as an external power what is left is an anthropomorphic life of meaning and readability. (DP 163–4)

Indeed, this logic of life is one which perhaps pervades organicist and vitalist thinking generally, to the extent at least that such thought conceives of life in terms of a logic of *self-maintenance* that renders (self)difference and the other – the technical or prosthetic but also (*a fortiori*) 'untimely' death or destruction – as fundamentally external, hence inessential, to life as such. In this organicist logic, all images of 'life', including those informing 'living meaning', that intentionality that is thought to constitute a world, inevitably proceed from an acceptance of the self's originary, determinate and continuous relation to itself, a relation untroubled by any *necessary* opening to the other. Yet it would suffice merely to register, for instance, the countless examples of camouflage and mimicry on the part of numerous species – both animal and botanical; for the purpose both of predation and of evasion – in order to admit the potential 'indeterminacy' of so-called 'operational' and 'effective' 'perceptual stimuli'.[34] Such physiognomic and ecological ruses speak both to the conflictual character of natural habitats and to a fundamental deficit in informational security, which together necessitate an *economy* of interpretation, even in the absence of any affirmation of that 'living' meaning which is imagined to bring a world into relief. Here the exteriorisation or prostheticisation of self through the formation of habit, the sociality of interspecies interaction, the preservation or cultivation of self and environment, hence the *institution* of an environment which sustains the organism or within which an organism might work to sustain itself – such phenomena speak to the *in-principle* selectivity and compensatory nature of perception, experience and praxis. And all this before we even begin to consider the strategic use by human agents of such 'artificial' objects as scarecrows, plastic owls, baits, recordings of animal noises, fences, electric lights and more in efforts to manage animal movement and behaviour. As thus *open* and *contested*, the elements or conditions of a given organism's environment can always, at the very least, *function* as elements or conditions of the environment of another, such that no environment can be entirely circumscribed, closed off from 'its' (or some other) 'outside'. Indeed, 'lack of a circumscribed and well-ordered environment' can be taken as a general condition of existence for all organisms to the extent that a given environment is never entirely closed off to the disruptive effects or forces of intervention, anthropogenic or otherwise (see Chapter 2), which is as much as to say that *no* animal is properly fit for this earth. Part of what *constitutes* an organism's environment, in other words, is the structural possibility that the organism in question can find itself *outside* 'that' environment, a structural possibility – itself neither organic nor inorganic, strictly speaking – which threatens from the outset that 'living' meaning that might otherwise be thought to characterise a creature's 'world'.³⁵

On this basis we might say of any 'environment', as Derrida has remarked of any 'context', that within it 'there is a margin of play, of difference, an opening ... [which] come[s] close to blurring or dangerously complicating the limits between inside and outside, in a word, the framing of a context'.³⁶ To admit this much, moreover, is to begin to confront the extent to which the divided temporality that defines structural openness to the future-to-come – a temporality which appears on the one hand to hold open the promise of a 'posthuman' zoopolitics-to-come while announcing, on the other, a certain inevitability in the form of anthropogenic climate change – may call for a significant *impolitic*, perhaps even *demoralising*, rethinking of the logics of contemporary eco-philosophical thought. For the possibility being rendered visible today in the form of rapid climate change is that environments, notwithstanding their status as 'natural' or 'physical' systems, are never free from the effects of 'writing', such that the circumscription and inhabitation of a given environment is marked by all the complications that Derrida attributes to the structure or operation of *(con)textuality*. Recast as a moment or dimension of a contextuality riven by this margin of play, that is, no environment could ever be considered entirely delimited. Any supposed 'circumscription', rather, could only ever be, as Derrida writes of contexts, 'relatively *firm*' – 'neither absolutely solid [*fermeté*] nor entirely closed [*fermeture*]' – and never 'simply identical to itself'.³⁷ For that reason, too, no organism could be said to 'have' a circumscribed and well-ordered environment, to have its 'proper place', which is to say, to inhabit or to occupy the 'centre' of an environment that were not itself structurally open to some outside, and therefore lacking a fixed centre.

What may follow from this (re)thinking of life 'as such' as thus *institutional, prosthetic* – as fundamentally in-ventive, as maintained or sustained by virtue of efforts that are always less than resolute, less than perfect, hence provisional and necessarily open to transformative eventualities, and therefore 'always partially undetermined' and only ever 'relatively firm'? What are the consequences of such a thought, for example, for the contemporary imperative to challenge anthropocentrism, and its presumption of human sovereignty and response, in the name of attending to life more generally? And what might these consequences mean, in turn, for attempts to think a (zoo)politics of climate change – whether of the Anthropocene or of environmental impact, more generally – that would exceed the (anthropocentric?) politics of blame (human responsibility) and of coordinated global action (human sovereignty)?

In the first instance, it becomes possible to recognise that it is not only anthropocentric ideals of human species survival – such as those implied in the value of sustainability, say – that remain informed by a (humanist) metaphysic of life which derives the norms of life from life's presumed interior law. The same might also be said of those vitalist or bio-philosophical accounts of ecological existence that conceive of the organism (nonhuman or otherwise) as an internally coherent 'organic structure, which maintains uninterrupted relations with exterior elements that it utilizes (by breathing and eating) in order to maintain or develop its own structure'.[38] As a *metaphysic*, such an idealised image of harmonious communion between an animal and 'its' environment (or world) would therefore remain complicit with the anthropocentrism that it might otherwise be called upon to challenge. To note this complicity is, first of all, to acknowledge the extent to which the critical hunt after anthropocentrism can proceed with any confidence only by turning tail on the animal-to-come, approaching the problem of carnophallogocentric violence in terms of a well-established axiology of (bad) human sovereignty and (good) ecological stability. Within such a schema, that is, response to the problem of anthropocentrism inevitably takes the form of analysing various actions, decisions or political positions on the seemingly secure basis of such critically endorsed values. Accordingly, the problem of anthropocentrism – whether in the guise of teleological humanism, anthropogenic climate change or carnophallogocentric violence more generally – presents itself as one masterable, solvable, through an application of well-defined concepts, an appearance which only *furthers* the image of human sovereignty that the critique of human exceptionalism otherwise hopes to dispel.

Yet if this observation brings out the residual anthropocentrism of certain strands of eco-philosophical and biopolitical thought, it also brings to the fore once again the abyssal, internally divided nature of 'the limit' between the human and the animal. For the homology of environmentality with contextuality testifies to the extent to which the *dynamis* that Virno identifies as the biological invariant of the *Homo sapiens* is not, strictly speaking, the 'prerogative' of that 'indefinite' species alone. Indeed, in view of the thought of zoopower developed earlier, such indefinite potentiality to differ could not be said to be the prerogative or property of *any* particular species, organism or form of life. Rather, it would be riven by that nonpower at the heart of power, hence 'owed' to nothing more 'meaningful' or 'substantial' than that 'gap' between so-called organism and so-called environment, the gap *within* such organisms and *within* environments. By virtue of such, this indefinite, strictly unlocatable potentiality would deny every creature access to what Virno calls a 'circumscribed and well-ordered environment in which to insert [itself] with innate expertise once and for all' (NH 97), making every environment something of a 'pseudoenvironment', a provisional, institutional space. Yet it is a form of climate change routinely identified as *anthropogenic* that – in a mode of manifestation akin to what Virno calls a natural-historical diagram – is rendering especially visible today certain variations in the *distribution, instantiation, implication* and *reserve* of that (nonhuman) potentiality. If it seems undeniable, moreover, that one could add to this list of phenomena made visible by anthropogenic climate change certain *limitations* to nonhuman potentiality, in the form of 'natural limits',[39] the extent to which such limitations are revealed in and as the very *mutability* of ecological and climatological systems may also suggest the need for these limitations to be read otherwise: to be engaged, that is, not simply according to the model of the limit, but rather in terms of the *problem* of response.

Undoubtedly the notion of reading limits otherwise might itself be read as foregrounding primarily epistemological or conceptual returns on a thinking of the animal-to-come, at the expense, say, of confronting the demand for action. Yet such interpretive practices are, on the contrary, all too concrete both in their operations and in their consequences. Take, for example, efforts to protect coral communities on the Great Barrier Reef from outbreaks of *Acanthaster planci*, the coral-eating crown-of-thorns starfish (COTS). Such efforts hinge on the maintenance of a COTS reproductive threshold density which can aid in coral recovery and adaptation to climate change-induced stresses, such as rising sea temperatures and ocean acidification.[40] Here an identified limit designates simultaneously a parameter of perceived ecological stability, understood in terms of coral reef health and resilience, and a threshold demarcating a plague-like outbreak from an ex-nominated baseline. Understood in such terms the limit all too readily operates as a law demanding enforcement, in the form of COTS 'control' programmes – direct injections of various toxins (bile salts, household vinegar or sodium bisulphate) into large numbers of individual starfish. Such parameters to normal COTS population density (hence to reef health) are read otherwise by the asteroids themselves, however, with studies of the reproductive and larval biology of *A. planci* as well as the dynamics of population recruitment, density and aggregation identifying the possibility that the starfish communities are 'naturally' prone to episodic outbreaks.[41] A significant increase in the frequency of these outbreaks has nevertheless been linked to elevated phytoplankton availability associated with the nutrient enrichment of reef waters, a condition which is in turn attributed to terrestrial run-off, driven by storms flooding sediment and nutrients from agricultural fertilisers into the ocean.[42] From a reef conservation perspective, such movements of nutrient-filled water – potentially exacerbated by climate change – enable the dangerous transgression of a critical limit which threatens further coral loss, but for the seastar populations these same developments produce a condition of abundance – of phytoplankton, an *A. planci* larval food source. Literally *fed* by commercial agriculture practices, the coral-eating starfish appear, therefore, in and as an ambivalent figure of monstrosity: an artificial by-product of industrial pollutants and a threat to the health of a natural wonder of the world. Yet the hypothesis that COTS populations are otherwise prone to 'outbreaks' testifies to the extent to which that species' status as a monstrosity is already assigned on the basis of the aesthetic and economic value that the Great Barrier Reef holds for the State of Queensland, a global tourism market, and much more besides.[43] And if ecosystem preservation strategies can be seen as so obviously informed by such anthropocentric priorities – even carnophallogocentrically and necropolitically driven by them, as current COTS population controls methods may show – what does this mean for attempts to mobilise a nonanthropocentric approach to coral reef 'management'?

If anthropocentrism is to be addressed as a problem, then, what this problem perhaps highlights is the need to engage it in such a way that *responding* to the problem is precisely what constitutes the problem. As Cary Wolfe has noted, 'just because we direct our attention to the study of nonhuman animals', or to forces and conditions of the nonhuman world generally, 'with the aim of exploring how they have been misunderstood and exploited, that does not mean that we are not continuing to be humanist – and therefore, by definition, anthropocentric'.[44] Accordingly, responding to the problem of anthropocentrism – taking anthropocentrism as a question rather than as a known value – would mean making a problem precisely of response: pursuing a thought of response defined, in our context at least, in view of the animal-to-come. Understood in this sense, the problem of anthropocentrism would present itself as the problem of thinking a response devoid of that (human) sovereignty and purpose which has always been attributed to it, which is to say, thinking the aporetic possibility of a response that is perhaps unrecognisable as a response or that does not lend itself to being experienced as a response. Indeed, following Derrida we might dare to consider such a way of thinking as the very kernel of responsibility:

> I will . . . venture to say that ethics, politics, and responsibility, *if there are any*, will only ever have begun with the experience and experiment of the aporia. When the path is clear and given, when a certain knowledge opens up the way in advance, the decision is already made, it might as well be said that there is none to make: irresponsibly, and in good conscience, one simply applies or implements a program. Perhaps, and this would be the objection, one never escapes the program. In that case, one must acknowledge this and stop talking with authority about moral or political responsibility. The condition of possibility of this thing called responsibility is a certain *experience and experiment of the possibility of the impossible: the testing of the aporia* from which one may invent the only *possible invention, the impossible invention*.[45]

In this respect, the operation of naming proposed by Isabelle Stengers, in her reflection on what she calls the 'coming barbarism', constitutes a perhaps more *inventive* response to the effects of global warming than does many a call for direct climate change action.[46] For in responding to impending environmental catastrophe, Stengers proposes not to call upon the human species as a global collective, a 'we' who could solve the climate crisis, but instead to name *the intrusion of Gaia* as an event that calls such a 'we' into question (CT 43). The name 'Gaia' recalls, of course, the famous work by James Lovelock and Lynn Margulis, who sought to characterise the biosphere as an 'ensemble of living organisms' capable of 'act[ing] as a single entity'.[47] And, in view of Colebrook's diagnosis of a certain 'posthumanist' metalepsis, such attributions of coherence and self-regulation to this planetary being would appear to have little to offer to the contemporary critique of anthropocentrism insofar as they remain entirely consistent with the modern, humanist metaphysic of life diagnosed by Foucault. But Stengers's account of Gaia is one that rather shatters that reassuring aura of a stable, nurturing and life-preserving being. For Gaia names, on Stengers's account, not a living 'mother Earth' but rather 'an assemblage of material processes that demand neither to be protected nor to be loved, and which cannot be moved by the public manifestation of our remorse' (CT 48). Indeed, 'Gaia, she who intrudes, *asks nothing of us*, not even a response to the question she imposes'; she is 'indifferent to the question "who is responsible?"' (CT 46). Crucially, though, Gaia designates not simply a way of conceiving a physical system or a material environment but also a specific *disruption* to the forms of knowledge and existence that have characterised centuries of human civilisation. Gaia names, then, the intrusion of 'an unprecedented or forgotten form of transcendence':

> The intrusion of this type of transcendence, which I am calling Gaia, makes a major unknown, *which is here to stay*, exist at the heart of our lives. This is perhaps the most difficult to conceptualize: no future can be foreseen in which she will give back to us the liberty of ignoring her. It is not a matter of a 'bad moment that will pass', followed by any kind of happy ending – in the shoddy sense of a 'problem solved'. We are no longer authorized to forget her. (CT 47)

As epistemological intrusion, Stengers's Gaia constitutes both a disturbance, a force of differing, as well as a call for a form of thinking and feeling that can break the monotony of thinking about climate change instrumentally, which is to say, always and solely as a problem to be solved. And from this fact stems a series of divergences – twists, perhaps – from the kind of thinking called forth by moves to construe anthropos in terms of its biological conditions and its status as a species. In contrast to Chakrabarty's pursuit of 'a figure of the universal', for example, Stengers's Gaia necessarily interrupts the search for any such conceptual certainties: 'the response to her intrusion will not admit, cannot admit, any guarantee, because Gaia is deaf to our ideas' (CT 84). And where Chakrabarty finds in the name of 'species' a call, upon 'us', to pursue a 'global approach to politics', Stengers is wary of making any such claim to the terms of the response:

> Do not ask me to sketch what other world may be able to come to terms, or compose, with Gaia. The response doesn't belong to us, that is to those who have provoked her intrusion and now decipher it through data, models, and simulations. Naming Gaia is naming a question, but emphatically not defining the terms of the answer, as such a definition would give us, us again, always us, the first and last word. Learning to compose will need many names, not a global one, the voices of many peoples, knowledges, and earthly practices. It belongs to a process of multifold creation, the terrible difficulty of which it would be foolish and dangerous to underestimate *but which it would be suicidal to think of as impossible*. There will be no response other than the barbaric if we do not learn to couple together multiple, divergent struggles and engagements in this process of creation, as hesitant and stammering as it may be. (CT 50)

Against the search for universals and the call for a global politics, then, the naming of Gaia's intrusion might give us pause for thought when claiming different forms of agency and responsibility on the part of 'the species'. Undoubtedly, various forms of human activity – each differentially constituted with respect to their relative orientations, interactions and impacts – have aggregated to exert a significant force or pressure on the geophysical and atmospheric conditions that define the Subatlantic age of the Holocene.⁴⁸ And certainly the need to respond in some way seems undeniable, if only because refusal to act would nevertheless constitute a response.⁴⁹ But the intrusion of Gaia, on Stengers's account, calls for a response – a mode of thinking and feeling – not from a global 'we' or 'us', but from 'many peoples, knowledges, and earthly practices'. Such a call implies, in the first instance, an injunction to look beyond the figural death of man, and even the literal – if potential – death of the species, in order to foreground their *decomposition*. For the 'political problem' with the figures of 'man', 'humanity' and the like derives not simply from their 'oppressive' nature, as Chakrabarty assumes,⁵⁰ but more significantly from the fact that these notions have been deployed to name a unity or coordination of purpose and action which has never really existed – the species' newfound geological agency notwithstanding. Wherever 'man' has been thought to be acting, that is, closer inspection has always revealed the circumscribed and contingent operations of *assemblages*. Hence the debates about whether to name the species or Capital as the geological agency whose actions have given rise to the Anthropocene. Hence too the variability and provisionality of those 'natural-historical diagrams' that expose the iterative, differential and still contemporary event of what Virno nevertheless wants to call 'anthropogenesis'. In this context, moreover, it is worth recalling that, as Vinciane Despret reminds us, the inhuman 'structures' to which Deleuze and Guattari give the name 'assemblages' take shape through and as distributions of agential, or interagential, force:

> Deleuze's translator, Brian Massumi, chose to translate *agencements* as 'assemblages'; I would rather opt for keeping the French word: *agencement*. First this term renders perceptible the intimate link between '*agencement*' and 'agency', and second, it insists upon an active process of attunement that is never fixed once and for all. An *agencement* is a rapport of forces that makes some beings capable of making other beings capable, in a plurivocal

manner, in such a way that the *agencement* resists being dismembered, resists clear-cut distribution. What constitutes the agent and the patient is distributed and redistributed incessantly.[51]

Despret recalls this point as part of a discussion of animal agency, but in the context both of the Anthropocene and of the animal-to-come it should be remembered that the range of 'beings' made capable in or by such assemblages extends to include not only animals but also (after Stengers) 'peoples, knowledges, and earthly practices' generally (CT 50). Artworks and animals, concepts and radiation, sun, sky and signification: the constellations of forces that flow through, in and out of 'an' assemblage resist being organised according to conventional taxonomies, least of all by such oppositions as natural and artificial, physical and institutional, living and inorganic, human and nonhuman, or even organism and environment. Yet debates about whether to name the species or Capital as the agency whose actions have given rise to the Anthropocene continue to attribute past, present and future geological and atmospheric transformations to a single anthropocentric force. And a certain kind of loopy thinking thereby confers upon a species, or dimension of a species, the power to act in concert, translating 'aggregated activity' into 'coordinated action' and giving 'us' the first and last word yet again.

By contrast, perhaps, the naming of Gaia as a form of intrusion, the call to attend to plays of nonpower in or as the (re)distribution of (nonhuman) potentiality or, indeed, 'im/potentiality' - such moves may grant the chance to conceive of a politics of the Anthropocene as a kind of zoopolitics produced or discovered in view of the animal-to-come. And, in that form, the question of thinking responsibility in relation to climate change – or, indeed, to any other form of carnophallogocentric violence – would perhaps have less to do with determining who or what is culpable, or even who or what is obliged to answer the call to action, than it has to do with the problem of thinking *nonhuman response*. While the concept of responsibility has always implied 'a sufficient knowledge or consciousness of what being *responsible* means',[52] hence a capacity to *respond* in view of that knowledge, what has proven to be the elusive and problematic attribution of responsibility to that 'open, porous' 'hyperobject' named the human species would appear to suggest that the question of responsibility is, in any event, never entirely *answerable* to that meaning or condition. Here, the apparent distinction between causal and formal (moral, legal) responsibility already suggests as much. But further than this, and notwithstanding the planet's apparent 'indifference' to the question of who is responsible, Gaia's intrusion, understood as a form of *response* to a history of human (co)existence, might be seen to enact a consequential form of nonhuman response, even a strange kind of 'being responsible'.

No doubt, such an observation risks authorising an anthropocentric stance insofar as it may appear to indulge certain forms of climate change denial, which try to attribute atmospheric changes to the routine operations of pre-existing earth systems processes. But the same would have to be said of Lovelock and Margulis's version of the Gaia hypothesis, and, indeed, many a call for climate change action, to the extent that they ascribe to earth systems processes their own *purposeful* logic. Heeding the strange relations between the force of anthropocentrism and the metaphysics of life, then, the thought of a nonhuman or other-than-human mode of 'being responsible' would have to be seen as a form of response unsecured by that sovereignty or that living meaning, that intentionality, which is so regularly called upon to animate calls for climate change action or environmental justice. And if it appears that such a questioning of life can only exacerbate anthropocentric denial of responsibility towards the nonhuman world, the move to account for 'responsibility' in this way might yet constitute a step towards rethinking the supposed distinction between reaction and response. For the thought of responsibility implies the necessary possibility of doing or acting *otherwise*. No being, no creature or subject, for example, that was incapable of acting otherwise than according to a predetermined or pre-programmed plan, of doing anything other than *reacting* 'mechanistically', could be said to be responsible as such. Indeed, on Derrida's account, the mechanistic – in the sense of 'automatic' (because programmatic) – reaction would mark, at best, the very absence of decision, hence the absence of responsibility. Yet the various 'questions', as Stengers puts it, that may come to be 'addressed to any of [Gaia's] constituent processes' – the interventions, the modifications, the intensifications and reductions, the couplings and separations – 'can bring into play a sometimes *unexpected response* involving them all' (CT 45).

In this regard, it is worth recalling that Lovelock and Margulis developed their Gaia hypothesis in order to account for 'the profoundly *anomalous* composition of the Earth's atmosphere when it is compared with that of the *expected* atmosphere of a planet interpolated between Mars and Venus'.[53] Their hypothesis – that 'the total ensemble of living organisms which constitute the biosphere can act as a single entity to regulate chemical composition, surface pH and possibly also climate' – thus served as a means of accounting for the fact that 'the biosphere and all of those parts of the Earth with which it actively interacts' appear to constitute an 'entity with properties that *could not be predicted* from the sum of its parts'.[54] To think of nonhuman entities, systems or forces (animals, species, ecosystems, weather events and more) as being responsible, therefore, is to think of them as potentially 'capable' of 'acting', of responding to environmental changes or interventions – hence initiating their own changes in turn – in ways that could not be calculated in advance via a logic either of reaction or of intention. To the extent that such initiatives emerge, moreover, as responses to anomalous or unexpected change, to a prior, hence unmasterable difference and otherness, response – 'human' or otherwise – would take place as the expression not of a form of sovereignty but rather of a dynamic contingency. To concede in this way such a mode of (nonhuman) 'response' would therefore be to make 'a major unknown' exist not only 'at the heart of our lives', as Stengers has put it, but moreover at the heart of all life as such. But it would also broach the rather impolitic, and perhaps impossible, thought of a nonhuman mode of '*ir*responsibility'. For the very incalculability of nonhuman response, the unpredictability of nonhuman initiative, would thereby exceed the parameters of a concept of causal responsibility. Such forms of initiative would be, in that sense, unaccountable even to Gaia's own laws, so to speak: always having the potential to act otherwise than they 'should'.

In this way, the question of what is *to come* of (and for) specific environments or ecological contexts may yet be open or opened to possibilities that are unanswerable to the conservative logics (in both senses of the term) of protection and preservation that so often inform the politics and management of ecosystems. According to such logics, the forms and possibilities characterising the futures of coral reefs, for example, must be derived from the internal law of life, from an idealised moment of uncompromised self-regulation, which would otherwise be only *threatened* by an intervention – perverse, if not monstrous – from without. By contrast, the thought of nonhuman response, of nonhuman (ir)responsibility, uncoupled from the metaphysics of life, might attend to coral reefs, among other ecological 'systems', rather as *agencements*, assemblages of entangled, provisional, institutional forces that could never be entirely closed to the outside. Figured as moments of force redistributed within such assemblages, moreover, 'agencies' of coral reef rehabilitation might come in surprising guises – in the guise, for instance, of the broadcast of 'healthy' reef soundscapes via underwater loudspeakers.[55] Or they might come in the guise of low-voltage electric current administered through steel frames fixed to denuded reef substrates. Indeed, use of electrolytic technology in marine ecosystem restoration has been trialled for a number of decades now, with some studies reporting remarkable increases in coral growth rates as well as improved resistance to stresses in other forms of marine life.[56] Working with the inherent openness of biological, ecological life to institutionality, hence 'artificial' supplementation, such developments gesture towards the time of what Dominique Lestel calls 'an artificial and communitary transspecies animality that develops in spaces shared with humans'.

Unanswerable to evolutionary laws or origins, these *agencements* 'constitute an *a posteriori* animality that is revealed through adventures that are always undertaken together', and which are 'inscribed in the cultural, organic and material genealogies that contaminate our own yet which nevertheless set down the conditions of existence'.[57]

Here, the thought of 'adventure', of a process set underway, in which nonhuman animals of various types may participate and respond, speaks to the role that such forms of life inevitably play in the ongoing transformation of the conditions of such life. Thus, potential forces of environmental rehabilitation might yet take the form of biological 'invasion', as hypothesised by marine biologist and Australian Laureate Fellow David Bellwood.[58] Writing with Christopher Goatley, Bellwood notes that, while Caribbean coral reef ecosystems are currently suffering from an excess of micro-algae and reduced herbivory, 'an invasion of Red Sea rabbitfishes is disrupting Mediterranean ecosystems by removing micro-algae'.[59] Consequently, he suggests, 'the future of Caribbean coral reefs may depend upon a rabbitfish invasion', a hypothesis which in turn raises the issue of active interventions.[60] Of course, biological invasions are routinely seen as ecological threats, and Bellwood is careful not to propose that deliberate steps be taken to translocate rabbitfishes from the Red Sea to the Caribbean. But the key point for him is that such movements 'seem to be just a matter of time', having been already initiated by the construction of the Suez Canal (enabling Lessepsian migration from the Red Sea to the Mediterranean) and by the aquarium trade's introduction of exotic fishes into diverse waters. Indeed, already 'approximately 20% of fish lineages in the Caribbean appear to have crossed the Atlantic from east to west'.[61] Exploiting various anthropogenic translocation mechanisms, in other words, species of fishes expand their geographic range to their advantage. And with such colonisations may come radical transformations of coral reef ecosystems - transformations that are often destructive, but which might also enable, potentially, the rehabilitation of rapidly collapsing Caribbean habitats into seemingly aberrant but otherwise 'healthy' and functional 'Mediterranean' ecosystems. Notwithstanding the power of the language of invasion to paint such developments as anathematic, therefore, the inevitability (perhaps even, in some cases, the desirability) of such movements underscores the need to attend to the new reality, to the previously unimagined futures, of such 'artificial and communitary transpecies' ecologies.[62]

While these and other approaches to rehabilitating coral reefs undoubtedly flirt with an instrumental (hence anthropocentric) view regarding the 'management' of more-than-human worlds – and while their efficacy and ecological impacts undoubtedly demand continued scrutiny[63] – the openness of these approaches to what may be called, in turn, the openness of nonhuman response itself helps to articulate what might be at stake in affirming a strange, aporetic mode of nonhuman responsibility. To be sure, 'responsibility' seems to have always (historically, conventionally) been thought as a burden or prerogative 'possessed' solely by the human animal, hence as attributable to nonhuman animals only via a kind of metaphoricity (anthropomorphism), or by way of a transgressive counter-normative act.[64] To that extent, a *trace* of anthropos perhaps remains inexpungible from any attempt to challenge the prevailing metaphysics of animals and animality – paradigmatically, Descartes's concept of the animal-machine, but also the thought of animals and the nonhuman world more generally as internally coherent entities, governed by life's interior law. Hence the anachronicity of an intellectual milieu in which the figure of the human, fatally disfigured by countless critical thrusts, is resurrected as that force which 'unwittingly' exercises its sovereignty over the nonhuman world – exercising a sovereignty *without* sovereignty, therefore. What has accordingly been thought as the sway of the human might, in that sense, be taken rather as the sway of that trace. For what the naming of Gaia's intrusion, the thought of a nonhuman (ir)responsibility and the promise of the animal-to-come collectively demonstrate is the extent to which every 'we' is already constituted, in part, by the differential agential force of any number of animal, geological and otherwise nonhuman entities, processes and events. With regard to thinking about what 'we' might do in the face of climate change, carnophallogocentrism and anthropocentrism more generally, therefore, the thought of the animal-to-come may help to underscore the possibility, if not the exigency, of recognising any such 'we' as already a co-creation, as it were.

In view of her unaccountability, then, responding to Gaia – understood as an epistemological intrusion as much as an existential one – would mean attending to the potential for human activities to 'put questions' to the assemblage of evolutionary, climatic and geophysical processes that define life as we know it. On a smaller scale, this would entail attending to the ongoing (re)distributions of that im/potentiality which underpins and animates the relations between organisms and 'their' environments. But, further, responding to Gaia, responding to the *problem* of anthropocentrism, would mean attending to the potential for such nonhuman agencies to be *uncooperative*, even unaccountable, foregrounding the possibility, if not the necessity, of negotiating, of 'learning to compose' with those agencies: working *with* such agencies, as distinct (in a sense) from working *on* them. Along these lines, moreover, what Virno thinks of, in his account of anthropogenesis, as 'the different socio-political expression that could be given, here and now' (NH 93) to the *dynamis* of the 'potential animal' can be understood to take shape in and as ambivalent moments rather of *zoo*-anthropo-genesis. Such forms of zoo-anthropogenesis would encompass not only those formations that Lestel discusses as 'hybrid communities',[65] including the 'artificial and communitary' transpecies relations discussed above, but also what Despret depicts as new articulations of 'withness' and 'being-with', 'new ways of being human with non-human' others.[66] If the thought of 'the animal-to-come' registers within critical reflection an imperative to acknowledge the fact and the future of animals and animality, in other words, this demand might be most immediately felt in the recognition that the first-person plural pronoun – that word which would refer to a collective subject not only of action or history but also of responsibility – contains within it the trace of an animal other that is a condition of its possibility. Inscribed within any 'we' is the scope or potential, that is, to refer to a broader, more distributed – yet necessarily differential and conflictual – agency, 'political' as well as 'biological', and perhaps much more besides.

What Hope for the Animal-To-Come?

At first blush, there would appear to be something profoundly ironic, if not a little disingenuous, about affirming the future of animality at a time when the very life and continued existence of countless animal species have been put into jeopardy by the ongoing environmental destruction enacted by the human animal. In an era of apparently irreversible anthropogenic climate change, what lies in store for far too many species is, in fact, no future at all. One might have cause to wonder with Claire Colebrook, then, whether a 'joyous affirmation of the living, of the multitude, of productivity, of the other or of pure potentiality and futurity' is the 'best mode of thinking and reading', when there is 'no shortage of data bombarding us daily about the inevitable end of the human organism', if not also many other forms of organic life.[1] Bound as it is to the 'infinite promise' inscribed within the structure or dimension of 'future-to-come', the thought of the animal-to-come perhaps means nothing in the absence of hope, in the absence of that 'absolutely undetermined messianic hope' at the heart of any promise. But to what extent could one speak with any confidence, hence with any sincerity, of the animal-*to-come*, when all contemporary signs point towards not the proliferation of forms of animality but an ever-increasing loss of biological diversity and the fate of mass extinction? What possible cause for hope could be fixed upon under such circumstances?

Insofar as this situation may be taken up as a philosophical question in addition to being a socio-political issue (pretending, for argument's sake, that the two modes are so precisely distinguishable), a response to the problem might be attempted by interrogating – or 'deconstructing' – the meaning or concept and even the possibility of hope itself. Here we could take our cue from Derrida's various readings or counter-readings of a range of cognate concepts – promise, event, future-to-come, the messianic, incoming, arrivant, hence justice, democracy, hospitality, faith, and more. Acknowledging the 'standard account' of hope as consisting in the conjunction of a desire for some outcome with the belief in that outcome's possibility,[2] we might note this structure's tacit inscription of some recourse to a horizon of expectation, and its presupposition of the possible arrival of the object of hope. Keeping in mind the irreducibility of responsibility and justice to calculability, we might go on to suggest conversely that any desire for that which is dispersed within or by the temporality of the future-to-come could only ever amount to a hoping for that which may never arrive. We might then supplement this account by drawing support or inspiration from some singular figure in the history of philosophy – Kierkegaard, for example[3] – in order to speculate on a more radical, aporetic hope, one whose necessary but fraught relations to some conception of the good or of justice, to the future and to the possibility of possibility, would reveal that a frustrated hope for the 'im-possible' would, in fact, be the only possible hope.[4]

A reinterpretation of hope along these lines would no doubt shed new light on this recently bereft concept and perhaps present it in a slightly more salutary fashion, serving to acknowledge the difficulty of the times and the frailty of action while giving cause for some hope nevertheless – putting a little hope back into hope, as it were, even if it took the perverse form of an unfulfillable, even inconceivable, hope. But if this impossible hope were to have any meaning, any consistency of force, it could never allow itself to serve as an excuse to avoid confronting the specific forms of violence perpetuated by the use of hope as a political value or strategy. For hope can all too easily take the form rather of a fantasy cultivated and mobilised by social powers for the purpose of bolstering hegemony. Capitalism, most obviously, thrives on 'its ability to maintain an *experience* of the *possibility* of upward social mobility', while various governments of the day further deploy ideologies of race and colonial authority to legitimate and compound unequal distributions of hope'.[5] Hopes, both 'personal' and 'political', can take the form of what Lauren Berlant calls 'cruel optimism', whereby 'the object/scene that ignites a sense of possibility actually makes it impossible to attain the expansive transformation for which a person or a people risks striving'.[6] In this way, hope becomes the mechanism by which even a would-be *progressive* politics defeats itself. For hope, as queer theorist Lee Edelman argues, all too frequently functions as the alibi by which a more fundamental status quo – 'reproductive futurism', in Edelman's terms; 'the absolute privilege of heteronormativity' – prevails.[7] Here, the value of hope gains both its apparent virtue and its oppressive force from its relation to a space of politics understood as the conflict of visions of 'a more desirable social order', a logic which remains 'conservative insofar as it works to *affirm* a structure, to *authenticate* a social order, which it then intends to transmit to the future in the form of its inner Child'.[8] That Child, as the seemingly incontestable index of all possible futures, of the future of life itself, 'remains the perpetual horizon of every acknowledged politics, the fantasmatic beneficiary of every political intervention', and thus becomes the sign under which everything that sits 'outside the consensus by which all politics confirms the absolute value of reproductive futurism' – queerness most immediately, but also any threat to the survival of the body politic – is thereby rendered as figuring a place 'of abjection'.[9]

The propensity for hope to submit to such betrayals – indeed, to be the very perpetrator of such (dis)simulative acts – provides reason enough to suspect its value in any critical reflection on the contemporary cultural condition, and doubly so when read in the context of what appear to be widescale practices of environmental destruction, biotic extinction and anthropogenocide. Indeed, in *that* context, one would perhaps feel justified in suspecting that any affirmation of hope at this late stage (in a concluding chapter which appears to be offering little in the way of conclusions) could not be anything but utterly *generic* – a modest expression of optimism against all odds, constructed in conformity with the scholarly expectation that critical works produced in the name of a marginalised or unheralded collective end on a note of positive affect. Such ruses can only compound the challenges (explored in the last chapter) that may be put to the authority or sovereignty of 'man', a posthumanist and postmodern questioning that already fuels much incredulity towards the value of hope. Thus for Jean-François Lyotard, a crisis of modernity is broached in the history of thought with the realisation that the 'human' is 'a highly unlikely material (that is, energetic) formation' dependent on the 'transitory ... conditions of terrestrial life' – and, further, that humans are not 'the motors of development' but are 'its products, vehicles, and witnesses'.[10] Such a realisation, in Lyotard's telling of this 'postmodern fable', inevitably signifies the 'the end of hopes', since 'hope is what belongs to a subject of history who promises him/herself – or to whom has been promised – a final perfection'.[11] Hope, in other words, is the privileged affect of that grand modern(ist) narrative of progress, which would install 'man' as master of his destiny. And in that sense hope would be the very obstacle to a form of thought oriented towards another kind of politics, one that might break (with) the value of reproductive futurism. As Colebrook and Weinstein put it in their reflection on the tensions engendered by the figure of the Anthropocene:

> Rather than looking hopefully to a day when these tensions are resolved either in a final moment of posthuman vanquishing of 'man' or [in] the triumph of human survival, we, following Lee Edelman, reject hope as a political strategy, in that, 'hope as affirmation is always affirmation of an order whose *refusal*

will register as unthinkable, irresponsible, inhumane'. Hope as all-too-thinkable imbricates 'us' in the heterosexist, masculinist logics at the highest order of humanism – for what is affirming hope other than bestowing an epic agential power in 'man', or returning to an 'anthropos' of a pre-postmodern, prefeminist, critique? Thus, relying upon hope would be to resurrect the presumption that 'man' as the fundamental unit [in intellectual work] is thinkable ... Rejecting hope ... takes us beyond the humanist Anthropocene logics to a position from which we might be able to begin recasting political positions in light of twenty-first-century crises.[12]

Following Lyotard, following Edelman, and following the problematisation of hope more generally, there would seem to be more than enough reasons, therefore, to view hope as irredeemably suspect.

But what is meant by 'following' here? What is it to come after? If one were to *follow* such critiques, for instance, by witnessing or diagnosing within them a certain kind of performative paradox, hence inflecting or infecting them with a small dose of hope – a sincere desire for or trust in this position that lies *beyond* all hope, or at any rate beyond any politics of hope – this move need not be seen as made in the naïve hope of negating or undermining the various critical points registered in the preceding problematisations. Indeed, such a move might rather be read as simply pursuing these problematisations in other directions. Taking Colebrook and Weinstein's question ('what is affirming hope other than bestowing an epic agential power in "man" ...?') as an example: what would follow from reading this formulation not as a vehicle for succinctly expressing what we can now see as the fundamental problem with hope, but rather from reading it in all sincerity, which is to say, precisely *as a question*?

Certainly, to the extent that the thought of the animal-to-come I've developed here has been construed from Derrida's logic of 'future-to-come' – hence from a certain 'experience' of a 'desert-like messianism (without content and without identifiable messiah)', a 'quasi-"messianism" so anxious, fragile, and impoverished' that it may even take the form of a 'despairing "messianism"' – that construction aims to recall a far less thinkable experience of hope than that cultivated by conventional humanisms.[13] And if a perhaps 'stronger' sense of hope may be said to have imposed itself at times in the course of my discussion, that inflection would seem to have arrived in response to what might be characterised as a rather limited, even pessimistic, reading of pessimism itself. Thus the pursuit of the animal-to-come has sought after, among other things, the possibility of a zoopolitics not grounded in or limited to a politics of protection. The latter – as a demand for the institution of juridico-political measures to protect animal beings of various kinds from an ever-dangerous, ever-brutal population of *human* animals – would appear to be a perfect illustration of Schmitt's dictum that 'all genuine political theories presuppose man to be evil, i.e. by no means an unproblematic but a dangerous and dynamic being'.[14] Yet Schmitt's appeal to 'evil' here is itself problematic, or at least misleading in its apparent univocity, to the extent that it constitutes for him simply a 'summary' conception, one that encompasses 'numerous modifications and variations',[15] including Helmut Plessner's characterisation of 'man' as "'primarily a being capable of creating distance" who in his essence is undetermined, unfathomable, and remains an "open question"'.[16]

In view of the nonpower at the heart of (zoo)power and Derrida's speculation on the 'limitrophic' practices or practising of 'human'-'animal' distinctions, we would no doubt want to be wary about attributing this force, this 'capability' of creating distance, to humanity or to the human animal as such. But we can see in any case that the political theories that Schmitt gathers under the banner of 'pessimistic anthropologies' cover two potentially different modes or moments of problematicity, a divergence which thus opens onto (at least) two contrasting dimensions of the political. In the first, 'politics' descends from a view of the human animal as fundamentally dangerous or brutal, hence in need of supplementation by political institutions intended specifically to curtail that danger and to protect itself and others from its violent or stupid acts. But against – or alongside – this view may stand a second image, one in which such dangerousness and dynamism mark the very chance or force of questioning, of creating distance, of being otherwise. The problematic of problematicity (so to speak) would thus lie in the potential for the logic of protection, insofar as it dominates the (bio)politics of animals and animality, to operate at the same time to protect or secure 'man' from that questioning which would risk or endanger the body politic itself. For it would be through such questioning, through such endangering of the body politic – in Edelman's terms, the social order and the politics of reproductive futurism – that something like a 'nonanthropocentric' 'posthumanism' might seek to challenge the authority and sway of that animal which calls itself 'human'. It would be precisely in dangerousness and dynamism, in other words, that one might find cause for hope for the animal-to-come.

This is as much as to suggest that hope for the animal-to-come is, ultimately, anything but *life*-affirming. Indeed, as a relation to a future-to-come which is irreducible to any 'future that can always reproduce the present',[17] hope would perhaps augur and even administer a certain opening to death and destruction. Notwithstanding the aura of creativity and productive possibility illuminating the thought of the animal-to-come, that is, moments of animal inventiveness, acts of animal initiative, and so forth inevitably announce the ending of certain possibilities. For such moments to be, precisely, occasions for the arrival of the (animal) other, they *must* coincide with a certain kind of disruption, discontinuity, destruction, even death – not least of all with disruption of those forms of anthropocentrism and carnophallogocentrism that would otherwise forestall or depreciate the (animal) other's arrival. But they may happen to coincide with the destruction of as yet unimagined and perhaps unimaginable others as well. The animal-to-come would thus be the bearer of 'death', bearing the 'capacity' to frustrate an organism's, a species' – a society's, an economy's – attempts to live on, or indeed any such attempts to ensure the *continuity* of life in general.[18] This bearance – which Derrida characterises in the second volume of *The Beast and the Sovereign* as a survivance 'in the sense of survival that is neither life nor death pure and simple', 'a survivance whose "sur-" is without superiority ... supremacy or sovereignty' – speaks to the 'inscription' of death within life, a 'weave of survival, like death in life or life in death'.[19] But it speaks also to that bearance which would 'sustain' *questioning*, would bear or carry or support the force of questioning, a trait that underscores again the problematic of problematicity, that divergence of dynamism and dangerousness that opens onto or into two potentially contrasting dimensions of the political.[20]

And it is in this context that the attempts at conceptual innovation (as it were) which I have explored in the course of thinking the animal-to-come might hope to register some political significance or effect. Distributed, institutional prosthetic animal-machine; heterochthonous in-vention of animal others; differantial nonpower at the heart of zoopower; animal action and new etho-mediatic public space; nonhuman (ir)responsibility and sovereignty without sovereignty – these formulations, as attempts first and foremost to think contemporary conditions, do not announce visions of a more desirable social order, let alone a final perfection, so much as multiply resources (so to speak) for disrupting or breaking with certain habits of thought. For this very reason, the zoopolitics announced by the thought of the animal-to-come points towards something other than a radically inclusive image of a (future) 'democracy-to-come', one which would be imagined as extending beyond humankind to encompass a 'parliament of the living'[21] more generally. Against or within or alongside this image, zoopolitics would name (among other things) the war or conflict of possibilities announced by these competing forces of carnophallogocentrism and antianthropocentrism, of domestication and invention, of cycle of life and frailty of action, of biopolitical protection and animal natality, of anthropogenesis and posthuman decomposition, of environmental degradation and nonhuman response. Just as much, it would name the war or conflict between the modes of destruction promised by each of these forces, the conflict between the ways or manners in which force or disposition must put an *end* to certain possibilities.

With the inevitability of conflict comes, no doubt, the possibility of choosing sides, as it were, hence the potential for action. But rather than follow this possibility (as the genre of social philosophy might prescribe) along the lines of a rekindled, if tempered, political optimism, the thought of the animal-to-come might lead us to wonder about what other forms or roles hope might take in this conflict, and about the kinds of questions those forms might pose to reflections on zoopolitics. For if the thought of the animal-to-come could be said to lead towards any specific form of action, it would perhaps be towards the introduction of something like multispecies thinking into the very construction of a concept, not least of all into the formation of political concepts. What may come, in other words, from thinking through specific instances of animal behaviour, specific events of animal interaction, as articulations of hope?

Can the common practice of food-caching, for example, the act of hiding away provisions for consumption at a later time, be understood, as Thom van Dooren asks, 'in the absence of something like hopefulness'?[22] If such a question, broached by van Dooren in his etho-ethnographic study of the critically endangered Mariana crow (*Corvus kubaryi*), immediately invites ethological investigations into the existence or otherwise of a 'capacity' for prospective thinking among corvids, say, the possibilities of a 'more-than-human' concept of hope are nevertheless irreducible to the presence or absence of such competencies. Certainly, food-caching speaks to a future-orientedness regardless of whether the behaviour is ultimately thought to derive from that mode of foresight (or 'episodic future thinking') that speaks to a degree of ipseity or intentionality, or rather from heritable 'fixed action patterns', such that the 'power' of prospection is attributable to the distributed agency of (co)evolutionary processes.[23] In the case of the Mariana crows' stashing of nuts from the Pacific almond tree (*Terminalia catappa*), moreover, the trick is also a practice whose fate is tied to forces, processes and decisions that have little to do with phenotypy. For the habit of provisioning and the very survival of the species are, as van Dooren demonstrates, intertwined with histories of colonisation, struggles for economic development and efforts at species conservation. If the future of the 'aga', as the crows are called by the indigenous Chamorro people, thus appears to rest on the outcome of a clash of visions – development *versus* conservation – it is nevertheless the case that the US Fish and Wildlife Service's registration of the Mariana crow as endangered has played its own part in exacerbating the decline of the species. For the listing, as van Dooren puts it, 'has pitted the aga against the people':

> Aga have been shot. They have been harassed and driven off land ... Put simply, they are now profoundly disliked by many. Not for any attribute or characteristic of the birds themselves; rather, in this case, they have become the epicenter of a complex and ongoing struggle over land ... In some cases their presence has very literally brought people's livelihoods to a halt. (WC 182)

Accordingly, van Dooren explains, many Chamorro people, 'knowing that aga like almonds, knowing that the birds perhaps rely on these nuts or at the very least are more likely to hang around where they are found', have taken to 'removing the trees wherever they find them' (WC 182).

The declining fortunes of the Mariana crow can therefore be taken to testify to the potentially counterproductive nature of hope. But in the aga's predilection for provisioning almonds van Dooren finds an occasion to register nevertheless the irreducibility of hope to such ideological, programmatic or governmental visions of social order. For the general activity of food-caching testifies to an active relation to a circumstance to come, a future that is equal parts promise and threat. Understood, that is, in the context of 'a world of uncertainty, a world in which food may well be scarce, caching is an effort to bring about the more desirable future in which one is not hungry' (WC 207). In this sense, van Dooren suggests, food-caching amounts to a practice of hope – literally of making provision –

that presents not as a quiescent relation to an abstract vision but rather as an attempt to '*cultivate* the conditions for a better future' (WC 209). Viewed from this perspective, moreover, 'hope is anything but a uniquely human pastime. These provisioning crows help us to see that we inhabit a world of multiplying futures, a world thick with both possibilities and with crafty, desirous, living beings working toward their fruition' (WC 207). To acknowledge these futures, moreover, is to do more than expand or multiply the possible objects of hope by including various nonhuman species among those for whom 'one' may hope. For '"hope" in a multispecies register', van Dooren insists, 'should be more than hope *for* other species (or even *with* a select few); it must also be an invitation and a challenge to learn to recognize radically other modes of hopefulness, diverse forms of future-orientedness, in which others – human and not – are working toward particular possibilities' (WC 212).

In this way, van Dooren opens the thought and experience of hope to the in-vention of 'more-than-human' modalities, giving a glimpse of what the thought of the animal-to-come, as I have been calling it, may yet bring to the possibilities of zoopolitics. If such a thought may sometimes take the guise of an affirmation of animal natality, plurality and potentiality, it would be rash or improvident to see in such appearances a simple affirmation of the creativity or autonomy, let alone virtue or felicity, of the nonhuman world. While van Dooren derives from the Mariana crow's acts of almond-caching a sense of hope as *ecological*, that is, such modes and experiences are at the same time never less than *institutional*. Certainly, the little biological literature that exists on the diet and behaviour of the *C. kubaryi* makes no reference to the Pacific almond, indicating the likelihood that access to the nuts is not essential to the birds' survival.[24] But what this perhaps means is that the Mariana local's removal of Pacific almond trees most immediately threatens not the survival of a species so much as the continued practising of a particular aga *custom*. Ultimately arbitrary, and perhaps even insignificant in the broader scheme of things, this wont, which, *as* cultural, is therefore not the aga's own, speaks nevertheless to the distribution of modes of existence – a mode of animality, to be sure, but also a mode of prospection – within and across a dispersed animal-machine. Hence the behaviour's fragility, its susceptibility to disruption, variation and even extinction, as van Dooren well demonstrates with his recounting of the historical forces that have shaped the aga's fortunes. But hence, too, its appropriability, interpretability, which is to say, the externalising prostheticity by virtue of which anyone might hope to derive some significance, some call for action, from that species' plight. Institutional as much as they are ecological, animal practices await technoprosthetic supplementation by any number of forces or agencies – human, animal or otherwise. Devoid of any essential, directly intuitable or seemingly incontestable justness or injustice, these animal practices remain open nevertheless to being read in such terms – or, indeed, to being read otherwise. And so remains the chance, therefore, to take them up in the name not of a zoopolitics premised on existing images of carnophallogocentrism, of anthropocentric monopolisation of violence, but perhaps of one informed by the novel possibilities produced within varied moments and contexts of 'human'-'animal' interaction, moments whose productivity does not and cannot be taken to embody only the plenitude of life, but must bear at the same time the force of a questioning that would subject all manner of dreams and aspirations to a certain encounter or moment of destruction, seizing them, therefore, in preparation for the invention, the in-coming, of a truly unhoped-for animal-to-come.

Notes

Zoopolitics in deconstruction?

1. Jacques Derrida and Elisabeth Roudinesco, *For What Tomorrow . . . A Dialogue* (Stanford: Stanford University Press, 2004), 64.
2. See for instance the work published in the journals *Environmental Ethics* (1979–), *The Trumpeter* (1983–), *Environmental Values* (1992–) and *Animal Welfare* (1992–). Arne Naess, an influential figure in the early years of environmental ethics, was, strictly speaking, a post-Kantian continental philosopher by virtue both of being Norwegian and of writing in the twentieth century, but he grounded his 'ecosophy' of deep ecology primarily in the ideas of Spinoza. For a discussion and development of deep ecology, as well as a guide to primary sources in this tradition, see Warwick Fox, *Towards a Transpersonal Ecology: Developing New Foundations for Environmentalism* (Dartington: Resurgence, 1995). Martin Heidegger gained some exposure in environmental ethics – particularly via Michael E. Zimmerman, 'Towards a Heideggerian Ethos of Radical Environmentalism', *Environmental Ethics* 5, no. 2 (Summer 1983): 99–131; see also Michael E. Zimmerman, *Heidegger's Confrontation with Modernity: Technology, Politics, and Art* (Bloomington and Indianapolis: Indiana University Press, 1990) – though his work

was not as influential in discussions of animal ethics. While being grounded in utilitarianism rather than a juridical model of rights, Peter Singer's *Animal Liberation: A New Ethics for Our Treatment of Animals* (London: HarperCollins, 1975) represents perhaps the founding philosophical work dedicated specifically to animals as an ethical question. In late twentieth-century philosophical engagements with the animal question, the major exception to the general Anglo-American apathy (indeed, antipathy) towards contemporary continental thought is Donna Haraway, *Primate Visions: Gender, Race, and Nature in the World of Modern Science* (New York: Routledge, 1989); and *Simians, Cyborgs and Women: The Reinvention of Nature* (New York: Routledge, 1991).
3. Matthew Calarco, *Zoographies: The Question of the Animal from Heidegger to Derrida* (New York: Columbia University Press, 2008), 1.
4. Harriet Ritvo, 'On the Animal Turn', *Daedalus* 136, no. 4 (Fall 2007): 118–22.
5. Thus Calarco, in *Zoographies*, reads the work of Heidegger, Agamben, Levinas and Derrida with a focus on the extent to which their respective critiques challenge the metaphysics of human subjectivity but do so without calling into question at the same time what Calarco identifies as an implicit anthropocentrism: the metaphysical conceits that have defined thinking about animals. Of the figures he discusses, it is clear that Calarco feels that Derrida offers the most deliberate and developed critique of metaphysical anthropocentrism. Nevertheless, in Calarco's view Derrida's 'thought does not offer a genuine challenge to this tradition and remains beholden to its logic and conceptuality' (137), because he 'resolutely refuses to abandon the human-animal distinction' (145).
6. Jacques Derrida, *The Animal That Therefore I Am*, ed. Marie-Louise Mallet, trans. David Wills (New York: Fordham University Press, 2008).
7. On the motif of 'to-come', see, for example, Jacques Derrida, 'Force of Law: The "Mystical Foundation of Authority"', trans. Mary Quaintance, in *Deconstruction and the Possibility of Justice*, ed. Drucilla Cornell, Michael Rosenfield and David Gray Carlson (New

York and London: Routledge, 1992), 3–67; *Specters of Marx: The State of the Debt, the Work of Mourning, and the New International*, trans. Peggy Kamuf (New York and London: Routledge, 1994); *Rogues: Two Essays on Reason*, trans. Pascale-Anne Brault and Michael Naas (Stanford: Stanford University Press, 2005). In these works, Derrida mentions in passing 'so-called "animal" life' (*Specters of Marx*, 85), 'what we still so confusedly call animals' ('Force of Law', 19). In doing so, he underscores a need to 'reconsider in its totality the metaphysico-anthropocentric axiomatic that dominates, in the West, the thought of the just and unjust' ('Force of Law', 19), as well as the 'rationality' of interrogating 'the conventionally accepted limits between the so-called human living being and the so-called animal one' (*Rogues*, 151). Likewise, in *The Animal That Therefore I Am*, Derrida observes, in passing, a reference in Kant to 'the future of the animal' (99) – a 'third epoch', when 'the chimpanzee might be able to say "I think" and accede to understanding' (98) – and underscores Kant's failure to draw out the consequences of that possibility. But Derrida himself travels no further down this path, other than noting the 'anthropomorphic and anthropocentric' nature of Kant's speculation. He thus never quite articulates the two problematics, and commentary on Derrida's work likewise bypasses that possibility. In developing this thought of the animal-to-come, I have found only two prior references to this articulation of animality and 'to-come'. In a brief endnote in his discussion of political speciation, animality, natality and defacement, Allen Feldman, 'Inhumanitas: Political Speciation, Animality, Natality, Defacement', in *In the Name of Humanity: The Government of Threat and Care*, ed. Ilana Feldman and Miriam Iris Ticktin (Durham, NC, and London: Duke University Press, 2010), 'paraphrases' Derrida to 'infer' an animal ethics that 'would be treated as a pure performative act suspended over an abyss that would presuppose a messianic animal-to-come' (149, n. 1). More recently, Dominique Lestel has proposed – albeit without reference to Derrida – to reflect on 'novel procedures of animalisation' and the 'hybridisation of real animals and prostheses' (among other phenomena) as gestures towards what he calls 'animality to come'; Dominique

Lestel, 'The Animality to Come', trans. Matthew Chrulew, *Ctrl-Z: New Media Philosophy* 6 (2016). I discuss Lestel's work and its various relations to Derrida's work in more detail in Chapter 1.
8. See Derrida, *Specters of Marx*: 'To haunt does not mean to be present, and it is necessary to introduce haunting into the very construction of a concept. Of every concept, beginning with the concepts of being and time. That is what we would be calling here a hauntology' (161). I discuss this notion of hauntology in more detail in Chapter 1.
9. Derrida, *Animal*, 29.
10. Derrida, *Animal*, 28. See Chapter 3 for instantiations of this 'ethical' reading.
11. Robert Briggs, 'Wild Thoughts: A Deconstructive Environmental Ethics?' *Environmental Ethics* 23, no. 2 (Summer 2001): 115–34; 'Following the animal-to-come', *Derrida Today* 12, no. 1 (2019): 20–40. The latter publication is a preliminary foray into the issues and possibilities that I explore in the chapters that follow. The former reads Derrida's work as a kind of environmental ethics (or rather as a complication of such) in a fashion that has also been attempted in the recently published collection *Eco-Deconstruction: Derrida and Environmental Philosophy*, ed. Matthias Fritsch, Philippe Lynes and David Wood (New York: Fordham University Press, 2018).
12. See the three special issues of *Angelaki: Journal of the Theoretical Humanities* (2014–15) produced by Brett Buchanan, Jeffery Bussolini and Matthew Chrulew, which provide introductions to and select translations of work by Lestel, Despret and Italian theorist Roberto Marchesini. 'Loosely defined under the umbrella of "philosophical ethology"', these works undertake 'philosophical investigations into the relationships between humans and animals in their cultural, material and symbolic dimensions', approaching 'the question of the animal and related problematics in posthumanism, animal studies and critical theory by engaging human/animal relations not merely as textual plays of language but as domains of bodily comportment and conduct'; Brett Buchanan, Jeffery Bussolini and Matthew Chrulew, 'General Introduction: Philosophical Ethology', *Angelaki: Journal of the Theoretical Humanities* 19, no. 3 (2014): 1. One of Vinciane

Despret's books has since been translated into English as *What Would Animals Say If We Asked the Right Questions?* trans. Brett Buchanan (Minneapolis: University of Minnesota Press, 2016).

13. See Cary Wolfe, *What is Posthumanism?* (Minneapolis: University of Minnesota Press, 2010): 'when we talk about posthumanism, we are not just talking about a thematics of the decentering of the human in relation to either evolutionary, ecological, or technological coordinates (though that is where the conversation usually begins and, all too often, ends); rather, I will insist that we are also talking about *how* thinking confronts that thematics, what thought has to become in the face of those challenges' (xvi).

14. Jacques Derrida, *Margins of Philosophy*, trans. Alan Bass (Sussex: Harvester Press, 1982), 123.

15. For sustained and erudite engagements with Derrida's reflections on the animal question and related issues (sovereignty, life, death, ecology), see David Farrell Krell, *Derrida and Our Animal Others: Derrida's Final Seminar, 'The Beast and the Sovereign'* (Bloomington and Indianapolis: Indiana University Press, 2013); Michael Naas, *The End of the World and Other Teachable Moments: Jacques Derrida's Final Seminar* (New York: Fordham University Press, 2015); and Philippe Lynes, *Futures of Life Death on Earth: Derrida's General Ecology* (London and New York: Rowman and Littlefield, 2018).

16. Jacques Derrida, *Life Death*, ed. Pascale-Anne Brault and Peggy Kamuf, trans. Pascale-Anne Brault and Michael Naas (Chicago: University of Chicago Press, 2020).

1 Following the animal-to-come . . .

1. Jacques Derrida, *The Animal That Therefore I Am*, ed. Marie-Louise Mallet, trans. David Wills (New York: Fordham University Press, 2008), 10. Hereafter cited in the text as A, followed by the page reference.

2. Martin Heidegger, *Being and Time*, trans. John Macquarrie and Edward Robinson (Oxford and Cambridge: Blackwell, 1962), 100.

3. Emmanuel Levinas, 'Ethics as First Philosophy', trans. Seán Hand and

Michael Templè, in *The Levinas Reader*, ed. Seán Hand (Blackwell: Oxford, 1989), 75–87.

4. Despite the centrality of the theme of 'the face' and the routine reference to '*the* other' and '*his* face', I leave open the possibility that Levinas's thought resists being reduced to a simple ethics of responsibility to the other understood exclusively as the other individual being, which is nevertheless how that thought is most regularly taken up when attempting to articulate a Levinasian account of the animal other. See for instance Matthew Calarco, *Zoographies: The Question of the Animal from Heidegger to Derrida* (New York: Columbia University Press, 2008), 55–77; and Peter Atterton, 'Levinas and Our Moral Responsibility Toward Other Animals', *Inquiry* 54, no. 6 (2011): 633–49. For one resource that might aid in pursuing this suspended question, see Mick Smith's reading of Levinas, alongside Iris Murdoch, Hannah Arendt and Giorgio Agamben, throughout *Against Ecological Sovereignty: Ethics, Biopolitics, and Saving the Natural World* (Minneapolis: University of Minnesota Press, 2011).

5. Derrida made explicit use of the motif of 'to-come' in a range of 'political' works presented and published from the late 1980s through to *Rogues: Two Essays on Reason*, trans. Pascale-Anne Brault and Michael Naas (Stanford: Stanford University Press, 2005). The text of *The Animal That Therefore I Am* was written for and presented at a conference on 'The Autobiographical Animal', which was held in Cerisy in 1997.

6. Jacques Derrida, 'Force of Law: The "Mystical Foundation of Authority"', trans. Mary Quaintance, in *Deconstruction and the Possibility of Justice*, ed. Drucilla Cornell, Michael Rosenfield and David Gray Carlson (New York and London: Routledge, 1992), 27. Hereafter cited in the text as FL, followed by the page reference.

7. Jacques Derrida, *Specters of Marx: The State of the Debt, the Work of Mourning, and the New International*, trans. Peggy Kamuf (New York and London: Routledge, 1994), 17, 64. Hereafter cited in the text as SM, followed by the page reference.

8. For an extended discussion of Derrida's 'concept' of 'democracy to come', including its relation to the aporetic structure of the promise,

see Samir Haddad, *Derrida and the Inheritance of Democracy* (Bloomington and Indianapolis: Indiana University Press, 2013), particularly chapter 3. It should be noted that English translations of *Specters of Marx* and *Rogues* use the formulation 'democracy to come'. I insert hyphens into this and similar formulations ('democracy-to-come', 'justice-to-come' and, ultimately, 'the animal-to-come') in order to provide a visual reminder of the fact that what is being named is not simply a future but the inscription of an eschatological relation to a non-present 'future', hence the inscription of non-presence, *within* the events or concepts at stake. In this way, I am following, as it were, the conventional practice of translating '*l'à-venir*' – which 'spaces out the ordinary word for the future, *avenir*, into the components of the infinitive: to come' (SM 177, translator's note) – as 'future-to-come', and I am grafting this 'spacing' onto or into the thought and practice of democracy, and so on.

9. 'Perhaps', Derrida says, because 'one must always say perhaps for justice' (FL 27). It is not a given, after all, that justice must always entail transformation – or, rather, that 'transformation' is itself self-evidently, self-identically just, desirable or even recognisable as such. I return to the question of the desirability, as it were, of this openness to or invention of the transformative event in the concluding pages of this book.

10. Any exhaustive evidencing of this fact would require citing virtually Derrida's entire bibliography. A list of the most instructive examples, however, would have to include Derrida's critique in *Of Grammatology*, trans. Gayatri Chakrabarty Spivak (Baltimore and London: Johns Hopkins University Press, 1976), of 'the inflation of language' and his supplementary account of writing's *comprehension* ('in all senses of the word') of language (6–10), whereby writing comes to designate 'action, movement, thought ... experience, affectivity'; activities within athletics, military and politics, 'in view of the techniques that govern those domains today'; 'the most elementary processes of information within the living cell'; 'the entire field of the cybernetic *program*'; and much more besides (9). See also Derrida's 'Scribble (Writing-Power)', trans. Cary Plotkin, *Yale French*

Studies 58 (1979): 117–47, in which he reads within (or, perhaps, into) Warburton's essay on the origin of language writing's constitution, as it were, of and as power, of and as the realm of action. Possibly the most significant challenge to the suggestion that Derrida equates writing with meaning and interpretation is 'Signature Event Context', in his *Limited Inc*, ed. Gerald Graff (Evanston: Northwestern University Press, 1988), 1–23, in which Derrida *begins* by questioning the idea that 'communication' is simply a 'semiotic operation' or 'linguistic exchange', relating to 'a semantic or conceptual content', and directs his analysis towards the sense of communication as 'nonsemantic movement', such as in the communication of a tremor or force (1). Here, in addition to rehearsing some of the arguments about 'action language' deployed in 'Scribble', Derrida engages (and complicates) J. L. Austin's speech act theory and its central notion of 'the performative' precisely because it offers a way of understanding 'communication' as something other than the communication of meaning – and, rather, as an 'act' or 'event' 'communicating a force through the impetus [*impulsion*] of a mark' (13 and ff.)

11. Derrida, *Limited Inc*, 9.
12. Derrida, *Limited Inc*, 134. At least two separate moments in *Of Grammatology* point already towards this need for another concept of institution. The first is Derrida's elaboration of 'the thesis of the arbitrariness of the sign' and concomitant suggestion that 'the very idea of institution – hence of the arbitrariness of the sign – is unthinkable before the possibility of writing and outside of its horizon. Quite simply, that is, outside of the horizon itself, outside the world as space of inscription, as the opening to the emission and to the spatial *distribution* of signs, to the *regulated play* of their differences, even if they are "phonic".' Writing thus 'disturbs' 'the opposition of nature and institution, of *physis* and *nomos*' (44). The second moment lies in the subsequent reading of 'culture' as original supplement of 'Nature' in Rousseau (144–52). I return to the question of culture in Chapter 2.
13. Lestel has articulated his thought in relation to Derrida in his 'The Infinite Debt of the Human Towards the Animal', trans. Matthew Chrulew, *Angelaki: Journal of the Theoretical Humanities* 19, no. 3

(2014): 171–81; and 'Like the Fingers of the Hand: Thinking the Human in the Texture of Animality', trans. Matthew Chrulew and Jeffrey Bussolini, in *French Thinking About Animals*, ed. Louisa Mackenzie and Stephanie Posthumus (East Lansing: Michigan State University Press, 2015), 61–73; hereafter cited in the text as LFH, followed by the page reference. In these discussions, he situates his thought as lying at the interface of Derrida's 'hermeneutico-interactionist posture' and the 'onto-evolutionary' (LFH 62) approach exemplified by Paul Shepard, *Thinking Animals: Animals and the Development of Human Intelligence* (New York: Viking, 1978).

14. It should be noted that many of the ideas I here cite from Lestel are formulated by him with reference specifically to Shepard, rather than to Derrida. However, in using these ideas to translate my argument about the 'institutionality' of human/animal existence, I am suggesting that a version of such 'onto-evolutionary' thinking is already implicit in Derrida's work, but also that, for reasons I advance below, the name 'onto-evolutionary' might not be the most appropriate and, indeed, may play a large part in preventing recognition of such thinking in Derrida's work. To put it another way: part of what I am doing in formulating the thought of the animal-to-come is constructing a version of Derrida that is able to account for what others want to account for when they speak of the 'onto-evolutionary' – but doing so in terms of this alternative (deconstructive) logic of institution.

15. Lestel, 'Infinite Debt', 178.

16. Lestel, 'Infinite Debt', 177.

17. 'The reference to the notion of *texture* signifies that the human/animal relation is not only social but also cognitive and above all metabolic' (LFH 71, n. 1). The metabolic significance of the term 'texture' may, to English ears, seem obscure, but it earns this nuance both from its etymology (the French terms *text*, *textuel*, *texture* and *tissu*, as with their English equivalents, derive from the Latin *texere*: 'to weave') and from France's contributions to medical science. French anatomist Marie-François-Xavier Bichal (1771–1802) first used *'tissu'* as the generic term for the different membranes contained within bodily organs, while Pierre Augustin Béclard noted in his *Elements of General*

Anatomy, trans. Robert Knox (Edinburgh: MacLachlan and Stewart, 1830 [Fr. 1823]) that the particles which make up bodily organs 'are interlaced and interwoven, on which account their arrangement is named texture' (2).

18. The reference here to '*zoē*' and '*bios*' is a nod towards Giorgio Agamben's tracing of the two contrasting terms for 'life' employed in classical Greek: '*zoē*, which expressed the simple fact of living common to all living beings (animals, men, or gods), and *bios*, which indicated the form or way of living proper to an individual or a group'; Giorgio Agamben, *Homo Sacer: Sovereign Power and Bare Life*, trans. Daniel Heller-Roazen (Stanford: Stanford University Press, 1998), 1. I return to Agamben in Chapters 3 and 4.

19. Such is the principle animating much recent work on 'biodeconstruction'. See Francesco Vitale, *Biodeconstruction: Jacques Derrida and the Life Sciences*, trans. Senatore Mauro (Albany: SUNY Press, 2018). See also 'After Biodeconstruction' the special issue of *CR: The New Centennial Review* focusing on Vitale's book, in particular Michael Naas, 'Learning to Read "Life Death" Finally: Francesco Vitale's Epigenetic Criticism' *CR: The New Centennial Review* 19, no. 3 (2019): 13–33.

20. See on this point Derrida's seemingly playful remark that 'everybody agrees on this point' regarding 'something like a discontinuity, rupture, or even abyss' between the so-called animal and the so-called human: 'one would have to be more asinine than any beast [*plus bête ques les bêtes*] to think otherwise. Even the animals know that (ask Abraham's ass or ram or the living beasts that Abel offered to God: they know what is about to happen to them when men say "Here I am" to God, then consent to sacrifice themselves, to sacrifice their sacrifice ...)' (A 30). See also Dinesh Wadiwel's argument that, in the second volume of the Beast and the Sovereign seminars, Derrida provides a reading of Heidegger's language of *Walten* as a means of arguing that 'humans are not innately superior to animals, but win their superiority through the application of force'; Dinesh Joseph Wadiwel, 'The Will for Self-Preservation: Locke and Derrida on Dominion, Property and Animals', *SubStance* 43, no. 2 (2014): 149. Jacques Derrida, *The*

Beast and the Sovereign, Volume II, ed. Michel Lisse, Marie-Louise Mallet and Ginette Michaud, trans. Geoffrey Bennington (Chicago and London: University of Chicago Press, 2011).

21. On the preference for 'let[ting] the human-animal distinction go', see Calarco, *Zoographies*, 145–9. By contrast, Derrida approaches this 'distinction' in terms of what he calls 'limitrophy', a term pointing towards 'what abuts onto limits but also what feeds, is fed, is cared for, raised and trained, what is cultivated on the edges of a limit ... *Limitrophy* is therefore my subject. Not just because it will concern what sprouts or grows at the limit, around the limit, by maintaining the limit, but also what *feeds the limit*, generates it, raises it, complicates it' (A 29).

22. René Descartes, *A Discourse on the Method of Correctly Conducting One's Reason and Seeking Truth in the Sciences*, trans. Ian Maclean (Oxford: Oxford University Press, 2006), 46. See John Cottingham, '"A Brute to the Brutes?" Descartes' Treatment of Animals', *Philosophy* 53 (1978): 551–9, for an engagement with various objections to Descartes's philosophical account of animals as automata.

23. Jacques Derrida, *Without Alibi*, ed. and trans. Peggy Kamuf (Stanford: Stanford University Press, 2002), 72, 74.

24. I return to the question of response in Chapter 5.

25. See Calarco, *Zoographies*, 126–36, for a discussion of the temptation to grant (certain) animals status as moral and legal subjects on the basis that animals are 'a subject of life' (Tom Regan, cited in Calarco, *Zoographies*, 130). Calarco goes on to account for some of the ethical pitfalls of this approach, to the extent that it enacts its own forms of violent exclusion and continues to participate in the structure of carnophallogocentrism that underpins the constitution of subjectivity as such. He thus seeks to identify some of the 'quasi-invisible constraints that guide animal ethics and politics in a seemingly predestined direction' (127). In linking notions of animal subjectivity – in the sense of a subject of 'experience', 'sensation', 'desire', perhaps even 'thought' – to the metaphysics of interiority, I am intending to signal and diverge from still other constraints and predestinations. This is not to suggest, however, that all attempts to speculate on animal subjectivity

are doomed to succumb to such constraints. For two reflections on animal subjectivity that in different ways articulate such 'subjectivity' in terms of prior and constituent relations to various phylogenetic, ecological, communicative and institutional 'outsides', see Roberto Marchesini, 'Philosophical Ethology and Animal Subjectivity', trans. Jeffrey Bussolini, *Angelaki: Journal of the Theoretical Humanities* 21, no. 1 (2016), 237–52; and Dominique Lestel, 'The Question of the Animal Subject: Thoughts on the Fourth Wound to Human Narcissism', trans. Hollis Taylor, *Angelaki: Journal of the Theoretical Humanities* 19, no. 3 (2014): 113–25. For a discussion of animal subjectivity that takes into account forces or structures of biopower and animal subjectification, see Matthew Chrulew, 'Animals as Biopolitical Subjects', in *Foucault and Animals*, ed. Matthew Chrulew and Dinesh Joseph Wadiwel (Leiden: Brill, 2017), 222–38.

26. Thomas Hobbes, *Leviathan* (London: Oxford University Press, 1909 [1651]). Jacques Derrida, *The Beast and the Sovereign, Volume I*, ed. Michel Lisse, Marie-Louise Mallet and Ginette Michaud, trans. Geoffrey Bennington (Chicago: University of Chicago Press, 2009); hereafter cited in the text as BSI, followed by the page reference.

27. As Hannah Arendt has remarked, in *The Promise of Politics*, ed. Jerome Kohn (New York: Schocken Books, 2005): 'Politics arises *between men*, and so quite *outside* of man. There is therefore no real political substance. Politics arises in what lies *between men* and is established as relationships. Hobbes understood this' (95). I return to Arendt in Chapter 4.

28. The thought of differance, which 'makes' im/possible the self-identity of any difference, implies the possibility that difference, division, divergence, and so on may appear in the form or relation of convergence. As irreducibly non-identical with itself, a moment of difference is never self-identically different, never self-identically (that) difference, but may also 'appear' in or as a moment of the same, as 'the differance of' the same. See Derrida's essay on 'Differance' in *Speech and Phenomena, and Other Essays on Husserl's Theory of Signs*, trans. David B. Allison (Evanston: Northwestern University Press, 1973), 129–60.

29. Dominique Lestel, 'The Animality to Come', trans. Matthew Chrulew, *Ctrl-Z: New Media Philosophy* 6 (2016): n.p.
30. Lestel, 'The Animality to Come', n.p.
31. Lestel, 'The Animality to Come', n.p.
32. In this regard, see Mick Smith, *Against Ecological Sovereignty*, and his fecund reading of (Bataille's reading of) the images painted, between fifteen and seventeen thousand years ago, on the walls of the Lascaux Cave in southwestern France – in particular the image of a bird-headed human figure standing alongside a bison, pierced by a spear presumably thrown in the act of hunting. Where Bataille, on Smith's account, sees in the painting 'the birth of humanity's ethical as well as artistic sensibilities' (3), Smith notes the residual teleological (and ultimately absolutist) impulse that underpins 'the decision to recognize the Lascaux people as nascent humanity', which 'can only work by recursively according them all of the qualities presumed necessary to be fully human from the beginning' (7). 'If we read Bataille against Bataille', however, 'then different, ethicopolitical possibilities emerge as Lascaux's images collide with the now. We can recognize that the birth of humanity – at least insofar as it operates as a regulatory idea(l), as a category of beings separated from and dominating other beings – is not an irreversible past event' but rather 'a continually renewed and altering creation . . . both metaphysical and politically partisan' (9). See also Georges Bataille, *Prehistoric Painting: Lascaux or the Birth of Art*, trans. Austryn Wainhouse (Lausanne: Skira, 1955).
33. Lestel, 'Infinite Debt', 174.

2 Specifically cultural

1. Satoshi Hirata, Kunio Watanabe and Masao Kawai, '"Sweet-Potato Washing" Revisited', in *Primate Origins of Human Cognition and Behavior*, ed. Tesuro Matsuzawa (Tokyo: Springer, 2001), 487–508. In addition to providing context and making further observations on the macaque research, Hirata et al. include an abridged version of Kawai's first publication of the research findings in 1964.

2. See, for instance, Frans B. M. de Waal, 'Silent Invasion: Imanishi's Primatology and Cultural Bias in Science', *Animal Cognition* 6, no. 4 (2003): 293–9; Robert M. Sapolsky, 'Culture in Animals: The Case of Non-human Primate Culture of Low Aggression and High Affiliation', *Social Forces* 85, no. 1 (2006): 217–33.
3. See Michael Krützen, Janet Mann, Michael R. Heithaus, Richard C. Connor, Lars Bejder and William B. Sherwin, 'Cultural Transmission of Tool Use in Bottlenose Dolphins', *Proceedings of the National Academy of Sciences of the United States of America* 102, no. 25 (2005): 8939–43; Lucas A. Bluff, Alex Kacelnik and Christian Rutz, 'Vocal Culture in New Caledonian Crows *Corvus moneduloides*', *Biological Journal of the Linnean Society* 101 (2010): 767–76; Michio Nakamura and Shigeo Uehara, 'Proximate Factors of Different Types of Grooming Hand-Clasp in Mahale Chimpanzees: Implications for Chimpanzee Social Customs', *Current Anthropology* 45, no. 1 (2004): 108–14. See Sapolsky, 'Culture in Animals', for a review of these and other examples.
4. Nakamura and Uehara, 'Proximate Factors', 108.
5. W. C. McGrew, 'Ten Dispatches from the Chimpanzee Wars', in *Animal Social Complexity: Intelligence, Culture, and Individualized Societies*, ed. Frans B. M. Waal and Peter L. Tyack (Cambridge, MA: Harvard University Press, 2003), 432–3.
6. McGrew, 'Ten Dispatches', 433, citing Edward Burnett Tylor, *Primitive Culture: Researches Into the Development of Mythology, Philosophy, Religion, Language, Art, and Custom*, Vol. 1, 6th edn (London: Murray, 1920 [1871]), 1.
7. McGrew, 'Ten Dispatches', 437.
8. See Raymond Williams, *Keywords: A Vocabulary of Culture and Society*, rev. edn (London: Fontana, 1983), 87–93. The 'metaphoricity' of this latter sense is debatable at least to the extent that Cicero had already spoken (first century BCE) of the cultivation of soul (*cultura animi*) by way of training in philosophy, a use which Williams notes but without reflecting on the significance of this use for his own claim that culture achieved the sense of intellectual cultivation 'by metaphor' across the sixteenth and seventeenth centuries.

9. Alec McHoul, *Semiotic Investigations: Towards an Effective Semiotics* (Lincoln and London: University of Nebraska Press, 1996), 45.
10. Giambattista Vico, *The First New Science*, ed. and trans. Leon Pompa (Cambridge and New York: Cambridge University Press, 2002 [It. 1725]), 10.
11. Thomas Hobbes, *Leviathan* (London: Oxford University Press, 1909 [1651]), 131, 133.
12. Vico, *First New Science*, 30.
13. Hobbes, *Leviathan*, 96.
14. Vico, *First New Science*, 11.
15. Johann Gottfried Herder, *Outlines of a Philosophy of the History of Mankind*, trans. T. O. Churchill (New York: Bergman Publishers, 1966 [Ger. 1784–91]), v. Translation modified.
16. Herder, *Outlines*, 166.
17. See Hirata et al., '"Sweet-Potato Washing" Revisited', 489–90.
18. W. C. McGrew and C. E. G. Tutin, 'Evidence for a Social Custom in Wild Chimpanzees?', *Man* 13, no. 2 (1978): 242.
19. McGrew and Tutin, 'Evidence for a Social Custom', 242.
20. McHoul, *Semiotic Investigations*, 47.
21. McHoul, *Semiotic Investigations*, 47.
22. Vico, *First New Science*, 16.
23. 'Imagine not, that I seek to derogate from the value of a mode of living, which Providence has employed as a principal instrument for leading man to civil society: for I myself eat the bread it has produced. But let justice be done to other ways of life, which, from the constitution of our Earth, have been destined, equally with agriculture, to contribute to the education of mankind'; Herder, *Outlines*, 207–8.
24. McHoul, *Semiotic Investigations*, 48.
25. McGrew, 'Ten Dispatches', 434.
26. McHoul, *Semiotic Investigations*, 48. Here we can see that the duplicity of the concept of culture manifests in relation not only to the *scope* of its reference, but also to its analytical function. The concept is routinely used, that is, to designate *both* a field of (culturally produced) artefacts, practices and behaviours *and* the capacity or force responsible for the production such artefacts, practices, behaviours.

The double duty the concept is called on to perform in such cases is taxonomic on the one hand (identifying given phenomena as cultural or not), and explicative on the other (accounting for the existence of such phenomena). Indeed, this is how McGrew can declare that Tylor's all-inclusive 'definition' of culture is useless for its inability to *explain* what it *designates* as cultural ('something that explains everything explains nothing').

27. A 'prerequisite of animal culture is that the behavior persists past its originators; transmission can be intra- or inter-generational and spreads as a function of kinship or proximity . . . Evidence [for animal culture] often takes the form of observing a distinctive behavior(s) in a group or population, detecting signs of its spread to new individuals, and a plausible argument about why this pattern does not reflect genetic or ecological factors'; Sapolsky, 'Culture in Animals', 218. 'Does culture equal tradition, and tradition equal culture? No, it is not that simple . . . Some information is transmitted genetically across generations. This is deucedly difficult to establish in the wild, where variables of nature and culture are confounded, even for behavior. Do generations of warthogs wear down a path to a waterhole because it is their cultural inclination, or because it is the most energetically efficient or least predator-risky route? Even if we were lucky enough to be there to see them tread a new trail, would it be from whimsy or from changed (but unseen to us) environmental contingencies?'; McGrew, 'Ten Dispatches', 429.
28. Jacques Derrida, *Psyche: Inventions of the Other, Volume I*, ed. Peggy Kamuf and Elizabeth Rottenberg (Stanford: Stanford University Press, 2007), 29.
29. Derrida, *Psyche I*, 24.
30. Derrida, *Psyche I*, 24.
31. Derrida, *Psyche I*, 22.
32. Derrida, *Psyche I*, 25.
33. McGrew, 'Ten Dispatches', 424.
34. To that extent, the valuing of the nature's self-sufficiency in the thought of (animal) culture is far from new. Indeed, there is a certain sense in which Enlightenment accounts of human activities were

driven by an implicit imperative to explain the *naturalness* ('providence') of cultural forms. Thus, confronted by the variety of laws, customs and the like that characterised the ancestral nations, Vico constructed his science of human practices on the idea that such variations amounted to historically (that is, developmentally) differentiated expressions of a fundamental, immutable natural law. And while Vico was thereby rejecting Hobbes's account of the natural condition of war of all against all, the English philosopher himself depicted the establishment of civil society as an imitation of natural achievements, nature being both the model of rational design and the *source* of the human capacity to imitate it: 'Nature (the Art whereby God hath made and governes the World) is by the *Art* of man, as in many other things, so in this also imitated, that it can make an Artificial Animal . . . imitating that Rationall and most excellent worke of Nature, *Man*'; Hobbes, *Leviathan*, 8. But where such accounts appear to draw a realm of culture visibly defined by its artificiality and variability – hence by a certain arbitrariness or indeterminacy – back *into* a sphere of natural phenomena explicable in terms of determinate or mechanistic processes, in the case of 'culture in animals' a reverse impulse seems to be in play – or would be, were it not for those expressions of normativity that continue to draw (animal) culture back into (animal) nature.

35. Herder, *Outlines*, 185.
36. Herder, *Outlines*, 164.
37. Herder, *Outlines*, 202–3.
38. Niall Lucy, *Beyond Semiotics: Text, Culture and Technology* (London and New York: Continuum, 2001), 23. Lucy adds that 'that seems about as deterministic as it could get' (23). Herder himself used his theory to provide explanations, with varying degrees of credibility, for the development even of complex social phenomena, tracing the institution of social structures premised on polygamy to the features of climate. See Herder *Outlines*, 211.
39. Sapolsky, 'Culture in Animals', 219.
40. Dominique Lestel, 'Dissolving Nature in Culture: Some Philosophical Stakes of the Question of Animal Cultures', trans. Jeffrey Bussolini,

Angelaki: Journal of the Theoretical Humanities 19, no. 3 (2014): 98. Hereafter cited in the text as DN, followed by the page reference.

41. See also the 'axiom' that Derrida lays out regarding culture in his engagement with the question of 'European cultural identity': *'what is proper to a culture is to not be identical to itself . . .* to be able to take the form of a subject only in the non-identity to itself or . . . only in the difference *with itself [avec soi]*. There is no culture or cultural identity without this difference *with itself . . .* self-difference, difference to itself [*différence à soi*], that which differs and diverges from itself, of itself'; Jacques Derrida, *The Other Heading: Reflections on Today's Europe*, trans. Pascale-Anne Brault and Michael B. Naas (Bloomington and Indianapolis: Indiana University Press, 1992), 9–10.

42. For a more sophisticated and detailed exploration of this structure or movement and the essential prostheticity of animal existence, see Cary Wolfe's reading of Derrida and Bernard Stiegler in the context of Humberto Maturana and Francisco Varela, in *Before the Law: Humans and Other Animals in a Biopolitical Frame* (Chicago: University of Chicago Press, 2013), 76–7.

43. See, for example, Kevin N. Laland, *Darwin's Unfinished Symphony: How Culture Made the Human Mind* (Princeton and Oxford: Princeton University Press, 2017), in which, alongside much more besides, Laland discusses the findings of research into the differing capacities for public-information use demonstrated by ninespine and threespine sticklebacks, two closely related species of fishes. Laland's monograph is a prodigious work, providing both a theory of the evolution of culture and cognition, supported by comprehensive reference to the existing literature, and a description of the experimental studies and mathematical modelling undertaken by his team of assistants and collaborators in the course of developing this theory. At the basis of his account is the idea that genetic evolution is underpinned by a 'cultural drive', a theory that is not radically divergent from Lestel's account of culture as intrinsic to the living, but which Laland derives from a hypothesis proposed by biochemist Allan Wilson: 'Wilson argued that the spread of behavioral innovations through cultural transmission led animals to exploit the environment

in new ways, and thereby increased the rate of genetic evolution. He suggested that the ability to devise novel solutions to life's challenges and to copy the good ideas of other animals would give individuals an advantage in the struggle to survive and reproduce' (114–15). Elaborating on this thesis and the hypothesis of a gene-culture co-evolutionary dynamic, Laland proposes that 'the widespread teaching exhibited by our hominen ancestors' (318) accounts, to a significant degree, for the 'uniqueness' of human cognition, as well as language and cultural acceleration, because teaching, 'which is rare in nature but universal in human societies', enables the kind of 'high fidelity information transmission' necessary for culture to ratchet up in complexity (317).

44. At time of writing, a web search for *cat adopts squirrel* returns results for at least three separate cases, including reputable news reports containing original interviews, images and video footage. It should also be noted that purring is not outside the normal range of vocalisations produced by squirrels.

45. Patrícia Izar, Michele P. Verderane, Elisabetta Visalberghi, Eduardo B. Ottoni, Marino Gomes de Olivera, Jeanne Shirley and Dorothy Fragaszy, 'Cross-genus Adoption of a Marmoset (*Callithrix jacchus*) by Wild Capuchin Monkeys (*Cebus libidinosus*): Case Report', *American Journal of Primatology* 68 (2006): 692–700.

46. Izar et al., 'Cross-genus Adoption', 695–6.

47. Izar et al., 'Cross-genus Adoption', 696.

48. Izar et al., 'Cross-genus Adoption', 697.

49. Izar et al., 'Cross-genus Adoption', 699.

50. The characterisation of this porosity as 'in-principle' is not Lestel's but mine. Lestel prefers to distinguish (even if only relatively so) 'porous' from 'closed' animal societies: 'the most complex animal societies are the porous and not the closed ones, just like human societies' (DN 93). If I insist on the in-principle porosity of (animal) 'cultures', it is not in order to declare that any and every animal society in fact evidences cultural exchange (as it were) with other (animal) societies, but rather to underscore the fact that *vis-à-vis* any such seemingly circumscribed 'culture' a certain moment of in-vention – in the form,

for example, of *intervention* – always remains possible, a point which I return to in Chapter 5.

51. It should be noted that McGrew acknowledges the complication of 'cross-species' instruction but, in the end, identifies it not as evidencing the very operations of 'culture' but rather as hopelessly compromising the possibility of understanding the *nature* (that is, evolutionary origins) of culture in animals: 'Riddle: When is social learning not really social learning? Answer: When human-reared apes are given "honorary" human status for the purpose of developmental cognitive studies. Thus, our closest relatives are put into experimental settings where humans are their models (and caretakers and surrogate parents and kin). Then, their ability to learn socially from human models is compared to similarly aged human children. The apes cannot win in such a setup. If they perform well, it is dismissed as "enculturation", that is, upgraded ability that is not generalizable to nonenculturated apes. If they perform badly, their inferiority is confirmed. Such an experimental design is sometimes termed "cross-fostering", but of course it is not, since no human child is ever taken from its kind and turned over to apes for rearing. It makes an interesting thought experiment: Who would show more social learning and cultural superiority, a human infant reared by an ape or an ape infant reared by a human? Arguably, the artificiality of both conditions means that little can be learned about evolved processes of social learning from them' ('Ten Dispatches', 428).

52. A web search for 'cat and dog friendships', for instance, will return countless results. For a slightly more formal report, albeit one which still falls well short of the evidential standards demanded by most sciences, see Donna J. Haraway, *When Species Meet* (Minneapolis: University of Minnesota Press, 2008), and her discussion of the 'off-category friendship' between Safi, an 'eighty-pound German shepherd–Belgian sheepdog mix', and Wister, a neighbour's donkey (232–4). I return to Haraway in Chapter 3.

53. For a discussion of the failures and 'successes' of one such rehabilitation and reintroduction programme, and a reflection on their implications for understanding animal culture, see Matthew Chrulew,

'Saving the Golden Lion Tamarin', in *Extinction Studies: Stories of Time, Death, and Generations*, ed. Deborah Bird Rose, Thom van Dooren and Matthew Chrulew (New York: Columbia University Press, 2017), 49–87.

54. See, for instance, Lisa Parks's discussion of animal-infrastructure relations, 'Mediating Animal-Infrastructure Relations', in *Being Material*, ed. Stefan Helmreich, Marie-Pier Boucher, Rebecca Uchill (Cambridge, MA: The MIT Press, 2019), 144–53. 'Over the past two decades, ospreys have transformed the horizontal mounting platforms of many cell towers into nesting sites. In the past these large, fish-eating birds, which often have a six-foot wingspan, established their nests in high-canopy or dead trees. Since they favor perches with a clear approach, the cell tower, which is usually fifty to two hundred feet high, has become an optimal nesting site. In Florida 45% of the state's cell towers are home to osprey nests. A Flint, Michigan newspaper headline attributes the species' revival in the area to cell tower installation, proclaiming: "Osprey return gets boost from cell towers". Cell towers have been described as "encouraging" ospreys to extend their breeding range into new areas, including densely populated urban regions near water' (145).
55. On the role of globalising 'urban-adaptable species' in the transformation of 'local' biospheres, see Michael L. McKinney, 'Urbanization as a Major Cause of Biotic Homogenization', *Biological Conservation* 127, no. 3 (2006): 247–60.
56. Derrida, *Psyche I*, 24.
57. Derrida, *Psyche I*, 25.
58. Derrida, *Psyche I*, 25.
59. Derrida, *Psyche I*, 46.

3 Zoopower

1. Jacques Derrida, *The Animal That Therefore I Am*, ed. Marie-Louise Mallet, trans. David Wills (New York: Fordham University Press, 2008), 27. Hereafter cited in the text as A, followed by the page reference.

2. Cary Wolfe, *Before the Law: Humans and Other Animals in a Biopolitical Frame* (Chicago and London: University of Chicago Press, 2013). Hereafter cited in the text as BL, followed by the page reference.
3. Giorgio Agamben, *Homo Sacer: Sovereign Power and Bare Life*, trans. Daniel Heller-Roazen (Stanford: Stanford University Press, 1998), 9. On the possibly irreconcilable differences between Foucault's and Agamben's respective accounts of biopolitics, see Jeffrey T. Nealon, *Plant Theory: Biopower and Vegetable Life* (Stanford: Stanford University Press, 2016), 14–27.
4. Agamben, *Homo Sacer*, 2; Hannah Arendt, *The Origins of Totalitarianism* (New York: Harcourt Brace Jovanovich, 1979), 296. Agamben's account of the exclusion of mere subsistence from political life in the classical world owes a great deal to Arendt's analysis in *The Human Condition*, 2nd edn (Chicago: University of Chicago Press, 1998 [1958]). I return to this work and this question of the sphere of politics in Chapter 4.
5. For an excellent development of this structure with specific reference to Derrida's *Beast and the Sovereign* seminars, see Patrick Llored, 'Zoopolitics', trans. Matthew Chrulew and Brett Buchanan, *SubStance* 43 no. 2 (2014): 115–23: 'For sovereignty to exist, it must appropriate the lives of nonhuman living beings: this could well be the sole definition of zoopolitics' (120). To the extent that my argument in this chapter and throughout can be reduced to a single goal, it lies in the attempt to produce another, very different, definition (and practice) of zoopolitics.
6. For a similar critique of the rights model (albeit without reference to biopolitics), see Kelly Oliver, 'What Is Wrong with (Animal) Rights?', *The Journal of Speculative Philosophy* 22, no. 3 (2008): 214–24.
7. Dominic LaCapra, *History and Its Limits: Human, Animal, Violence* (Ithaca: Cornell University Press, 2009), 166; cited in BL 27.
8. It should go without saying that these diverse commentaries take this interpretation of Derrida in different directions, connecting it with a variety of other questions and directing it towards novel ends. For just a few examples, see Leonard Lawlor, *This Is Not Sufficient: An Essay*

on *Animality and Human Nature in Derrida* (New York: Columbia University Press, 2007); Matthew Calarco, *Zoographies: The Question of the Animal from Heidegger to Derrida* (New York: Columbia University Press, 2008); and Donna J. Haraway, *When Species Meet* (Minneapolis: University of Minnesota Press, 2008), hereafter cited in the text as WSM, followed by the page reference.

9. In 'translating' the ethical reading of passivity in these terms, I pay homage to John D. Caputo and his exemplary account of what it might mean to speak of (an) ethics in deconstruction, which he calls rather a 'poetics of obligation'; John D. Caputo, *Against Ethics: Contributions to a Poetics of Obligation with Constant Reference to Deconstruction* (Bloomington and Indianapolis: Indiana University Press, 1993). On Caputo's account – published well before the recent readings of Derrida's reference to suffering as a matter of highlighting animal vulnerability – obligation is 'a feeling, the feeling of being bound (*ligare, ob-ligare, re-ligare*), an element of my feeling *Befindlichkeit*, but I cannot get on top of it, scale its heights, catch a glimpse of its rising up. It comes at me, comes over me, overtakes me, seizes hold of me' (7). 'The whole idea of a poetics of obligation is to find an idiom for the fact (as it were) that we are laid hold of by others, seized and laid claim to, that the fullness of freedom is hollowed out by the hollow eyes of those who suffer' (32). 'The power of obligation varies directly with the powerlessness of the one who calls for help, which is the power of powerlessness' (5). For discussions of Caputo's poetics of obligation, see Robert Briggs, 'Genealogy, Transcendence, Obligation: Questioning (the Question of) Ethics', *Discourse: An Interdisciplinary Philosophical Journal* 3 (1997): 1–12; Robert Briggs, 'Wild Thoughts: A Deconstructive Environmental Ethics?', *Environmental Ethics* 23, no. 2 (Summer 2001): 115–34. One particularly interesting exception to the (effectively) neo-Levinasian reading of 'nonpower' in terms of a deconstructive ethics of alterity can be found in Oisín Keohane's reading of Derrida's nonpower alongside Heidegger's 'unpower' (*das Machtlose*, which Keohane proposes to translate as 'mightlessness'), and demonstration of the range of inflections or associations that Derrida gives to *impouvoir*

across a number of his works; Oisín Keohane, 'The Impossible Force of "Mightlessness": Translating Derrida's *impouvoir* and Heidegger's *Machtlose*', in *Heidegger, Levinas, Derrida: The Question of Difference*, ed. L. Foran and R. Uljée, *Contributions to Phenomenology* 86 (2016): 117–32.

10. Michel Foucault, *The History of Sexuality, Volume 1: An Introduction*, trans. Robert Hurley (New York: Pantheon, 1978 [1976]).
11. Jacques Derrida, *Of Grammatology*, trans. Gayatri Chakrabarty Spivak (Baltimore and London: Johns Hopkins University Press, 1976), 63.
12. Derrida, *Of Grammatology*, 66.
13. Derrida, *Of Grammatology*, 66.
14. Derrida, *Of Grammatology*, 7.
15. Jacques Derrida, 'Scribble (Writing-Power)', trans. Cary Plotkin, *Yale French Studies* 58 (1979): 117.
16. Derrida, 'Scribble', 117.
17. Derrida, 'Scribble', 144.
18. Michel Foucault, *Discipline and Punish: The Birth of the Prison*, trans. Alan Sheridan (London: Penguin, 1991 [1975]), 26–8; Michel Foucault, *Power/Knowledge: Selected Interviews and Other Writings*, ed. Colin Gordon (Brighton: Harvester, 1980).
19. Jacques Derrida, 'Differance', in *Speech and Phenomena, and Other Essays on Husserl's Theory of Signs*, trans. David B. Allison (Evanston: Northwestern University Press, 1973), 148.
20. Jacques Derrida, *Limited, Inc* (Evanston: Northwestern University Press, 1988), 149.
21. 'It seems to me that power must be understood in the first instance as the multiplicity of force relations immanent in the sphere in which they operate and which constitute their own organization; as the process which, through ceaseless struggles and confrontations, transforms, strengthens, or reverses them; as the support which these force relations find in one another, thus forming a chain or a system, or on the contrary, the disjunctions and contradictions which isolate them from one another; and lastly, as the strategies in which they take effect, whose general design or institutional crystallization is embodied in the state apparatus, in the formulation of the law, in various

social hegemonies. Power's condition of possibility, or in any case the viewpoint which permits one to understand its exercise, even in its "peripheral" effects, and which also makes it possible to use its mechanisms as a grid of intelligibility of the social order . . . is the moving substrate of force relations which, by virtue of their inequality, constantly engender states of power, but the latter are always local and unstable.' Foucault, *History of Sexuality, Volume 1*, 92–3.

22. In 'Beyond the Power Principle', trans. Elizabeth Rottenberg, *The Undecidable Unconscious: A Journal of Deconstruction and Psychoanalysis* 2 (2015): 7–17, a lecture presented a few months after Foucault's death but not published until 2015, Derrida presented a reading of *The History of Sexuality* which raised the question of how it might deal with Freud's account of 'a death drive that was no doubt not simply alien to the drive for power or the drive for mastery' (16). Adopting a conciliatory tone perhaps appropriate to what functioned, effectively, as a memorial to Foucault, Derrida expressed his wonder at what kind of a response Foucault would give to this complication: 'I would presume that, in a sentence that I will not construct for him, he would have proposed associating or dissociating, gathering in order to send them away – both mastery and death, death and the master' (16). In any event, in 'The Subject and Power', in *Power (Essential Works Vol. 3)*, ed. James D. Faubion (New York: New Press, 2000 [1982]), 326–48, Foucault can be said to have previously articulated his own version of Derrida's complication or reservation: 'Do we need a theory of power? Since a theory assumes a prior objectification, it cannot be asserted as a basis for analytical work. But this analytical work cannot proceed without an ongoing conceptualization. And this conceptualization implies critical thought – a constant checking' (327).

23. Michel Foucault, 'My Body, This Paper, This Fire', trans. Geoffrey Bennington, *Oxford Literary Review* 4, no. 1 (1979): 27; Foucault, *Power/Knowledge*, 114.

24. Jacques Derrida, *Rogues: Two Essays on Reason*, trans. Pascale-Anne Brault and Michael Naas (Stanford: Stanford University Press, 2005), 11.

25. At any rate, Derrida's reference to 'an assemblage' invites association of this account of ipseity with Deleuze and Guattari's thought of 'assemblages', suggesting that ipseity in Derrida's analysis need not be seen as limited to autopoietic entities; Gilles Deleuze and Félix Guattari, *A Thousand Plateaus: Capitalism and Schizophrenia*, trans. Brian Massumi (Minneapolis: University of Minnesota Press, 1987).
26. Jacques Derrida, *The Beast and the Sovereign, Volume I*, ed. Michel Lisse, Marie-Louise Mallet and Ginette Michaud, trans. Geoffrey Bennington (Chicago and London: University of Chicago Press, 2009), 183.
27. Jacques Derrida, *The Beast and the Sovereign, Volume II*, ed. Michel Lisse, Marie-Louise Mallet and Ginette Michaud, trans. Geoffrey Bennington (Chicago and London: University of Chicago Press, 2011), 88.
28. Derrida, *Beast and the Sovereign II*, 88.
29. Derrida, *Of Grammatology*, 44; Derrida, *Limited Inc*, 134.
30. Derrida, *Beast and the Sovereign II*, 149; emphasis added.
31. Derrida, *Beast and the Sovereign I*, 44. 'All genuine political theories presuppose man to be evil, i.e., by no means an unproblematic but a dangerous and dynamic being'; Carl Schmitt, *The Concept of the Political*, exp. ed., trans. George Schwab (Chicago: University of Chicago Press, 2007), 61.
32. Schmitt, *Concept of the Political*, 65.
33. Schmitt, *Concept of the Political*, 52.
34. Derrida, *Beast and the Sovereign I*, 39.
35. Here the political 'protection' of indigenous peoples in 'formerly' colonial states stands out as a stark example. See Thor Kerr and Shaphan Cox, 'Media, Machines and Might: Reproducing Western Australia's Violent State of Aboriginal Protection', *Somatechnics* 6, no. 1 (2016): 89–105, for an analysis of how state violence against sovereign Aboriginal people in Western Australia is allowed to 'proceed unchallenged through discourses of private capital accumulation and public Aboriginal protection' (89).
36. Antonio Negri and Cesare Casarino, 'It's a Powerful Life: A Conversation on Contemporary Philosophy', *Cultural Critique* 57

(Spring 2004): 174. For an examination of the potential of Agamben's and Negri's respective theories to respond to the subjection of animals within regimes of biopower, see Matthew Chrulew, 'Animals in Biopolitical Theory: Between Agamben and Negri', *New Formations* 76 (2012): 53–67.

37. David Farrell Krell, *Derrida and Our Animal Others: Derrida's Final Seminar, 'The Beast and the Sovereign'* (Bloomington and Indianapolis: Indiana University Press, 2013), 146.

38. Krell, *Derrida*, 145–6.

39. Cary Wolfe, 'Flesh and Finitude: Thinking Animals in (Post)Humanist Philosophy', *SubStance* 37, no. 3 (2008): 28. Wolfe also reproduces a version of this argument in *Before the Law*, as part of his critique of arguments that 'the distinctly human is constituted precisely by a radical *not* being-able that is barred to other creatures . . . This essential "(not) being-able" is not the prerogative or even the place, you might say, of either the subject or indeed of "the human", since it is to be located elsewhere, in an alterity that is not just radically extra-subjective, and not just radically ahuman, but also, in fact, radically *inorganic*: namely, in the prosthetic relation to the externality and technicity of trace' (78). In the view of Vinciane Despret, moreover, Wolfe's account avoids reducing animals to the status of victim insofar as it 'resituates these lives claiming to bear grief in the concrete and everyday dimensions of interspecific relations, dimensions that create a particular form of "common vulnerability"'; Vinciane Despret, *What Would Animals Say If We Asked the Right Questions?* trans. Brett Buchanan (Minneapolis: University of Minnesota Press, 2016), 86.

40. It remains possible that this project would amount to what Wolfe (citing Stanley Cavell) depicts as so much use of 'metaphysics to get out of the moral of the ordinary, out of our ordinary moral obligations' (Cavell cited in Wolfe, 'Flesh and Finitude', 32). That this is an argument not entirely without foundation would be impossible to deny – and who, in any case, would want to be seen arguing against such a charge? Perhaps only someone as 'bold' as Nietzsche, whose variable, differential, but nonetheless indisputable influence on Derrida's thinking is at risk, I would argue, of being underplayed

in the more generally accepted reading of Derrida's 'nonpower' in ethical terms as 'vulnerability'.

41. For a collection of investigations adopting a more nuanced perspective – drawn explicitly from Foucault's work – on the complexities of power in a differential history of human-animal relations, see Matthew Chrulew and Dinesh Joseph Wadiwel, eds, *Foucault and Animals* (Leiden: Brill, 2017).
42. Foucault, *Discipline and Punish*, 26.
43. Foucault, *Discipline and Punish*, 27.
44. Jocelyne Porcher, *Vivre avec les animaux. Une utopie pour le 21ème siècle* (Paris: Editions La Découverte, 2011); Jocelyne Porcher and Tiphaine Schmitt, 'Dairy Cows: Workers in the Shadows?', *Society and Animals* 20 (2012): 39–60. As Porcher's *Vivre avec les animaux* is not available in English, I limit my discussion of her work to the paper co-authored by Schmitt, and to those parts of her book that Vinciane Despret cites and discusses in *What Would Animals Say?*
45. Cited in Despret, *What Would Animals Say?*, 178. For one influential discussion of the exploitative nature of profit-oriented animal farming, see Barbara Noske's discussion of the 'animal industrial complex', in *Beyond Boundaries: Humans and Animals* (New York: Black Rose Books, 1996), 22–39.
46. Porcher and Schmitt, 'Dairy Cows', 43.
47. Despret, *What Would Animals Say?*, 180–1.
48. Porcher and Schmitt, 'Dairy Cows', 41.
49. Porcher and Schmitt's discussion of the cows' responses to the introduction of 'an unusual procedure' – the application of lithotham (sea algae) in each of the cow's stalls, whereas ordinarily it would be applied only to the floor outside of the stalls – is particularly enlightening in this regard: 'The cows' behavior faced with this new procedure tell us a great deal about them. Those who tested it first were clearly disconcerted and were unable to anticipate what [the farmer] was expecting from them. The others, however, immediately understood, based on their observation, and took the initiative of leaving [their stalls] of their own accord' ('Dairy Cows', 51).
50. Foucault, 'Subject and Power', 341.

51. 'I have good reasons for judging that Cayenne loves to do agility; she plants her bum in front of the gate to the practice yard with fierce intent until I let her in to work patterns with me. On the mornings when we are driving to a trial, she tracks the gear and stays by the car with command in her eye. It's not just the pleasure of an excursion or access to a play space. We do nothing else in the agility yard but work on the obstacle patterns; that is the yard she wants access to' (WSM 220).
52. Derrida, *Limited Inc*, 149.
53. Peter Sloterdijk, 'Rules for the Human Zoo: A Response to the *Letter on Humanism*', trans. Mary Varney Rorty, *Environment and Planning D: Society and Space* 27 (2009): 21.
54. To that extent, the ambiguity of reference in the possessive pronoun opening the final sentence in the passage cited above – 'their attachment to houses'; whose attachment? 'Men's' or the 'pets'? – is particularly suggestive of paths to explore in historicising the animal-to-come. In following those paths, we might prefer to be cautious about sourcing an 'age of pets' to the adoption of housing, and to investigate, for example, the forms of human-dingo relations that may have characterised the semi-nomadic life of Aboriginal Australian communities. At any rate, Sloterdijk's passage warrants further analysis alongside Derrida's remarks concerning 'the becoming-livestock of the beast', in which 'the appropriation, breaking-in, and domestication of tamed livestock are human socialization' (A 96), as well as alongside Derrida's interrogation of the Heideggerian motif of the 'at home', which invites the question of what 'living with the animal', 'cohabiting with the animal' means (A 145).
55. Sloterdijk, 'Rules', 20.
56. For example, see Brian Hare and Michael Tomasello, 'Human-like Social Skills in Dogs?' *Trends in Cognitive Sciences* 9, no. 9 (September 2005): 339–444. Hare and Tomasello review several studies (including a number of their own) of the abilities of canines to read human communicative and social behaviours, comparing and contrasting these with findings from similar investigations into the abilities of chimpanzees, wolves (canid ancestors), and both domesticated and

undomesticated foxes. Their review suggests that 'the unusual social skills of dogs arose as a result of domestication and represent a case of convergent evolution with humans (i.e. similar derived traits in distantly related species)' (441).

57. Dominique Lestel, 'How Chimpanzees have Domesticated Humans: Towards an Anthropology of Human-Animal Communication', trans. Jonathan Benthall, *Anthropology Today* 14, no. 3 (1998): 13. Hereafter cited in the text as HCD, followed by the page reference.
58. Derrida, *Beast and the Sovereign II*, 88.
59. Jacques Derrida, *Specters of Marx: The State of the Debt, the Work of Mourning, and the New International*, trans. Peggy Kamuf (New York and London: Routledge, 1994), 89.
60. Derrida, *Beast and the Sovereign II*, 131.

4 Political animals

1. Cary Wolfe, *Before the Law: Humans and Other Animals in a Biopolitical Frame* (Chicago and London: University of Chicago Press, 2013), 10.
2. Jacques Derrida, *The Beast and the Sovereign, Volume I*, ed. Michel Lisse, Marie-Louise Mallet and Ginette Michaud, trans. Geoffrey Bennington (Chicago and London: University of Chicago Press, 2009), 16.
3. Hannah Arendt, *The Human Condition*, 2nd edn (Chicago: University of Chicago Press, 1998 [1958]). Hereafter cited in the text as HC, followed by the page reference.
4. Giorgio Agamben, *Homo Sacer: Sovereign Power and Bare Life*, trans. Daniel Heller-Roazen (Stanford: Stanford University Press, 1998), 4.
5. Agamben, *Homo Sacer*, 187.
6. Agamben, *Homo Sacer*, 6.
7. Hannah Arendt, *The Promise of Politics*, ed. Jerome Kohn (New York: Schocken Books, 2005), 127. The internal references are to Kenneth Burke, *Attitudes Toward History*, 3rd edn (Berkeley: University of California Press, 1984 [1937]), 4; and to Plato, *Seventh Letter*, 325d.
8. Jacques Derrida, *The Animal That Therefore I Am*, ed. Marie-Louise

Mallet, trans. David Wills (New York: Fordham University Press, 2008), 18. The portmanteau 'asinanity' is translator David Wills's ingenious solution to the problem of translating Derrida's use of the terms *bête* and *bêtise*. The noun *bête* can mean 'beast' or 'animal', but as an adjective means 'stupid', which Wills translates as 'asinine' in order 'to retain some connotation of animality'. It is in order to retain that same polyvalence and association that Wills takes the liberty of coining 'asinanity' as a translation for *bêtise* (an 'idiocy', a 'stupid thing'). See Derrida, *Animal*, 162–3, n. 6.

9. Hannah Arendt, *On Violence* (San Diego, New York and London: Harcourt Brace Jovanovich, 1970), 82.
10. I say 'more ambivalently' in view of Arendt's appeal to this (lost) distinction between *physis* and *nomos* as part of her explicit critique of a certain kind of anthropocentrism, expressed or enabled by modern science and technology: 'The modern age, with its growing world-alienation, has led to a situation where man, wherever he goes, encounters only himself. All the processes of the earth and the universe have revealed themselves either as man-made or as potentially man-made'; Hannah Arendt, *Between Past and Present: Six Exercises in Political Thought* (New York: The Viking Press, 1961), 89.
11. Arendt, *The Promise of Politics*, 111–12.
12. See Oskar Pfungst, *Clever Hans (The Horse of Mr Von Osten): A Contribution to Experimental Animal and Human Psychology*, trans. from German by Carl L. Rahn (New York: Henry Holt and Co., 1911). For a critical reading of Pfungst's study, see Vinciane Despret, *Hans, le cheval qui savait compter* (Éditions du Seuil: Paris, 2004). The final section of this work has been translated as Vinciane Despret, 'Who Made Clever Hans Stupid?', trans. Matthew Chrulew, *Angelaki: Journal of the Theoretical Humanities* 20, no. 2 (2015): 77–85.
13. Vinciane Despret, 'The Body We Care For: Figures of Anthropo-zoo-genesis', *Body and Society* 10, no. 2–3 (2004): 111–34.
14. Despret, 'Body We Care For', 111.
15. 'Unlike human behavior – which the Greeks, like all civilized people, judged according to "moral standards", taking into account motives and intentions on the one hand and aims and consequences on the

other – action can be judged only by the criterion of greatness because it is in its nature to break through the commonly accepted and reach into the extraordinary, where whatever is true in common and everyday life no longer applies because everything that exists is unique and *sui generis*' (HC 205).

16. Despret, 'Body We Care For', 115.
17. Despret, 'Who Made Clever Hans Stupid?', 81.
18. Despret, 'Body We Care For', 115–16.
19. Despret, 'Body We Care For', 117.
20. Brett Buchanan, Matthew Chrulew and Jeffery Bussolini, 'Vinciane Despret', *Angelaki: Journal of the Theoretical Humanities* 20, no.2 (2015): 1–3.
21. For Despret's account of her relationship with '*real* philosophy', see 'Why "I Had Not Read Derrida": Often Too Close, Always Too Far Away', trans. Greta D'Amico and Stephanie Posthumus, in *French Thinking About Animals*, ed. Louisa Mackenzie and Stephanie Posthumus (East Lansing: Michigan State University Press, 2015), 91–104.
22. Vinciane Despret, *What Would Animals Say If We Asked the Right Questions?* trans. Brett Buchanan (Minneapolis: University of Minnesota Press, 2016), 89. Hereafter cited in the text as WW, followed by the page reference.
23. Among many other illuminating examples discussed by Despret (WW 89–90) is the story first recounted by Vicki Hearne that experienced laboratory-based ethologists routinely advise young scientists not to work with cats. The problem, according to these experienced researchers, is that, while cats often easily pass various intelligence tests, they will subsequently refuse to cooperate in further testing, even to the point of starving themselves. Consequently, the informal advice is not to use cats, because 'they'll screw up the data'; Vicki Hearne, *Adam's Task: Calling Animals by Name* (New York: Skyhorse Publishing, 2007), 225. As Despret suggests, then, the whole research process – from research design, through experimental protocol, to the exercise of writing up results in formal scientific articles – operates in such a way as to make these forms of resistance or initiative invisible:

'the entire device is carried out in such a way that it blocks the possibility that the animal could show how he takes a position with respect to what is asked of him' (WW 91). 'That an animal actively resists or demonstrates his disinterest could certainly lead us to explore [this other] possibility: maybe he is *not* interested? The solution is usually more simple: cats, parrots, and others will simply be excluded [from the findings]' (WW 91).

24. For original research investigating counting abilities in honeybees, see Marie Dacke and Mandyam V. Srinivasan, 'Evidence for Counting in Insects', *Animal Cognition* 11 (2008): 683–9. News stories reporting on such apiological research were published in *The Telegraph* (UK) and *The New York Times*, among many other outlets across the globe.

25. Jürgen Habermas has, of course, provided the paradigmatic account of this transformation to the public sphere, in *The Structural Transformation of the Public Sphere: An Inquiry into a Category of Bourgeois Society*, trans. Thomas Burger with Frederick Lawrence (Cambridge: Polity Press, 1989). Indeed, Habermas's depiction of the rise of the bourgeois public sphere paints a far more nuanced account of the role of the media of speech and writing in its formation. For Habermas, the periodical press amounted to one condition, another being the emergence of new sites of sociality, such as coffee houses and salons, which together constituted a forum for the public use of reason, particularly debate over the political issues of the day. In this sense, his model of the public sphere remains intrinsically dialogical, which is to say, centred on speech and discussion, rather than appearance and action. For updated assessments of the theory of the public sphere, ones which elaborate on the increasingly mediatised nature of the contemporary public sphere as a space of visibility beyond the locale, see John Hartley, *The Politics of Pictures: The Creation of the Public in the Age of Popular Media* (London and New York: Routledge, 1992), 28–41; and John B. Thompson, *The Media and Modernity: A Social Theory of the Media* (Cambridge: Polity Press, 1995). Thompson's argument for the need to develop a politics based on the 'reinvention of publicness' has significant overlaps with the account I am developing here.

26. Jacques Derrida and Bernard Stiegler, *Echographies of Television:*

Filmed Interviews, trans. Jennifer Bajorek (Cambridge: Polity Press, 2002), 36, 3.
27. See Robert Briggs, 'Teletechnology', in *Derrida: Key Concepts*, ed. Claire Colebrook (London and New York: Routledge, 2015), 58–67.
28. Derrida, in Derrida and Stiegler, *Echographies*, 40.
29. Derrida, in Derrida and Stiegler, *Echographies*, 3.
30. Derrida and Stiegler, *Echographies*, 164.
31. Derrida and Stiegler, *Echographies*, 164.
32. As I have said elsewhere, 'the concept of artifactuality (as with teletechnology) refuses or complicates the apparent ontological distinction between the "reality" that we experience or perceive and the "media" that we read or watch, particularly as that distinction is reproduced in the notion of "representation"'; Briggs, 'Teletechnology', 63.
33. Hannah Arendt, *On Violence* (San Diego, New York and London: Harcourt Brace Javanovich, 1970), 4. One might further note the extent to which contemporary social media are readily often understood to be defined by the imperatives of an 'attention economy', first postulated by Michael H. Goldhaber, 'The Attention Economy and the Net', *First Monday* 2 (April 1997): n.p. Notwithstanding the apparent recency of 'the attention economy', communication in the Greek *polis* can likewise be understood to be structured by the (economic) variable of attention. See Robert Briggs, 'Who Knows? Humanities Research in "Computerized Societies"', *Ctrl-Z: New Media Philosophy* 5 (2015).
34. Derrida, in Derrida and Stiegler, *Echographies*, 38.
35. For an online republication of Despret's discussion which has embedded within the text many of the videos she discusses, see Vinciane Despret, 'Y for YouTube', trans. Brett Buchanan, *Ctrl-Z: New Media Philosophy* 6 (2016), http://www.ctrl-z.net.au//journal?slug=contents
36. In *The Promise of Politics*, Arendt distinguishes 'the meaning of politics' from political goals, 'which are never more than guidelines or directives by which we orient ourselves', and 'ends', which, like the ends that rule work and fabrication, operate 'under the sign of brute force', rather than freedom, and so are an anathema to politics. The 'meaning' of politics, by contrast, is precisely the *maintenance* of that 'in-between space' in which political action takes place (193).

37. For this reason, the (so to speak) Derridean reading of (animal) natality developed here differs – in emphasis rather than in substance – from the 'Derridean natality' that Allen Feldman derives from a genealogy of Derrida's encounter with the animal gaze which runs through Arendt's thought of natality to Levinas's ethical relation to the face'; Feldman, 'Inhumanitas: Political Speciation, Animality, Natality, Defacement', in *In the Name of Humanity: The Government of Threat and Care*, ed. Ilana Feldman and Miriam Iris Ticktin (Durham, NC, and London: Duke University Press, 2010), pp. 115–50. Feldman effectively problematises the residual metaphysics and anthropocentrism pervading both Arendt's and Levinas's respective arguments on the way to producing a complex image of (animal) appearance as always already 'inherited as a political relation' (145). Where Feldman's emphasis is on theorising an ethics of the face and of de-facement, I am less concerned here with formulating or justifying ethical stances than with merely attending to (hence multiplying) the possible forms and sites in which events of animal natality may be found.

38. Pertaining to this form or sense of animal action, the zoopolitical possibility revealed here therefore exceeds both the 'politics of recognition' that is sometimes thought to characterise the concerns of 'multiculturalism' and various 'new social movements' – see Charles Taylor, 'The Politics of Recognition', in *Multiculturalism*, ed. Amy Gutman (Princeton: Princeton University Press, 1994), 25–73 – and perhaps even the forms of witnessing that might enable what Kelly Oliver calls 'the recognition of what is beyond recognition'; Kelly Oliver, 'Witnessing and Testimony', *Parallax* 10, no. 1 (2004): 79–88. In reference to Hegelian theories of the struggle for recognition, Oliver argues that 'if recognition is conceived as being conferred on others by the dominant group, then it merely repeats the dynamic of hierarchies, privilege, and domination', and therefore 'do[es] no more than replicate the master-slave' hierarchy in a new form (79). On her account, 'victims of oppression, slavery and torture', for example, 'are not merely seeking visibility and recognition, but . . . are also seeking witnesses to horrors beyond recognition' (79). In the context of animal politics, the recently begun 'Save Movement' (thesavemovement.org) – a loose

collective of globally dispersed groups that 'bear witness' to farm animals about to be slaughtered – would perhaps be exemplary of the kind of witnessing implied by Oliver's argument. However, if it is not quite apposite to read the forms or possibilities of publicly appearing animal action outlined above as demands for recognition – not least of all because it is no straightforward matter here (if not also everywhere) to identify the 'subject' who has issued the demand – neither is it particularly fitting to depict such action as either issuing from or testifying to 'horrors beyond recognition'. If the new etho-media practices outlined here can be understood to intersect with Oliver's project, then, it is perhaps insofar as those practices further the 're-evaluation' of recognition by pointing to a 'beyond recognition' that remains unrecognisable in and to a politics concerned with 'oppression and victimization' (80). See also Kelly Oliver, *Witnessing: Beyond Recognition* (Minneapolis: University of Minnesota Press, 2001).

39. See, for instance, Evgeny Morozov's critique of 'cyber-utopianism' and 'Internet-centrism', where he notes how 'the decentralized nature of [online] communications' puts oppositional movements in a position of having 'to compete with the much funnier videos of cats flushing the toilet'; *The Net Delusion: The Dark Side of Internet Freedom* (New York: Public Affairs, 2011), 55. Morozov's concern is primarily with fighting political authoritarianism, and the scope of his critique of the internet's failings in this struggle extends to encompass online political debate and digital activism (or 'slacktivism') in addition to 'hedonistic' uses of the digital networked technologies. He would thus appear to be sceptical of conventional accounts of the nature and operations of politics, but his proposed remedy for what he calls 'the Net Delusion' shows that his critique is ultimately one of technology and not of the idea of politics as defined by deliberation, policymaking and governance.

5 Responding (after anthropos)

1. Jacques Derrida, *The Other Heading: Reflections on Today's Europe*, trans. Pascale-Anne Brault and Michael B. Naas (Bloomington and Indianapolis: Indiana University Press, 1992), 53.

2. Claire Colebrook and Jami Weinstein, 'Anthropocene Feminisms: Rethinking the Unthinkable', *philoSOPHIA* 5, no. 2 (Summer 2015): 167–8. In making these observations, Colebrook and Weinstein cite and reiterate points made by Donna Haraway in a 2014 lecture at the University of California, Santa Cruz, 'Anthropocene, Capitalocene, Chthulucene: Staying with the Trouble'.
3. Colebrook and Weinstein, 'Anthropocene Feminisms', 167.
4. Paolo Virno, 'Natural-Historical Diagrams: The "New Global" Movement and the Biological Invariant', *Cosmos and History: The Journal of Natural and Social Philosophy* 5, no. 1 (2009): 93. Hereafter cited in the text as NH, followed by the page reference.
5. In this respect, it should be noted that Virno's reference to the 'eternal' is not quite as metaphysical as it may sound: 'by "eternal" I simply mean that which displays a high degree of invariance, not being subject to social and cultural transformation' (NH 94).
6. Jason Read, 'Anthropocene and Anthropogenesis: Philosophical Anthropology and the Ends of Man', *The South Atlantic Quarterly* 116, no. 2 (2017): 267.
7. Dipesh Chakrabarty, 'The Climate of History: Four Theses', *Critical Inquiry* 35, no. 4 (2009): 221.
8. Chakrabarty, 'Climate of History', 213.
9. Chakrabarty, 'Climate of History', 217.
10. Chakrabarty, 'Climate of History', 221.
11. Slavoj Žižek, *Living in the End Times* (London: Verso, 2010), 330–6; Jason W. Moore, 'Anthropocene or Capitalocene? Nature, History, and the Crisis of Capitalism', in *Anthropocene or Capitalocene? Nature, History, and the Crisis of Capitalism*, ed. Jason Moore (Oakland: PM Press, 2016), 1–11.
12. Timothy Morton, *Dark Ecology: For a Logic of Future Coexistence* (New York: Columbia University Press, 2016), 23.
13. Morton, *Dark Ecology*, 14–15.
14. Morton, *Dark Ecology*, 36, 24, 23.
15. Chakrabarty, 'Climate of History', 216.
16. Chakrabarty, 'Climate of History', 221.
17. Chakrabarty, 'Climate of History', 222, emphasis added.

18. Jacques Derrida, *Margins of Philosophy*, trans. Alan Bass (Sussex: Harvester Press, 1982), 123. The specific essay in question is 'The Ends of Man', which Derrida originally presented in 1968.
19. Derrida, *Margins of Philosophy*, 117.
20. Thus, in Hegel, the *Phenomenology of Spirit*'s succession of anthropology and its delimitation of the figure and the finitude of man are thought through an appeal to the truth of man guaranteed by 'a teleology in the first person plural', the 'we' that unites 'absolute knowledge and anthropology', 'God and man', 'onto-theo-teleology and humanism'; Derrida, *Margins of Philosophy*, 121. In Husserl, 'the end of man (as a factual anthropological limit) is announced to thought from the vantage of the end of man (as a determined opening or the infinity of a *telos*)' (123). And, in Heidegger, more subtly, the exemplarity of man, the priority of *Dasein* – which, 'though *not* man, is nevertheless *nothing other* than man' (127) – in its proximity to Being 'inscribes the so-called formal structure of the question of Being within the horizon of metaphysics' (125).
21. Derrida, *Margins of Philosophy*, 134.
22. Derrida, *Margins of Philosophy*, 135.
23. Derrida, *Margins of Philosophy*, 135.
24. Morton, *Dark Ecology*, 5–6.
25. Morton, *Dark Ecology*, 7.
26. Claire Colebrook, *Death of the PostHuman: Essays on Extinction, Volume 1* (Open Humanities Press, 2016), 169. Hereafter cited in the text as DP, followed by the page reference.
27. Michel Foucault, *The Order of Things: An Archaeology of the Human Sciences* (London: Tavistock, 1970), 317.
28. Foucault, *Order of Things*, 318.
29. 'Even though [man] is not conceived as the end-product of evolution, he is recognized to be one extremity of a long series'; Foucault, *Order of Things*, 313.
30. For an overview of the effects of climate change not only on the 'viability' of a range of animal species but also on their forms of behaviours, habits, and so on, see Andrew Sih, Maud C. O. Ferrari and David J. Harris, 'Evolution and Behavioural Responses to Human-induced

Rapid Environmental Change', *Evolutionary Applications* 4 (2011): 367–87.

31. See, for instance, David E. Cooper, 'The Idea of Environment', in *The Environment in Question: Ethics and Global Issues*, ed. David E. Cooper and Joy A. Palmer (London and New York: Routledge, 1992), 167. 'An environment is what a creature knows – and knows in a certain way' (169). 'To speak in the language of phenomenology, [an animal's] relation [to its environment] is an "intentional" one. An environment, that is, is something *for* a creature, a field of meanings or significance. It is not simply that its environment matters to the creature. A badger set, after all, might matter a good deal to a zoology student without thereby belonging to his environment. The point is rather, first, that the items in one's environment are those which are brought into relief, "lit up", through occupying places in one's everyday practices . . . In calling an environment a field of significance I mean, second, that the items within it signify or point to one another, thereby forming a network of meanings. It is this which confers cohesion, a certain "wholeness", on an environment . . . Heidegger describes a person's world – for example, a farm with its equipment, inhabitants and surroundings – as constituting a "referential totality" . . . Animals, too, dwell in fields of significance; the droppings at the entrance to the tunnel indicate a fox, which signifies a threat to the badger's young, whose squealing expresses hunger, which refers the badger to the berries behind that tree, the scent on which means the recent presence of a fox . . .' (169–70).

32. Virno attributes 'worlds' only to the human (as indefinite) animal, characterising such worlds alternately as 'pseudo-environments' and 'culture', phenomena which on his account are nevertheless biological: 'The world is not a particularly vast and varied environment, nor is it the class of all possible environments: rather there is a world *only* where an environment is wanting. Social and political praxis provisionally compensates for this lack, building *pseudo-environments* within which omnilateral and indiscriminate stimuli are selected in view of advantageous actions . . . As a device which is itself biological

(that is, functional to the preservation of the species), culture aims at stabilizing the "indefinite animal"' (NH 98).

33. 'Throughout the Classical age, life was the province of an ontology which dealt in the same way with all material beings, all of which were subject to extension, weight, and movement; and it was in this sense that all the sciences of nature, and especially that of living beings, had a profound mechanistic vocation; from Cuvier onward [that is, on the threshold of modern thought], living beings escape, in the first instance at least, the general laws of extensive being; biological being becomes regional and autonomous; life, on the confines of being, is what is exterior to it and also, at the same time, what manifests itself within it. And though the question of its relations with the non-living, or that of its physico-chemical determinations, does arise, it does so not along the lines of a "mechanism" stubbornly clinging to its Classical modalities, but in an entirely new way, in order to articulate two natures one upon the other'; Foucault, *Order of Things*, 273.

34. See John Skelhorn and Candy Rowe, 'Cognition and the Evolution of Camouflage', *Proceedings of the Royal Society B: Biological Sciences* 283 (2016). In examining animal cognition as a selective pressure driving evolution, Skelhorn and Rowe question the prevalence of mechanistic assumptions in many explanations of camouflage, and identify research which highlights the many environmental factors and cues that feed into search and avoidance decisions made both by predators and prey, including strategic assessments of camouflage efficacy.

35. For an early rehearsal of this in-principle argument concerning the non-delimitability of environments, as well as the reading of 'environment' in terms of 'context' and 'writing' that follows from here, see my 'Wild Thoughts: A Deconstructive Environmental Ethics?' *Environmental Ethics* 23, no. 2 (Summer 2001): 115–34. For some more recent derivations of comparable arguments from Derrida's work, see several of the chapters in the recently published collection *Eco-Deconstruction: Derrida and Environmental Philosophy*, ed. Matthias Fritsch, Philippe Lynes and David Wood (New York: Fordham University Press, 2018), particularly the chapters by

Matthias Fritsch (279–302) and Viki Kirby (121–40), as well as the Introduction by the collection's editors (1–26). My argument here that no animal is fit for 'its' environment offers a potential counterpoint to the conclusion that Kirby draws from her discussion of (among other things) evolutionary principles in the context of Derrida's notion of writing: casting 'the environment as a force that speciates, a force that individuates *itself*, she argues that 'the sense of fitness ... is a sort of ontological tautology wherein existence of whatever sort, its very specificity, is exemplary of universal possibilities' (130).

36. Jacques Derrida, *Limited, Inc*, ed. Gerald Graff (Evanston: Northwestern University Press, 1988), 151.
37. Derrida, *Limited Inc*, 151.
38. Foucault, *Order of Things*, 273.
39. See, for instance, Read's suggestion that 'the Anthropocene can be in part understood as a kind of multiplication of natural limits, as oceans, the atmosphere, and various ecosystems reveal their irreducibility to abstract nature' ('Anthropocene and Anthropogenesis', 270–1).
40. See Udo Engelhardt, *Outbreaks of the Crown-of-Thorns Starfish on the Great Barrier Reef: Current Status, Emerging Trends and Developing Issues of Concern* (Cairns: WWF-Australia, 2018). Episodes of COTS outbreaks have been identified as one of the main drivers, alongside mass coral bleaching and storm damage, of declining hard coral cover across the Great Barrier Reef since 1985. The Great Barrier Reef, located in the Coral Sea off the coast of Queensland, Australia, is the world's largest coral reef system. It has been under the care and protection of the Great Barrier Reef Marine Park Authority since 1975, when it was established as a protected marine park, and was World Heritage-listed in 1981. Notwithstanding these measures geared towards preserving the reef, a study published in 2012 found that coral cover reduced by 50.7 per cent over 1985–2012; Glenn De'ath, Katharina E. Fabricius, Hugh Sweatman and Marji Puotinen, 'The 27-year Decline of Coral Cover on the Great Barrier Reef and its Causes', *Proceedings of the National Academy of Sciences of the United States of America* 109, no. 44 (2012): 17995–9.
41. Hence what is sometimes referred to as the 'natural causes thesis'

regarding COTS outbreaks. Engelhardt, *Outbreaks*, 7. On the reproductive and larval biology of *A. planci*, see J. S. Lucas, 'Reproductive and Larval Biology of *Acanthaster planci* in Great Barrier Reef Waters', *Micronesica* 9, no. 2 (1973): 197–203; R. C. Babcock and C. N. Mundy, 'Reproductive Biology, Spawning and Field Fertilization Rates of *Acanthaster planci*', *Australian Journal of Marine Freshwater Research* 43 (1992): 525–34. On population dynamics, see Jacob G. D. Rogers, Éva E. Pláganyi and Russell C. Babcock, 'Aggregation, Allee Effects and Critical Thresholds for the Management of the Crown-of-Thorns Starfish *Acanthaster planci*', *Marine Ecology Progress Series* 578 (August 2017): 99–114; and Babcock and Mundy, 'Reproductive Biology'. In view of the 'metaphors' of reading and interpretation deployed throughout this chapter, it is worth noting that Babcock and Mundy hypothesise olfaction to play an important role in *A. planci* spawning synchony. More recent research has identified putative COTS olfactory receptors, suggesting that chemosensation may be a critical signalling process in COTS aggregation, spawning and reproduction. See Rebecca E. Roberts, Cherie A. Motti, Kenneth W. Baughman, Noriyuki Satoh, Michael R. Hall and Scott F. Cummins, 'Identification of Putative Olfactory G-Protein Coupled Receptors in Crown-of-Thorns Starfish, *Acanthaster planci*', *BMC Genomics* 18 (2017).

42. K. E. Fabricius, K. Okaji and G. De'ath, 'Three Lines of Evidence to Link Outbreaks of the Crown-of-Thorns Seastar *Acanthaster planci* to the Release of Larval Food Limitation', *Coral Reefs* 29 (2010): 593–605. Engelhardt, *Outbreaks*, singles out high levels of dissolved inorganic nitrogen in reef waters, caused by run-off from nitrogen-fertilised sugarcane farms in coastal catchments, as a key promoter and exacerbator of COTS outbreaks (5). See also Grant Fraser, Ken Rohde and Mark Silburn, 'Fertiliser Management Effects on Dissolved Inorganic Nitrogen in Runoff from Australian Sugarcane Farms', *Environmental Monitoring and Assessment* 189 (2017).

43. In this way, we might also read episodes of COTS outbreak as examples of what Nicole Shukin calls 'living reminders of irredeemable events in the history of capitalism'; Nicole Shukin, 'Capitalism', in *The*

Edinburgh Companion to Animal Studies, ed. Lynne Turner, Undine Sellbach and Ron Broglio (Edinburgh: Edinburgh University Press, 2018), 110. In her study of contemporary, neoliberal capitalism's differential valuing of forms of animal life, Shukin diagnoses the ways in which neoliberal cultures of capitalism come to 'speculate, imaginatively and financially, in animal life as remedy and redeemer of a sinful system whose regulated growth has thrown planet Earth into profound ecological disaster' (96). In this way, she foregrounds 'the cunning of capitalism, which works with and through rather than against a spirit of animal liberation' (108). In a provocative conclusion to her argument, however, Shukin identifies (after Ron Broglio) the emergence of radioactive wild boars in regions affected by nuclear disaster (Chernobyl and Fukushima), whose 'flourishing', she argues, 'antagonises rather than serves the equivalence neoliberalism seeks between life and capital' (109), thereby demonstrating that life isn't 'simply captive to intensifying practices of capitalist enclosure' (110). While agricultural run-off perhaps pales into insignificance alongside nuclear disaster, we might nevertheless consider COTS outbreaks as a case of 'animals rudely interject[ing] themselves within the present as unwelcome reminders of a past disaster', and as arguably functioning 'as agents of a historical consciousness', as Shukin puts it, 'to undermine nothing less than the cunning of capitalism itself' (110).

44. Cary Wolfe, *What is Posthumanism?* (Minneapolis: University of Minnesota Press, 2010), 99.
45. Derrida, *Other Heading*, 41.
46. Isabelle Stengers, *In Catastrophic Times: Resisting the Coming Barbarism*, trans. Andrew Goffey (Open Humanities Press, 2015). Hereafter cited in the text as CT, followed by the page reference.
47. James Lovelock and Lynn Margulis, 'Atmospheric Homeostasis By and For the Biosphere: The Gaia Hypothesis', *Tellus* XXVI, no. 1–2 (1974): 2–10.
48. Here, the force of scale and the phenomena (if they could be called such) of scale effects warrant particular consideration. See Derek Woods, 'Scale Critique for the Anthropocene', *Minnesota Review* 83 (2014): 133–42; Timothy Clark, 'Scale as a Force of Deconstruction',

in *Eco-Deconstruction: Derrida and Environmental Philosophy*, ed. Matthias Fritsch, Philippe Lynes and David Wood (New York: Fordham University Press, 2018), 81–97. As Clark notes, 'scale effects are an elusive and underconceptualized form of agency', albeit one which is becoming only more prominent today (85).

49. Understood, that is, on the model of Jean-François Lyotard's proposition that 'silence is a phrase'. See *The Differend: Phrases in Dispute*, trans. Georges Van Den Abbeele (Minneapolis: University of Minnesota Press, 1988), xii.

50. Chakrabarty, 'Climate of History', 221.

51. Vinciane Despret, 'From Secret Agents to Interagency', *History and Theory* 52 (December 2013): 38. Gilles Deleuze and Felix Guattari, *A Thousand Plateaus: Capitalism and Schizophrenia*, trans. Brian Massumi (Minneapolis: University of Minnesota Press, 1987). Although I cannot pursue the question here, this depiction of assemblages as 'rapports of forces' perhaps warrants a second reading in terms of what I have nicknamed 'zoopower' (in Chapter 3), given Derrida's association, in *Rogues*, of 'ipseity' with 'the sovereign and reappropriating gathering of self in the simultaneity of an *assemblage* [emphasis added] or assembly'; Jacques Derrida, *Rogues: Two Essays on Reason*, trans. Pascale-Anne Brault and Michael Naas (Stanford: Stanford University Press, 2005), 11. See Woods, 'Scale Critique', for an attempt to divide 'the *anthropos* of "Anthropocene" and "anthropogenic" ... among scale domains' (138) by underscoring that figure's distribution and redistribution (to use Despret's terms) within a broader assemblage.

52. Jacques Derrida, *The Gift of Death*, trans. David Wills (Chicago and London: University of Chicago Press, 1995), 25.

53. Lovelock and Margulis, 'Atmospheric Homeostasis', 2, emphases added.

54. Lovelock and Margulis, 'Atmospheric Homeostasis', 3, emphasis added.

55. Timothy A. C. Gordon et al., 'Acoustic Enrichment Can Enhance Fish Community Development on Degraded Coral Reef Habitat', *Nature Communications* 10 (2019).

56. Thomas J. Goreau, 'Electrical Stimulation Greatly Increases

Settlement, Growth, Survival, and Stress Resistance of Marine Organisms', *Natural Resources* 5 (2014): 527–37. Baruch Rinkevich, 'Conservation of Coral Reefs through Active Restoration Measures: Recent Approaches and Last Decade Progress', *Environmental Science and Technology* 39, no. 12 (2005): 4333–42.

57. Dominique Lestel, 'The Animality to Come', trans. Matthew Chrulew, *Ctrl-Z: New Media Philosophy* 6 (2016).
58. David Roy Bellwood and Christopher Harry Robert Goatley, 'Can Biological Invasions Save Caribbean Coral Reefs?', *Current Biology* 27 (9 January 2017): R13–R14.
59. Bellwood and Goatley, 'Can Biological Invasions?', R13.
60. Bellwood and Goatley, 'Can Biological Invasions?', R13, R14.
61. Bellwood and Goatley, 'Can Biological Invasions?', R14.
62. The resistance with which such thoughts can be met, and the challenge they pose to conservative logics of life, is perhaps indicated by Bellwood's remark at the Australia Research Council's Coral Reef Futures Symposium 2018 that his discussion of biological invasions was the 'least popular paper' that he had ever published. See Liberty Lawson's discussion of Bellwood's presentation, 'Coral Futures: Finding a Compromise' (4 October 2018), published by the Sydney Environment Institute, https://sei.sydney.edu.au/opinion/coral-futures-finding-compromise/
63. The evidence for the success of electrical stimulation of coral growth, for instance, has been questioned by some. See Makoto Omori, 'Coral Restoration Research and Technical Developments: What We Have Learned So Far', *Marine Biology Research* 15, no. 7 (2019): 377–409.
64. Though see Despret's account of animal cooperation in scenes of work and industry (discussed in Chapter 3), where she broaches a sense of animal responsibility that overlaps in significant ways with the one being developed here: 'Thinking that farmers and cows share the conditions of work ... obliges us to consider the way that they mutually respond, how they are responsible in the relationship – here *responsible* does not mean that they must accept the causes but that they must respond to the consequences and that their responses are part of the consequences. If animals do not cooperate, the work is

impossible'; Vinciane Despret, *What Would Animals Say If We Asked the Right Questions?*, trans. Brett Buchanan (Minneapolis: University of Minnesota Press, 2016), 182.

65. Dominique Lestel, 'Hybrid Communities', trans. Brett Buchanan, *Angelaki: Journal of the Theoretical Humanities* 19, no. 3 (2014): 61–73. See also the discussion of Lestel's work in Chapter 3, where the acquisition of a communicative competence on the part of primates (some primates at least; specifically, those raised in facilities devoted to researching such competencies) is analysed in terms of the transactional, biopolitical hybrid community that defines the experimental situation itself.

66. Vinciane Despret, 'The Body We Care For: Figures of Anthropo-zoogenesis', *Body and Society* 10, no. 2–3 (2004): 130. Such articulations, for Despret, even include – perhaps especially include – 'experimental situations' in which 'the experimenter, far from keeping himself in the background, involves himself: he involves his body, he involves his knowledge, his responsibility and his future' (130).

What hope for the animal-to-come?

1. Colebrook, *Death of the PostHuman: Essays on Extinction, Volume 1* (Open Humanities Press, 2016), 38.
2. Claudia Blösser and Titus Stahl, 'The Moral Psychology of Hope: An Introduction', in *The Moral Psychology of Hope*, ed. Claudia Blösser and Titus Stahl (London: Rowman and Littlefield, 2019), 1–11.
3. Søren Kierkegaard, *Works of Love*, trans. David F. Swenson and Lillian Marvin Swenson (Princeton: Princeton University Press, 1946): 'Hoping lays hold upon the future, on the possibility, which . . . as distinguished from reality, is always a duality – the possibility of progress or retrogression, of building up or tearing down, of good or of evil. The eternal "*is*", but when the eternal touches on the temporal, or is in the temporal, they do not meet each other in the "present", for then the present would itself be the eternal. The present, the moment, is so swiftly past that it does not really exist except as a dividing line . . . Hence when the eternal is in the temporal it is in the future (for

the present cannot lay hold on it, and the past is past) or in the possibility. The past is the actual, the future the possible; the eternal is the everlastingly eternal; in time the eternal is the possible, the future' (201). 'To lay hold expectantly on the possibility of the good is *to hope*, which just for this reason cannot be any temporal expectation, but is an eternal hope. To lay hold expectantly on the possibility of evil is *to fear*. But the one who hopes as well as the one who fears is expectant. Yet as soon as the choice is made, the possible is changed, for the possibility of the good is eternal. It is only in the moment of contact that the doubleness of the possible is equal. By the decision to choose hope one decides, therefore, infinitely more than it seems, for it is an eternal decision. Only in the mere possibility, hence for the merely or indifferently expectant, are the possibilities of good and evil equal; [only] in the making of a distinction (and choice is the making of a distinction) is the possibility of the good more than possibility, for it is eternal' (202). For the hoped-for possibility to remain eternal, it must remain a possibility, which is to say, must never arrive, since in being actualised it would cease to be possible and would be rather actual. But the possibility that could never become actual would for that reason not be a possibility, since it would be impossible as such. Hope, as hope for the good or for justice, for the properly good and the properly just – which is to say, for the eternally just – is hope for the impossible. And if the possible is changed in the making of the choice, if the good becomes more than possible in the choice for hope (over fear), it becomes at the same time less than possible insofar as the choice for hope could only ever take the form of an impossible hope for an impossible unpresentable (justice-to-come).

4. The 'im-possible' names, for Derrida, 'what must remain (in a nonnegative fashion) foreign to the order of my possibilities, to the order of the "I can", ipseity, the theoretical, the descriptive, the constative, and the performative (inasmuch as this latter still implies a power for some "I" guaranteed by conventions that neutralize the pure eventfulness of the event, and inasmuch as the eventfulness of the to-come exceeds this sphere of the performative)'; Jacques Derrida, *Rogues: Two Essays on Reason*, trans. Pascale-Anne Brault and Michael Naas (Stanford:

Stanford University Press, 2005), 84. An im-possible hope would, in that sense, be not so much a hope for an impossible outcome as some kind of orientation, as it were – neither an affect nor a performance, neither an experience nor an action – with respect to the future-to-come, one which exceeds the order of what 'I can' do, of what 'I can' master, comprehend, affirm or reject, and perhaps even feel.
5. Ghassan Hage, *Against Paranoid Nationalism: Searching for Hope in a Shrinking Society* (Annandale, NSW: Pluto Press, 2003), 13.
6. Lauren Berlant, *Cruel Optimism* (Durham, NC: Duke University Press, 2011), 2.
7. Lee Edelman, *No Future: Queer Theory and the Death Drive* (Durham, NC: Duke University Press, 2004), 2.
8. Edelmam, *No Future*, 2–3.
9. Edelmam, *No Future*, 4.
10. Jean-François Lyotard, *Postmodern Fables*, trans. Georges Van Den Abbeele (Minneapolis: University of Minnesota Press, 1997), 99–100.
11. Lyotard, *Postmodern Fables*, 100, 99.
12. Claire Colebrook and Jami Weinstein, 'Anthropocene Feminisms: Rethinking the Unthinkable', *philoSOPHIA* 5, no. 2 (Summer 2015), 176–7. The embedded quotation is from Edelman, *No Future*, 4 (Colebrook and Weinstein's emphasis).
13. Derrida, *Specters of Marx: The State of the Debt, the Work of Mourning, and the New International*, trans. Peggy Kamuf (New York and London: Routledge, 1994), 29, 168–9. In this regard, it is worth recalling, too, Derrida's insistence, in *Rogues*, on the 'aporetic difficulty' of the promise, whereby the temporal structure of 'to-come' registers as 'a question of autoimmunity, of a *double bind* of threat and chance, not alternatively or by turns promise and/or threat but threat *in* the promise itself' (82). 'Hope' would here name the relation to (this) promise/threat.
14. Carl Schmitt, *The Concept of the Political*, exp. ed., trans. George Schwab (Chicago: University of Chicago Press, 2007), 61.
15. Schmitt, *Concept of the Political*, 58.
16. Schmitt, *Concept of the Political*, 60, citing Plessner's *Macht und menschliche Natur*.

17. Derrida, 'Force of Law: The "Mystical Foundation of Authority"', trans. Mary Quaintance, in *Deconstruction and the Possibility of Justice*, ed. Drucilla Cornell, Michael Rosenfield and David Gray Carlson (New York and London: Routledge, 1992), 27.
18. Here I perhaps risk diverging from Derrida's insistence that deconstruction pursues a question of 'survivance', a questioning that proceeds *in him* 'from an unconditional affirmation of life' such that deconstruction 'is not a discourse of death, but, on the contrary, the affirmation of a living being who prefers living and thus surviving to death'; Jacques Derrida, *Learning to Live Finally*, trans. Pascale-Anne Brault and Michael Naas (Hoboken: Melville House Publishing, 2007), 52. At the risk, in turn, of downplaying the potential significance of this apparent 'contradiction', I must defer engagement with this problem, which is too complex to take up in any detail here, to another occasion. In lieu of a more developed account, I will note simply that it is life understood as sovereignty over differance, an ultimately risk-free life in which all death (as difference) could ideally be mastered by a self-sufficient, self-organising life – and not the 'life beyond life' (52) that articulates Derrida's thought of 'survivance' – that the thought of the animal-to-come calls into question by registering this relation between invention and death. Derrida's notion of 'survivance' has become central in many recent explorations of his work in relation to questions of life, animality, bio-philosophy and ecology. Philippe Lynes presents an extended and sophisticated account of the 'concept' and its implications for thinking about life, death, extinction and a general ecology, in *Futures of Life Death on Earth: Derrida's General Ecology* (London and New York: Rowman and Littlefield, 2018).
19. Jacques Derrida, *The Beast and the Sovereign, Volume II*, ed. Michel Lisse, Marie-Louise Mallet and Ginette Michaud, trans. Geoffrey Bennington (Chicago and London: University of Chicago Press, 2011), 130, 131, 132.
20. In the fourth session of *Beast and the Sovereign II*, Derrida cites Heidegger's reference (in *The Fundamental Concepts of Metaphysics*) to philosophy or philosophising (insofar as it is 'our own human activity') as 'a drive to be at home everywhere, a demand, not blind and

without direction, but one which awakens us to . . . questions' (107–8) and re-reads it in terms of Heidegger's prior characterisation of 'our being' as a *Getriebenheit*, a 'being pushed' (101). In this way, Derrida reads the awakening to questioning in terms of the 'limit concept' of 'the drive' understood as 'a movement, a process, a tendency, a force' that 'pushes, but where it pushes there is not yet either drive or push, or pulse, or being pushed, or a being doing the pushing' (102). What Heidegger goes on to name as *Dasein*, therefore, is in Derrida's reading the 'force to bear [such] questioning', the 'force of bearing, of enduring, the force to support and prepare the birth of these questions' (107).

21. This phrase comes from David Wood, 'Specters of Derrida: On the Way to Econstruction', in *Ecospirit: Religions and Philosophies for the Earth*, ed. Laurel Kearns and Catherine Keller (New York: Fordham University Press, 2007). I cite it here for the way that it encapsulates a readily available – indeed, *seductive* – way of thinking about the possible connections between Derrida's democracy-to-come and animals or living beings more generally, but one whose vocabulary risks confirming the institutions and processes of the modern state as *the* site of politics, reducing zoopolitics to the inclusion of nonhuman others within otherwise conventional operations of modern government and judiciary. This is not to suggest, however, that Wood is unappreciative of the role that disruption and conflict would play in any such zoopolitics. For immediately preceding his introduction of the idea(l) of a 'parliament of the living', he writes: 'Genuinely trying to represent the interests of a species, or a region, et cetera, sets a standard that a court can take seriously. This is not to say that there will not be countless impossible cases, aporias, dilemmas, conflicts of interest. But that is true of the earth itself – nature is as much a battle zone as a cooperative community' (285).
22. Thom van Dooren, *The Wake of Crows: Living and Dying in Shared Worlds* (New York: Columbia University Press, 2019), 207. Hereafter cited in the text as WC, followed by the page reference.
23. On the distinctions between these and other kinds of future-oriented behaviour, see C. R. Raby and N. S. Clayton, 'Prospective Cognition in

Animals', *Behavioral Processes* 80, no. 3 (2009): 314–24. Van Dooren discusses this taxonomy along with several studies focused specifically on caching behaviour in corvids (WC 203–6).

24. Joe T. Marshall, Jr, 'The Endemic Avifauna of Saipan, Tinian, Guam and Palau', *The Condor* 51, no. 5 (1949): 216; J. Mark Jenkins, *The Native Forest Birds of Guam* (Washington: The American Ornithologists' Union, 1983), 26–32; Diana F. Tomback, 'Observations on the Behavior and Ecology of the Mariana Crow', *The Condor* 88, no. 3 (1986): 399–400.

Bibliography

Agamben, Giorgio. *Homo Sacer: Sovereign Power and Bare Life*. Translated by Daniel Heller-Roazen. Stanford: Stanford University Press, 1998.

Arendt, Hannah. *Between Past and Present: Six Exercises in Political Thought*. New York: The Viking Press, 1961.

Arendt, Hannah. *On Violence*. San Diego, New York and London: Harcourt Brace Jovanovich, 1970.

Arendt, Hannah. *The Human Condition*, 2nd edn. Chicago: University of Chicago Press, 1998 [1958].

Arendt, Hannah. *The Origins of Totalitarianism*. New York: Harcourt Brace Jovanovich, 1979.

Arendt, Hannah. *The Promise of Politics*. Edited by Jerome Kohn. New York: Schocken Books, 2005.

Atterton, Peter. 'Levinas and Our Moral Responsibility Toward Other Animals'. *Inquiry* 54, no. 6 (2011): 633–49.

Babcock, R. C. and C. N. Mundy, 'Reproductive Biology, Spawning and Field Fertilization Rates of *Acanthaster planci*'. *Australian Journal of Marine Freshwater Research* 43 (1992): 525–34.

Bataille, Georges. *Prehistoric Painting: Lascaux or the Birth of Art*. Translated by Austryn Wainhouse. Lausanne: Skira, 1955.

Béclard, Augustin. *Elements of General Anatomy*. Translated by

Robert Knox. Edinburgh: MacLachlan and Stewart, 1830 [Fr. 1823].

Bellwood, David Roy and Christopher Harry Robert Goatley. 'Can Biological Invasions Save Caribbean Coral Reefs?' *Current Biology* 27 (9 January 2017): R13–R14.

Berlant, Lauren. *Cruel Optimism*. Durham, NC: Duke University Press, 2011.

Blösser, Claudia and Titus Stahl. 'The Moral Psychology of Hope: An Introduction'. In *The Moral Psychology of Hope*, ed. Claudia Blösser and Titus Stahl, 1–11. London: Rowman and Littlefield, 2019.

Bluff, Lucas A., Alex Kacelnik and Christian Rutz. 'Vocal Culture in New Caledonian Crows *Corvus moneduloides*'. *Biological Journal of the Linnean Society* 101 (2010): 767–76.

Briggs, Robert. 'Following the Animal-To-Come'. *Derrida Today* 12, no. 1 (2019): 20–40.

Briggs, Robert. 'Genealogy, Transcendence, Obligation: Questioning (the Question of) Ethics'. *Discourse: An Interdisciplinary Philosophical Journal* 3 (1997): 1–12.

Briggs, Robert. 'Teletechnology'. In *Derrida: Key Concepts*, ed. Claire Colebrook, 58–67. London and New York: Routledge, 2015.

Briggs, Robert. 'Who Knows? Humanities Research in "Computerized Societies"'. *Ctrl-Z: New Media Philosophy* 5 (2015), http://www.ctrl-z.net.au//journal?slug=briggs-who-knows

Briggs, Robert. 'Wild Thoughts: A Deconstructive Environmental Ethics?' *Environmental Ethics* 23, no. 2 (Summer 2001): 115–34.

Buchanan, Brett, Jeffery Bussolini and Matthew Chrulew. 'General Introduction: Philosophical Ethology'. *Angelaki: Journal of the Theoretical Humanities* 19, no. 3 (2014): 1–3.

Buchanan, Brett, Matthew Chrulew and Jeffery Bussolini. 'Vinciane Despret'. *Angelaki: Journal of the Theoretical Humanities* 20, no. 2 (2015): 1–3.

Burke, Kenneth. *Attitudes Toward History*, 3rd edn. Berkeley: University of California Press, 1984 [1937].

Calarco, Matthew. *Zoographies: The Question of the Animal from Heidegger to Derrida*. New York: Columbia University Press, 2008.

Caputo, John D. *Against Ethics: Contributions to a Poetics of Obligation with Constant Reference to Deconstruction*. Bloomington and Indianapolis: Indiana University Press, 1993.

Chakrabarty, Dipesh. 'The Climate of History: Four Theses'. *Critical Inquiry* 35, no. 4 (2009): 197–222.

Chrulew, Matthew. 'Animals as Biopolitical Subjects'. In *Foucault and Animals*, ed. Matthew Chrulew and Dinesh Joseph Wadiwel, 222–38. Leiden: Brill, 2017.

Chrulew, Matthew. 'Animals in Biopolitical Theory: Between Agamben and Negri'. *New Formations* 76 (2012): 53–67.

Chrulew, Matthew. 'From Zoo to Zoöpolis: Effectively Enacting Eden'. In *Metamorphoses of the Zoo: Animal Encounter after Noah*, ed. Ralph R. Acampora, 193–220. Lanham: Lexington Books, 2010.

Chrulew, Matthew. 'Saving the Golden Lion Tamarin'. In *Extinction Studies: Stories of Time, Death, and Generations*, ed. Deborah Bird Rose, Thom van Dooren and Matthew Chrulew, 49–87. New York: Columbia University Press, 2017.

Chrulew, Matthew. '"The art of both caring and locking up": Biopolitical Thresholds in the Zoological Garden'. *SubStance* 43, no. 2 (2014): 124–47.

Chrulew, Matthew and Dinesh Joseph Wadiwel, eds. *Foucault and Animals*. Leiden, Brill, 2017.

Clark, Timothy. 'Scale as a Force of Deconstruction'. In *Eco-Deconstruction: Derrida and Environmental Philosophy*, ed. Matthias Fritsch, Philippe Lynes and David Wood, 81–97. New York: Fordham University Press, 2018.

Colebrook, Claire. *Death of the PostHuman: Essays on Extinction, Volume 1*. Open Humanities Press, 2016.

Colebrook, Claire and Jami Weinstein. 'Anthropocene Feminisms: Rethinking the Unthinkable'. *philoSOPHIA* 5, no. 2 (Summer 2015): 167–78.

Cooper, David E. 'The Idea of Environment'. In *The Environment in Question: Ethics and Global Issues*, ed. David E. Cooper and Joy A. Palmer, 165–80. London and New York: Routledge, 1992.

Cottingham, John. '"A Brute to the Brutes?" Descartes' Treatment of Animals'. *Philosophy* 53 (1978): 551–59.

Dacke, Marie and Mandyam V. Srinivasan. 'Evidence for Counting in Insects'. *Animal Cognition* 11 (2008): 683–9.

de Waal, Frans B. M. 'Silent Invasion: Imanishi's Primatology and Cultural Bias in Science'. *Animal Cognition* 6, no. 4 (2003): 293–9.

De'ath, Glenn, Katharina E. Fabricius, Hugh Sweatman and Marji Puotinen. 'The 27-year Decline of Coral Cover on the Great Barrier Reef and its Causes'. *Proceedings of the National Academy of Sciences of the United States of America* 109, no. 44 (2012): 17995–9.

Deleuze, Gilles and Félix Guattari. *A Thousand Plateaus: Capitalism and Schizophrenia*. Translated by Brian Massumi. Minneapolis: University of Minnesota Press, 1987.

Derrida, Jacques. 'Beyond the Power Principle'. Translated by Elizabeth Rottenberg. *The Undecidable Unconscious: A Journal of Deconstruction and Psychoanalysis* 2 (2015): 7–17.

Derrida, Jacques. 'Differance'. In *Speech and Phenomena, and Other Essays on Husserl's Theory of Signs*. Translated by David B. Allison, 129–60. Evanston: Northwestern University Press, 1973.

Derrida, Jacques. 'Force of Law: The "Mystical Foundation of Authority"'. Translated by Mary Quaintance. In *Deconstruction and the Possibility of Justice*, ed. Drucilla Cornell, Michael Rosenfield and David Gray Carlson, 3–67. New York and London: Routledge, 1992.

Derrida, Jacques. 'Scribble (Writing-Power)'. Translated by Cary Plotkin. *Yale French Studies* 58 (1979): 117–47.

Derrida, Jacques. *Learning to Live Finally*. Translated by Pascale-Anne Brault and Michael Naas. Hoboken: Melville House Publishing, 2007.

Derrida, Jacques. *Life Death*. Edited by Pascale-Anne Brault and

Peggy Kamuf. Translated by Pascale-Anne Brault and Michael Naas. Chicago: University of Chicago Press, 2020.

Derrida, Jacques. *Limited, Inc.* Evanston: Northwestern University Press, 1988.

Derrida, Jacques. *Margins of Philosophy*. Translated by Alan Bass. Sussex: Harvester Press, 1982.

Derrida, Jacques. *Of Grammatology*. Translated by Gayatri Spivak. Baltimore and London: Johns Hopkins University Press, 1976.

Derrida, Jacques. *Psyche: Inventions of the Other, Volume I*. Edited by Peggy Kamuf and Elizabeth Rottenberg. Stanford: Stanford University Press, 2007.

Derrida, Jacques. *Rogues: Two Essays on Reason*. Translated by Pascale-Anne Brault and Michael Naas. Stanford: Stanford University Press, 2005.

Derrida, Jacques. *Specters of Marx: The State of the Debt, the Work of Mourning, and the New International*. Translated by Peggy Kamuf. New York and London: Routledge, 1994.

Derrida, Jacques. *The Animal That Therefore I Am*. Edited by Marie-Louise Mallet. Translated by David Wills. New York: Fordham University Press, 2008.

Derrida, Jacques. *The Beast and the Sovereign, Volume I*. Edited by Michel Lisse, Marie-Louise Mallet and Ginette Michaud. Translated by Geoffrey Bennington. Chicago and London: University of Chicago Press, 2009.

Derrida, Jacques. *The Beast and the Sovereign, Volume II*. Edited by Michel Lisse, Marie-Louise Mallet and Ginette Michaud. Translated by Geoffrey Bennington. Chicago and London: University of Chicago Press, 2011.

Derrida, Jacques. *The Gift of Death*. Translated by David Wills. Chicago and London: University of Chicago Press, 1995.

Derrida, Jacques. *The Other Heading: Reflections on Today's Europe*. Translated by Pascale-Anne Brault and Michael B. Naas. Bloomington and Indianapolis: Indiana University Press, 1992.

Derrida, Jacques. *Without Alibi*. Edited and translated by Peggy Kamuf. Stanford: Stanford University Press, 2002.

Derrida, Jacques and Elisabeth Roudinesco. *For What Tomorrow... A Dialogue*. Translated by Jeff Fort. Stanford: Stanford University Press, 2004.

Derrida, Jacques and Bernard Steigler. *Echographies of Television: Filmed Interviews*. Translated by Jennifer Bajorek. Cambridge: Polity Press, 2002.

Descartes, René. *A Discourse on the Method of Correctly Conducting One's Reason and Seeking Truth in the Sciences*. Translated by Ian Maclean. Oxford: Oxford University Press, 2006.

Despret, Vinciane. 'From Secret Agents to Interagency'. *History and Theory* 52 (December 2013): 29–44.

Despret, Vinciane. 'The Body We Care For: Figures of Anthropo-zoo-genesis'. *Body and Society* 10, no. 2–3 (2004): 111–34.

Despret, Vinciane. 'Who Made Clever Hans Stupid?' Translated by Matthew Chrulew. *Angelaki: Journal of the Theoretical Humanities* 20, no. 2 (2015): 77–85.

Despret, Vinciane. 'Why "I Had Not Read Derrida": Often Too Close, Always Too Far Away'. Translated by Greta D'Amico and Stephanie Posthumus. In *French Thinking About Animals*, ed. Louisa Mackenzie and Stephanie Posthumus, 91–104. East Lansing: Michigan State University Press, 2015.

Despret, Vinciane. 'Y for YouTube'. Translated by Brett Buchanan. *Ctrl-Z: New Media Philosophy* 6 (2016), http://www.ctrl-z.net.au//journal?slug=despret-y-for-youtube

Despret, Vinciane. *Hans, le cheval qui savait compter*. Paris: Éditions du Seuil, 2004.

Despret, Vinciane. *What Would Animals Say If We Asked the Right Questions?* Translated by Brett Buchanan. Minneapolis: University of Minnesota Press, 2016.

Edelman, Lee. *No Future: Queer Theory and the Death Drive*. Durham, NC: Duke University Press, 2004.

Engelhardt, Udo. *Outbreaks of the Crown-of-Thorns Starfish on the Great Barrier Reef: Current Status, Emerging Trends and Developing Issues of Concern*. Cairns: WWF-Australia, 2018.

Fabricius, K. E., K. Okaji and G. De'ath. 'Three Lines of Evidence to Link Outbreaks of the Crown-of-Thorns Seastar *Acanthaster planci* to the Release of Larval Food Limitation'. *Coral Reefs* 29 (2010): 593–605.

Feldman, Allen. 'Inhumanitas: Political Speciation, Animality, Natality, Defacement'. In *In the Name of Humanity: The Government of Threat and Care*, ed. Ilana Feldman and Miriam Iris Ticktin, 115–50. Durham, NC, and London: Duke University Press, 2010.

Foucault, Michel. 'My Body, This Paper, This Fire'. Translated by Geoffrey Bennington. *Oxford Literary Review* 4, no. 1 (1979): 9–28.

Foucault, Michel. 'The Subject and Power'. In *Power (Essential Works Vol. 3)*, ed. James D. Faubion, 326–48. New York: New Press, 2000 [1982].

Foucault, Michel. *Discipline and Punish: The Birth of the Prison*. Translated by Alan Sheridan. London: Penguin, 1991 [1975].

Foucault, Michel. *Power/Knowledge: Selected Interviews and Other Writings*. Edited by Colin Gordon. Brighton: Harvester, 1980.

Foucault, Michel. *The History of Sexuality, Volume 1: An Introduction*. Translated by Robert Hurley. New York: Pantheon, 1978 [1976].

Foucault, Michel. *The Order of Things: An Archaeology of the Human Sciences*. London: Tavistock, 1970.

Fox, Warwick. *Towards a Transpersonal Ecology: Developing New Foundations for Environmentalism*. Dartington: Resurgence, 1995.

Fraser, Grant, Ken Rohde and Mark Silburn. 'Fertiliser Management Effects on Dissolved Inorganic Nitrogen in Runoff from Australian Sugarcane Farms'. *Environmental Monitoring and Assessment* 189 (2017), https://doi.org/10.1007/s10661-017-6115-z

Fritsch, Matthias, Philippe Lynes and David Wood, eds. *Eco-Deconstruction: Derrida and Environmental Philosophy*. New York: Fordham University Press, 2018.

Goldhaber, Michael H. 'The Attention Economy and the Net'. *First Monday* 2 (April 1997), https://firstmonday.org/article/view/519/440

Gordon, Timothy A. C., Andrew N. Radford, Isla K. Davidson, Kasey Barnes, Kieran McCloskey, Sophie L. Nedelec, Mark G. Meekan, Mark I. McCormick and Stephen D. Simpson. 'Acoustic Enrichment Can Enhance Fish Community Development on Degraded Coral Reef Habitat'. *Nature Communications* 10, no. 1 (2019).

Goreau, Thomas J. 'Electrical Stimulation Greatly Increases Settlement, Growth, Survival, and Stress Resistance of Marine Organisms'. *Natural Resources* 5 (2014): 527–37.

Habermas, Jürgen. *The Structural Transformation of the Public Sphere: An Inquiry into a Category of Bourgeois Society*. Translated by Thomas Burger with Frederick Lawrence. Cambridge: Polity Press, 1989.

Haddad, Samir. *Derrida and the Inheritance of Democracy*. Bloomington and Indianapolis: Indiana University Press, 2013.

Hage, Ghassan. *Against Paranoid Nationalism: Searching for Hope in a Shrinking Society*. Annandale, NSW: Pluto Press, 2003.

Haraway, Donna. *Primate Visions: Gender, Race, and Nature in the World of Modern Science*. New York: Routledge, 1989.

Haraway, Donna. *Simians, Cyborgs and Women: The Reinvention of Nature*. New York: Routledge, 1991.

Haraway, Donna J. *When Species Meet*. Minneapolis: University of Minnesota Press, 2008.

Hare, Brian and Michael Tomasello. 'Human-like Social Skills in Dogs?' *Trends in Cognitive Sciences* 9, no. 9 (September 2005): 339–444.

Hartley, John. *The Politics of Pictures: The Creation of the Public in the Age of Popular Media*. London and New York: Routledge, 1992.

Hearne, Vicki. *Adam's Task: Calling Animals by Name*. New York: Skyhorse Publishing, 2007.

Heidegger, Martin. *Being and Time*. Translated by John Macquarrie and Edward Robinson. Oxford and Cambridge: Blackwell, 1962.

Herder, Johann Gottfried. *Outlines of a Philosophy of the History of Mankind*. Translated by T. O. Churchill. New York: Bergman Publishers, 1966 [Ger. 1784–91].

Hirata, Satoshi, Kunio Watanabe and Masao Kawai, '"Sweet-Potato Washing" Revisited'. In *Primate Origins of Human Cognition and Behavior*, ed. Tesuro Matsuzawa, 487–508. Tokyo: Springer, 2001.

Hobbes, Thomas. *Leviathan*. London: Oxford University Press, 1909 [1651].

Izar, Patrícia, Michele P. Verderane, Elisabetta Visalberghi, Eduardo B. Ottoni, Marino Gomes de Olivera, Jeanne Shirley and Dorothy Fragaszy. 'Cross-genus Adoption of a Marmoset (*Callithrix jacchus*) by Wild Capuchin Monkeys (*Cebus libidinosus*): Case Report'. *American Journal of Primatology* 68 (2006): 692–700.

Jenkins, J. Mark. *The Native Forest Birds of Guam*. Washington: The American Ornithologists' Union, 1983.

Keohane, Oisín. 'The Impossible Force of "Mightlessness": Translating Derrida's *impouvoir* and Heidegger's *Machtlose*'. In *Heidegger, Levinas, Derrida: The Question of Difference*, ed. L. Foran and R. Uljée. *Contributions to Phenomenology* 86 (2016): 117–32.

Kerr, Thor and Shaphan Cox. 'Media, Machines and Might: Reproducing Western Australia's Violent State of Aboriginal Protection'. *Somatechnics* 6, no. 1 (2016): 89–105.

Kierkegaard, Søren. *Works of Love*. Translated by David F. Swenson and Lillian Marvin Swenson. Princeton: Princeton University Press, 1946.

Krell, David Farrell. *Derrida and Our Animal Others: Derrida's Final Seminar, 'The Beast and the Sovereign'*. Bloomington and Indianapolis: Indiana University Press, 2013.

Krützen, Michael, Janet Mann, Michael R. Heithaus, Richard C. Connor, Lars Bejder and William B. Sherwin. 'Cultural Transmission of Tool Use in Bottlenose Dolphins'. *Proceedings of the National Academy of Sciences of the United States of America* 102, no. 25 (2005): 8939–43.

LaCapra, Dominic. *History and Its Limits: Human, Animal, Violence*. Ithaca: Cornell University Press, 2009.

Laland, Kevin N. *Darwin's Unfinished Symphony: How Culture Made the Human Mind*. Princeton and Oxford: Princeton University Press, 2017.

Lawlor, Leonard. *This Is Not Sufficient: An Essay on Animality and Human Nature in Derrida*. New York: Columbia University Press, 2007.

Lestel, Dominique. 'Dissolving Nature in Culture: Some Philosophical Stakes of the Question of Animal Cultures'. Translated by Jeffrey Bussolini. *Angelaki: Journal of the Theoretical Humanities* 19, no. 3 (2014): 93–110.

Lestel, Dominique. 'How Chimpanzees have Domesticated Humans: Towards an Anthropology of Human-Animal Communication'. Translated by Jonathan Benthall. *Anthropology Today* 14, no. 3 (1998): 12–15.

Lestel, Dominique. 'Hybrid Communities'. Translated by Brett Buchanan. *Angelaki: Journal of the Theoretical Humanities* 19, no. 3 (2014): 61–73.

Lestel, Dominique. 'Like the Fingers of the Hand: Thinking the Human in the Texture of Animality'. Translated by Matthew Chrulew and Jeffrey Bussolini. In *French Thinking About Animals*, ed. Louisa Mackenzie and Stephanie Posthumus, 61–73. East Lansing: Michigan State University Press, 2015.

Lestel, Dominique. 'The Animality to Come'. Translated by Matthew Chrulew. *Ctrl-Z: New Media Philosophy* 6 (2016), http://www.ctrl-z.net.au//journal?slug=lestel-the-animality-to-come

Lestel, Dominique. 'The Infinite Debt of the Human Towards the Animal'. Translated by Matthew Chrulew. *Angelaki: Journal of the Theoretical Humanities* 19, no. 3 (2014): 171–81.

Lestel, Dominique. 'The Question of the Animal Subject: Thoughts on the Fourth Wound to Human Narcissism'. Translated by Hollis Taylor. *Angelaki: Journal of the Theoretical Humanities* 19, no. 3 (2014): 113–25.

Levinas, Emmanuel. 'Ethics as First Philosophy'. Translated by Seán Hand and Michael Templè. In *The Levinas Reader*, ed. Seán Hand, 75–87. Oxford: Blackwell, 1989.

Llored, Patrick. 'Zoopolitics'. Translated by Matthew Chrulew and Brett Buchanan. *SubStance* 43, no. 2 (2014): 115–23.

Lovelock, James and Lynn Margulis. 'Atmospheric Homeostasis by and for the Biosphere: The Gaia Hypothesis'. *Tellus* 26, no. 1–2 (1974): 2–10.

Lucas, J. S. 'Reproductive and Larval Biology of *Acanthaster planci* in Great Barrier Reef Waters'. *Micronesica* 9, no. 2 (1973): 197–203.

Lucy, Niall. *Beyond Semiotics: Text, Culture and Technology*. London and New York: Continuum, 2001.

Lynes, Philippe. *Futures of Life Death on Earth: Derrida's General Ecology*. London and New York: Rowman and Littlefield, 2018.

Lyotard, Jean-François. *Postmodern Fables*. Translated by Georges Van Den Abbeele. Minneapolis: University of Minnesota Press, 1997.

Lyotard, Jean-François. *The Differend: Phrases in Dispute*. Translated by Georges Van Den Abbeele. Minneapolis: University of Minnesota Press, 1988.

McGrew, W. C. 'Ten Dispatches from the Chimpanzee Wars'. In *Animal Social Complexity: Intelligence, Culture, and Individualized Societies*, ed. Frans B. M. Waal and Peter L. Tyack, 419–43. Cambridge, MA: Harvard University Press, 2003.

McGrew, W. C. and C. E. G. Tutin. 'Evidence for a Social Custom in Wild Chimpanzees?' *Man* 13, no. 2 (1978): 234–51.

McHoul, Alec. *Semiotic Investigations: Towards an Effective Semiotics*. Lincoln and London: University of Nebraska Press, 1996.

McKinney, Michael L. 'Urbanization as a Major Cause of Biotic Homogenization'. *Biological Conservation* 127, no. 3 (2006): 247–60.

Marchesini, Roberto. 'Philosophical Ethology and Animal Subjectivity'. Translated by Jeffrey Bussolini. *Angelaki: Journal of the Theoretical Humanities* 21, no. 1 (2016): 237–52.

Marshall, Jr, Joe T. 'The Endemic Avifauna of Saipan, Tinian, Guam and Palau'. *The Condor* 51, no. 5 (1949): 200–21.

Moore, Jason W. 'Anthropocene or Capitalocene? Nature, History, and the Crisis of Capitalism'. In *Anthropocene or Capitalocene? Nature, History, and the Crisis of Capitalism*, ed. Jason Moore, 1–11. Oakland: PM Press, 2016.

Morozov, Evgeny. *The Net Delusion: The Dark Side of Internet Freedom*. New York: Public Affairs, 2011.

Morton, Timothy. *Dark Ecology: For a Logic of Future Coexistence*. New York: Columbia University Press, 2016.

Naas, Michael. 'Learning to Read "Life Death" Finally: Francesco Vitale's Epigenetic Criticism'. *CR: The New Centennial Review* 19, no. 3 (2019): 13–33.

Naas, Michael. *The End of the World and Other Teachable Moments: Jacques Derrida's Final Seminar*. New York: Fordham University Press, 2015.

Nakamura, Michio and Shigeo Uehara. 'Proximate Factors of Different Types of Grooming Hand-Clasp in Mahale Chimpanzees: Implications for Chimpanzee Social Customs'. *Current Anthropology* 45, no.1 (2004): 108–14.

Nealon, Jeffrey T. *Plant Theory: Biopower and Vegetable Life*. Stanford: Stanford University Press, 2016.

Negri, Antonio and Cesare Casarino. 'It's a Powerful Life: A Conversation on Contemporary Philosophy'. *Cultural Critique* 57 (Spring 2004): 151–83.

Noske, Barbara. *Beyond Boundaries: Humans and Animals*. New York: Black Rose Books, 1996.

Oliver, Kelly. 'What Is Wrong with (Animal) Rights?' *The Journal of Speculative Philosophy* 22, no. 3 (2008): 214–24.

Oliver, Kelly. 'Witnessing and Testimony'. *Parallax* 10, no. 1 (2004): 79–88.

Oliver, Kelly. *Witnessing: Beyond Recognition*. Minneapolis: University of Minnesota Press, 2001.

Omori, Makoto. 'Coral Restoration Research and Technical Developments: What We Have Learned So Far'. *Marine Biology Research* 15, no. 7 (2019): 377–409.

Parks, Lisa. 'Mediating Animal-Infrastructure Relations'. In *Being*

Material, ed. Stefan Helmreich, Marie-Pier Boucher and Rebecca Uchill, 144–53. Cambridge, MA: The MIT Press, 2019.

Pfungst, Oskar. *Clever Hans (The Horse of Mr Von Osten): A Contribution to Experimental Animal and Human Psychology*. Translated by Carl L. Rahn. New York: Henry Holt and Co., 1911.

Porcher, Jocelyne. *Vivre avec les animaux. Une utopie pour le 21ème siècle*. Paris: Editions La Découverte, 2011.

Porcher, Jocelyne and Tiphaine Schmitt. 'Dairy Cows: Workers in the Shadows?' *Society and Animals* 20 (2012): 39–60.

Raby, C. R. and N. S. Clayton. 'Prospective Cognition in Animals'. *Behavioral Processes* 80, no. 3 (2009): 314–24.

Read, Jason. 'Anthropocene and Anthropogenesis: Philosophical Anthropology and the Ends of Man'. *The South Atlantic Quarterly* 116, no. 2 (2017): 257–73.

Rinkevich, Baruch. 'Conservation of Coral Reefs through Active Restoration Measures: Recent Approaches and Last Decade Progress'. *Environmental Science and Technology* 39, no. 12 (2005): 4333–42.

Ritvo, Harriet. 'On the Animal Turn'. *Daedalus* 136, no. 4 (Fall 2007): 118–22.

Roberts, Rebecca E., Cherie A. Motti, Kenneth W. Baughman, Noriyuki Satoh, Michael R. Hall and Scott F. Cummins. 'Identification of Putative Olfactory G-Protein Coupled Receptors in Crown-of-Thorns Starfish, *Acanthaster planci*'. *BMC Genomics* 18 (2017), https://doi.org/10.1186/s12864-017-3793-4

Rogers, Jacob G. D., Éva E. Pláganyi and Russell C. Babcock. 'Aggregation, Allee Effects and Critical Thresholds for the Management of the Crown-of-Thorns Starfish *Acanthaster planci*'. *Marine Ecology Progress Series* 578 (August 2017): 99–114.

Sapolsky, Robert M. 'Culture in Animals: The Case of Non-human Primate Culture of Low Aggression and High Affiliation'. *Social Forces* 85, no. 1 (2006): 217–33.

Schmitt, Carl. *The Concept of the Political*, exp. ed. Translated by George Schwab. Chicago: University of Chicago Press, 2007.

Shepard, Paul. *Thinking Animals: Animals and the Development of Human Intelligence*. New York: Viking, 1978.

Shukin, Nicole. 'Capitalism'. In *The Edinburgh Companion to Animal Studies*, ed. Lynne Turner, Undine Sellbach and Ron Broglio, 94–114. Edinburgh: Edinburgh University Press, 2018.

Sih, Andrew, Maud C. O. Ferrari and David J. Harris. 'Evolution and Behavioural Responses to Human-induced Rapid Environmental Change'. *Evolutionary Applications* 4 (2011): 367–87.

Singer, Peter. *Animal Liberation: A New Ethics for Our Treatment of Animals*. London: HarperCollins, 1975.

Skelhorn, John and Candy Rowe. 'Cognition and the Evolution of Camouflage'. *Proceedings of the Royal Society B: Biological Sciences* 283 (2016), https://doi.org/10.1098/rspb.2015.2890

Sloterdijk, Peter. 'Rules for the Human Zoo: A Response to the *Letter on Humanism*'. Translated by Mary Varney Rorty. *Environment and Planning D: Society and Space* 27 (2009): 12–28.

Smith, Mick. *Against Ecological Sovereignty: Ethics, Biopolitics, and Saving the Natural World*. Minneapolis: University of Minnesota Press, 2011.

Stengers, Isabelle. *In Catastrophic Times: Resisting the Coming Barbarism*. Translated by Andrew Goffey. Open Humanities Press, 2015.

Taylor, Charles. 'The Politics of Recognition'. In *Multiculturalism*, ed. Amy Gutman, 25–73. Princeton: Princeton University Press, 1994.

Thompson, John B. *The Media and Modernity: A Social Theory of the Media*. Cambridge: Polity Press, 1995.

Tomback, Diana F. 'Observations on the Behavior and Ecology of the Mariana Crow'. *The Condor* 88, no. 3 (1986): 399–400.

Tylor, Edward Burnett. *Primitive Culture: Researches Into the Development of Mythology, Philosophy, Religion, Language, Art, and Custom*, Vol. 1, 6th edn. London: Murray, 1920 [1871].

van Dooren, Thom. *The Wake of Crows: Living and Dying in Shared Worlds*. New York: Columbia University Press, 2019.

Vico, Giambattista. *The First New Science*. Edited and translated by

Leon Pompa. Cambridge and New York: Cambridge University Press, 2002 [It. 1725].

Virno, Paolo. 'Natural-Historical Diagrams: The "New Global" Movement and the Biological Invariant'. *Cosmos and History: The Journal of Natural and Social Philosophy* 5, no. 1 (2009): 92–104.

Vitale, Francesco. *Biodeconstruction: Jacques Derrida and the Life Sciences*. Translated by Senatore Mauro. Albany: SUNY Press, 2018.

Wadiwel, Dinesh Joseph. 'The Will for Self-Preservation: Locke and Derrida on Dominion, Property and Animals'. *SubStance* 43, no. 2 (2014): 148–61.

Williams, Raymond. *Keywords: A Vocabulary of Culture and Society*, rev. edn. London: Fontana, 1983.

Wolfe, Cary. 'Flesh and Finitude: Thinking Animals in (Post) Humanist Philosophy'. *SubStance* 37, no. 3 (2008): 8–36.

Wolfe, Cary. *Before the Law: Humans and Other Animals in a Biopolitical Frame*. Chicago and London: University of Chicago Press, 2013.

Wolfe, Cary. *What is Posthumanism?* Minneapolis: University of Minnesota Press, 2010.

Wood, David. 'Specters of Derrida: On the Way to Econstruction'. In *Ecospirit: Religions and Philosophies for the Earth*, ed. Laurel Kearns and Catherine Keller, 264–87. New York: Fordham University Press, 2007.

Woods, Derek. 'Scale Critique for the Anthropocene'. *Minnesota Review* 83 (2014): 133–42.

Zimmerman, Michael E. 'Towards a Heideggerian Ethos of Radical Environmentalism'. *Environmental Ethics* 5, no. 2 (Summer 1983): 99–131.

Zimmerman, Michael E. *Heidegger's Confrontation with Modernity: Technology, Politics, and Art*. Bloomington and Indianapolis: Indiana University Press, 1990.

Žižek, Slavoj. *Living in the End Times*. London: Verso, 2010.

Index

action, 7, 16, 20, 33, 129, 141, 142, 154, 167, 174–5n, 215n
animal (nonhuman), 27–8, 83, 90–1, 103–6, 108–9, 115–20, 163, 202–3n
climate change, 131, 133, 135, 140, 144, 148, 149
culture, 35, 44, 47, 52, 126, 206n
frailty of, 97, 99, 116, 117–18, 157, 163
great deeds, 96, 97, 99, 102–5, 109, 115–16, 198–9n
Greek experience, 95–102, 115–16
political, 13, 39, 95–109, 115–20, 164, 200n, 201n
prostheticity of, 74–5, 83, 89–90
sovereign(ty), 27–8, 39–40, 52, 63, 90, 96, 99, 131, 140, 147–8
teletechnological conditions, 113, 115–20
see also agency; power; response
affect, 66, 75, 88, 118, 127, 159, 174, 215n
Agamben, Giorgio, 2, 6, 62–4, 65, 66, 78, 90, 95, 169n, 173n, 177n, 189n, 194n; *see also* zoē and bios
agency
animal (nonhuman), 33, 56, 57, 73, 83, 90, 147–8, 151–2, 153–5
distributed, prosthetic, 103, 111, 118–19, 147–8, 151, 154–5, 164, 167
geological, 127–8, 147
human (species), 90, 102–3, 127–9, 131, 133, 138, 146–7, 160, 210n
zoopower, 70–7
see also assemblage; ipseity; response

alterity, 14, 15–16, 62, 194n; *see also* animal other
animal culture, 35–8, 41–4, 46–7, 48–61, 87–9, 164–7, 183–4n, 185–6n, 186–7n; *see also* culture
animal other, 4, 14, 33, 51, 60–1, 62, 65–6, 79, 93, 119, 154–5, 156, 162, 163, 166, 173n, 180n, 190n, 217n
animalisation, 30, 87, 95, 170
animality
human, 8, 22–4, 26–7, 29–33, 123–9, 136, 151–2, 156, 162, 180n, 206–7n
institutionality of, 3, 6, 7, 18–34, 53–4, 59–60, 117, 151–2, 167, 176n
modalities/modes, 6, 21, 23, 28, 31–4, 54, 58, 114, 156, 166–7
politics, 7, 13, 26–9, 80, 34, 53, 80, 90–1, 92–3, 95, 102, 121, 128–9, 154, 162
textual field, 3, 22–4, 29, 32, 58, 176n
transformability, 15, 18–19, 29–33, 58, 60, 90, 95, 117, 152–3
transpecies, 30–1, 151–4
see also animal-machine; human-animal distinction; human-animal interaction; life; species
animal-machine
Cartesian concept, 25–6, 27, 44, 77, 83, 137, 153
institutional, 26–9, 31, 60, 77, 89, 120, 163, 167
transformation, 25–6, 29, 31, 60, 89–90

animals
  apes, 36, 41, 56, 57, 59, 64, 87–9, 170n, 187n, 196n
  boars, 210n
  cats, 14, 33, 54, 114, 199–200n, 203n
  coral, 142–3, 151–3, 208n, 221n
  cows, 82–3, 195n
  crown-of-thorns starfish, 142–3, 208–9n
  crows, 36, 164–7
  dogs, 84–6, 114, 187n, 196–7n
  elephants, 108, 114
  honeybees, 109, 200n
  horses, 34, 103–5, 109
  magpies, 108
  monkeys, 35–6, 41, 46, 47, 48, 49, 54–5, 114, 180n
  octopuses, 114
  ospreys, 188n
  parrots, 30, 200n
  rabbitfishes, 152–3
  rats, 59, 106–7
  squirrels, 54, 186n
  sticklebacks, 53, 185n
animals, individual, 2, 4, 26, 29, 51–2, 82, 114–15, 173n
  Alex (parrot), 30
  Cayenne (Australian Shepherd), 84–5, 196n
  Clever Hans (horse), 103–5, 109
  Derrida's cat, 14, 33
  Imo (Japanese macaque), 35
  Kac's fluorescent rabbit, 30
  Kanzi (bonobo), 30, 88
  Lucy (chimpanzee), 56
animal-to-come, 2–3, 18–19, 22, 25–6, 28–34, 36, 53, 59–61, 81, 85, 90–1, 92, 95, 100–1, 119–20, 121–3, 135, 139, 140–1, 142, 144, 148, 153–5, 156–67, 170n, 174n, 176n, 196n, 216n
Anthropocene, 8, 122–3, 127–33, 140, 147–8, 159–60, 208n, 211n; *see also* climate change
anthropocentrism
  axiology (prejudice), 2, 8, 31, 34, 140–1, 143
  critique, 7–8, 92, 122–3, 129–30, 131–5, 141, 169n, 198n
  nonanthropocentrism (anti-), 18, 28, 143, 162, 163
  philosophical, 7, 41, 92, 100, 137, 169n, 170n, 202n
  political, 65, 90, 94
  post-anthropocentrism, 129, 133

power, 31, 85, 90, 91, 148, 149, 167
problem, 8, 122–3, 129, 140–1, 143–4, 154–5
scientific, 50, 60, 142–3, 153
see also human exceptionalism; humanism; metaphysics
anthropogenesis (humanisation), 8, 31–2, 36, 56–7, 87, 123–7, 128–9, 147, 154–5, 163, 213n; *see also* domestication
anthropology (discipline), 2, 38, 41–2, 88, 107, 123
appearance, 28, 34, 67, 83, 89, 133, 166, 179
  animal, 30, 35, 93–5, 103, 106–9, 114–20, 121, 143, 202–3n
  media, 109–20, 200n, 202–3n
  political, 95, 97, 99–100, 101, 109–13, 115–20, 121, 125, 141, 200n, 202–3n
Arendt, Hannah, 6, 63, 94–104, 109, 111–13, 115–18, 173n, 179n, 198n, 202n
  conformism, 102–3, 105, 107
  distinctness, 97, 98, 102–3, 105, 107
  frailty of action, 115–16
  natality, 97–8, 102, 115–16
  ontological priority of appearance, 101–2, 109, 111–13
  original meaning of politics, 95–101, 116, 117, 118–19, 201n
  zoë/bios distinction, 95, 98, 189n
  see also action
Aristotle, 27
assemblage (*agencement*), 72–3, 147–8, 151–2, 154, 193n, 211n; *see also* agency
authority, 20, 38, 53, 60, 63, 72, 84, 90, 93, 103, 104, 109, 122, 128, 144, 158, 159, 162; *see also* sovereignty
auto-affection, 74–5
autopoiesis, 14, 18, 29, 34, 193n

Bajorek, Jennifer, 111
bare life, 63–4, 65, 78, 95; *see also* Agamben
bearing (bearance), 32, 66, 162–3, 167, 217n, 194n, 203n
beast (bestiality) *see* animality
Bellwood, David, 152, 212n
Bentham, Jeremy, 14, 62, 65–6
Berlant, Lauren, 158
biopolitics, 62–6, 76–80, 81, 85, 89, 91, 92–3, 95, 98, 128, 134, 141, 163, 189n, 294n, 213n; *see also* bare life; Agamben; Wolfe; zoopolitics

Calarco, Matthew, 169n, 178n
capital(ism), 123, 126–7, 128–9, 130, 147, 148, 158, 209–10n
Caputo, John D., 190n
Chakrabarty, Dipesh, 127–8, 130–1, 133, 146–7
choice, 39, 42, 44, 51, 63, 96, 106, 214n; *see also* decision
civilisation, 38–40, 48, 85, 87, 123, 127–8, 145, 196n, 198n
climate change (global warming, environmental destruction), 34, 47, 122, 127–8, 130–1, 133, 135–6, 139–43, 144–7, 148–50, 152, 156, 158–9, 205n; *see also* Anthropocene
Colebrook, Claire, 122, 133–7, 145, 156, 159–60
conflict (agonistics), 40, 52, 68, 71, 82–3, 94, 117, 138, 156, 158, 163–4, 210n, 217n
context, 28, 31, 45, 55, 59, 82, 90, 102, 107–8, 126, 136–41, 151, 165, 167, 207–8n; *see also* environment; exteriority; institution(ality); textuality
convention, 20–2, 53, 60–1, 84–5, 153, 214n
culture
  acculturation, 56–8, 87–9, 187n
  animal, 35–8, 41–4, 46–7, 48–61, 87–9, 164–7, 183–8n
  civilisation, 106–7
  concept, 3, 7, 21, 34, 35–61, 182–3n
  environment, 44, 47–8, 56–8, 126, 183n, 185–6n, 206–7n
  human culture, 37–42, 47–8, 55–9, 87–8, 90, 126–7, 183–4n, 185–7n, 206–7n, 210n
  human prerogative, 36–7, 39, 42, 51, 126, 136, 141
  nature/culture distinction, 21–2, 42, 43–4, 46–7, 51–2, 175n, 183–4n, 185–6n
  pseudo-environment, 126, 136, 141, 206n
  science of culture, 36–8, 40, 42, 53, 134, 184n
  transmission, 36, 44, 46–7, 50–1, 54, 55, 58, 59, 183n, 185–6n
  see also civilisation; habit(uation); humanism; invention

death, 64, 121–2, 138, 147, 159, 162–4, 172n, 192n, 216n; *see also* extinction; mortality
decision, 16, 52, 82, 144, 150, 180n, 207n, 214n
  sovereign, 39–40, 63, 95, 119
deconstruction, 2–3, 6–7, 8–9, 13, 15, 19, 21–2, 23, 28, 60, 72, 75, 76, 77, 94, 157, 176n, 190n
  biodeconstruction, 9, 177n
  eco-deconstruction, 171n, 207–8n, 211n, 216n, 217n
  see also Derrida
Deleuze, Gilles, 147, 193n
democracy-to-come, 2, 15–18, 32, 79, 117, 119–20, 122, 157, 163, 173–4n, 217n
Derrida, Jacques
  The Animal That Therefore I Am, 2, 4, 11–15, 22, 24–5, 29, 62, 65–6, 70–2, 76, 170n, 173n, 177n, 178n, 196n, 197–8n
  animal-machine, 25–9
  artifactuality, 111–13
  Beast and the Sovereign, 26–9, 74, 163, 177n, 189n, 216–17n
  différance, 29, 67–8, 71, 179n, 216n
  ethics, 1, 4, 14, 19, 32, 33, 62, 65–6, 75–6, 80, 144, 170n, 171n, 190n, 194–5n, 202n
  fear (terror), 27–8, 78–9
  Foucault, 65, 66–7, 68–70, 77, 192
  Heidegger, 21–2, 132, 169n, 177n, 190–1n, 196n, 205n, 216–17n
  Hobbes, 26–8, 78
  invention, 21–2, 44–5, 60–1, 74–5, 144, 174n, 216n
  ipseity, 71–5, 94, 193n, 211n, 214–15n
  justice, 2, 4, 15, 16–18, 65, 76–7, 80, 157, 174n
  meaning, 13, 20, 69–70, 72, 76, 86, 93, 131–2, 138–9, 174–5n
  metaphysics (humanism), 2, 8, 15, 17, 18, 23, 25, 60, 131–2, 169n, 170n, 194n, 202n, 205n
  politics (democracy), 13, 15–18, 24–5, 26–9, 32–3, 62, 64–6, 72, 75–80, 91, 93–4, 100, 110–12, 122, 139, 144, 157, 160–3, 170n, 173–4n, 202n, 217n
  power (force), 3, 4, 20–1, 24, 28–9, 62, 64, 66–80, 86, 91, 94, 100, 111, 132, 161, 163, 174–5n, 177n, 190–1n, 192n, 208n, 211n, 214–15n, 216–17n
  response (responsibility), 4, 14, 16, 25, 33, 65–6, 73, 74–5, 76, 121, 144, 149–50, 157, 192n

INDEX | 237

Rogues, 72, 170n, 173n, 174n, 211n, 214–15n
sovereignty, 26–9, 72–3, 79, 122, 131–2, 144, 162–3, 177n, 189n, 216n
Specters of Marx, 15–16, 32–4, 170n, 171n, 174n
suffering (vulnerability), 4, 14, 32–3, 62, 65–6, 68, 70, 74–80, 91, 190n, 194–5n
survivance, 91, 163, 216n
textuality, 3, 22–4, 70, 139–40
see also deconstruction; following; hauntology; limitrophy; nonpower; teletechnology; to-come; writing
Descartes, René, 2, 12, 14, 25–6, 178n; see also animal-machine
Despret, Vinciane, 5–6, 82–3, 103–9, 112, 114–18, 119, 147–8, 154, 171–2n, 194n, 199–200n, 201n, 211n, 212–13n
destruction, 122, 136, 138, 152–3, 156, 159, 162–4, 167; see also climate change; death
domestication, 31, 46, 81–90, 114, 121, 163, 196–7n

Earth systems (atmospheric, geochemical, biosphere), 122, 127, 131, 145–50, 198n, 208n; see also Gaia
Edelman, Lee, 158, 159–60, 162
endangered species, 57, 114, 134–5, 164–5
environment, 136–41
  concept of culture, 44, 47–9, 58–60, 183n, 185–6n
  context, 59, 126, 136, 139–40, 141, 151–2, 159, 207–8n
  human ('pseudo-environment'), 124–5, 126, 136, 141
  humanised (anthropogenic change), 56–7, 59, 74–5, 122, 127–8, 138, 151–2, 154, 156, 159, 163
  world, 74, 126, 136–9, 140, 206n
  see also Anthropocene; climate change; exteriority
Esposito, Roberto, 62
ethics (moral obligations), 1, 4–5, 8, 14, 19, 31, 32, 33, 42, 50, 51, 62, 65–6, 75–6, 80, 91, 130–1, 134, 139, 144, 149, 168–9, 170n, 171n, 173n, 178n, 180n, 190n, 194–5n, 198–9n, 202n; see also animal other; justice; responsibility
event, 3, 12, 15–17, 25, 29–32, 45, 66, 71, 94, 102, 107, 115–16, 118, 144, 147, 175n, 180n, 202n, 209n, 214n; see also future; history; transformation
everydayness, 42, 98, 102, 115, 119, 194n, 206n
evolution, 12, 22–3, 29, 30–2, 52–3, 71, 81, 83, 87, 125, 127–8, 151–2, 154, 172n, 176n, 185–6n, 187n, 196–7n, 205n, 207n, 208n; see also anthropogenesis
experiment, 31, 49–50, 65, 87–8, 104–9, 144, 197n, 198n, 199–200n, 213n
exploitation, 24, 54, 81–3, 85, 89, 126–7, 143, 152, 185–6n, 195n
exteriority (outside), 21, 26–8, 45–6, 50, 51–52, 54, 55, 60, 68, 73–4, 86, 89–90, 137–40, 151, 158, 167, 175n, 179n, 194n, 207n; see also context; environment; institution(ality); invention
extinction, 59, 115, 121–2, 127–8, 135, 156–7, 159, 167, 188n, 216n

farming (agriculture), 38, 65, 74, 81–3, 130, 143, 182n, 195n, 202–3n, 206n, 209n, 212–13n
fate (destiny), 34, 64, 122, 124–5, 131, 134–5, 156–7, 159, 164, 178n, 182n; see also future; to-come
fear, 27–8, 77–80, 94, 107, 213–14n
Feldman, Allen, 170n, 202n
finitude see mortality
following, 4, 7, 9–10, 11–15, 17–19, 28, 34, 59, 62, 65–6, 101–2, 109, 117, 129, 134, 159–60, 174n, 196n; see also ontology
force, 39, 44, 68–74, 76–80, 81–3, 87, 107, 111, 139, 157–8, 163–4, 179n, 182n, 191–2n, 201n
anthropocentrism (human exceptionalism), 3, 7–8, 15, 20–1, 132, 148, 149, 153, 163, 177n
differing (differential), 68–9, 70–1, 73, 77, 81–2, 84–5, 101, 135, 145–8, 153–4, 211n
environmental (geological), 74, 128–30, 148, 150–2, 208n
questioning, 59, 73, 80, 91, 103, 119, 135, 145–6, 161–3, 167, 216–17n
writing, 20–1, 68, 71–2, 174–5n, 208n
see also assemblage; power
Foucault, Michel, 6, 62–3, 65, 67, 68–70, 73, 77, 81–2, 83, 86, 133–4, 137, 145, 189n, 191–2n, 195n, 205n, 207n

freedom, 52, 63–4, 72–3, 77, 86, 93, 96–7, 98, 113, 119, 125, 128, 190n, 201n
future, 2, 15–18, 29–34, 53, 60, 87, 91, 92, 113, 119, 121–2, 128, 135, 139, 145, 148, 151–5, 156–67, 170n, 174n, 212n, 213–14n, 215n, 217–18n; *see also* fate; history; hope; to-come

Gaia, 144–51, 153–4
genealogy, 41, 73, 78–9, 101, 152, 202n; *see also* hauntology; history
global warming *see* climate change
globalisation (global action), 34, 59, 109–13, 118, 122, 131, 133, 135, 140, 143, 144, 146–7, 188n, 202–3n; *see also* climate change; teletechnology

Habermas, Jürgen, 200n
habit(uation), 35, 38, 46–8, 52–4, 57–9, 75, 81, 104–5, 114–15, 126–7, 138, 163, 164–5, 205n; *see also* convention; culture
Haraway, Donna, 6, 84–6, 122, 169n, 187n, 204n
hauntology, 3, 7, 32–4, 36, 59–61, 70–1, 76, 90, 95, 101, 104, 111–14, 120, 122, 171n; *see also* deconstruction; genealogy
Hearne, Vicki, 199n
Hegel, G. W. F., 125, 132, 202n, 205n
Heidegger, Martin, 2, 13–14, 22, 80, 87, 122, 132, 168n, 169n, 177n, 190n, 196n, 205n, 206n, 216–17n
Herder, Johann Gottfried, 40, 41, 42, 47–9, 50, 182n, 184n
history
  anthropogenesis, 32–3, 123–7, 128–9, 154–5
  culture, 7, 30, 38–45, 47, 59–61, 87, 124, 126–7, 183–4n, 210n
  eternal, 40, 42, 123–5
  human-animal interaction, 23–4, 29–32, 81, 85–7, 114–15, 164–7
  natural, 47, 123, 125–30, 141–2, 147, 183–4n
  see also event; future; genealogy; hauntology; otherwise; transformation
Hobbes, Thomas, 6, 26–8, 39–40, 78, 90, 179n, 184n
hope, 6, 16, 24, 79–80, 133, 141, 156–67, 213–14n, 215n; *see also* future

human animal *see* animality; anthropogenesis
human-animal distinction (difference), 2–4, 7–8, 9, 13, 19–25, 29–30, 34, 37, 41, 58–61, 92–3, 97, 120, 136–7, 141, 161, 169n, 177n, 178n, 194n; *see also* human exceptionalism; institution(ality)
human-animal interaction, 24, 29–31, 53–4, 55–8, 81, 83, 88, 103, 114–15, 116–17, 138, 164–7, 199n; *see also* domestication; hybrid communities
human exceptionalism (chauvinism), 2, 3, 7, 9, 20–1, 33, 36, 37, 51, 58–9, 71–2, 79, 85, 100–1, 122–3, 129, 133, 136–7, 141
humanism (anthropologism), 2, 21–2, 31–2, 60–1, 65, 87, 92–3, 94, 101, 122–3, 128–33, 137, 140–1, 143, 145, 160–1; *see also* anthropocentrism; 'man'
Husserl, Edmund, 132, 205n
hybrid communities, 88–90, 154–5

immortality *see* mortality
immunity *see* protection
inhuman, 20, 32, 147
initiative, 60, 82–3, 90, 98–9, 102, 105, 107, 109, 116, 117–18, 119, 150–1, 152, 162, 195n, 199–200n; *see also* natality
innateness (inborn), 25, 27, 29, 51, 54, 71, 73–4, 89, 123–4, 126, 141, 177n; *see also* metaphysics; reaction
instinct *see* innateness
institution(ality)
  animality, 3, 6, 7, 18–34, 53–4, 59–60, 117, 151–2, 167, 176n
  behaviour, 27–9, 51–4, 59–60, 77, 84–5, 89, 106–8, 120, 138, 166–7
  deconstruction (question) of, 4, 7, 9, 19–24, 26–9, 60, 75, 77, 94, 175n, 176n
  environment, 59–60, 126–7, 138–42, 151–3
  human-animal distinction (difference), 3, 4, 6, 19–24, 29–30, 59–60, 93, 95, 119–20, 161
  invention, 21–2, 44–5, 60–1, 107–8
  life (*zoē*), 9, 23–4, 75, 94–5, 120, 138, 140, 141, 151–3, 167
  opposition to nature, 18, 21–2, 27, 75, 148, 175n
  political (government, state), 18, 26–8,

39–40, 63–4, 90, 92–5, 101, 117–18, 119–20, 161–2, 191–2n, 217n
  sovereignty, 26–9, 39, 63–4, 77–80, 89, 90–1, 95, 101–2, 119, 140–1, 163
    see also animal-machine; convention; culture; habit; textuality; prostheticity; writing
  intervention, 24–5, 51, 138–9, 150–2, 158, 186–7n
  invention, 21, 32, 34, 44–6, 58, 60–1, 74–5, 107–8, 110, 119, 144, 163, 174n, 200n, 216n
  animal, 35–6, 49–50, 60–1, 83–4, 90–1, 107–8, 114–15, 162
  ipseity, 71–5, 81, 83, 89–90, 94, 164, 193n, 211n, 214–15n; see also sovereign(ty)

justice, 4, 5, 39, 42, 119, 149, 157, 167, 182n, 214n
  biopolitical, 65, 76–7, 79–81, 94, 118
  justice-to-come, 2, 15, 16–18, 157, 174n, 214n

Kac, Eduardo, 30
Kant, Immanuel, 170n
Kawai, Masao, 41, 180n
Kierkegaard, Søren, 157, 213–14n
Krell, David Farrell, 79–80

Laland, Kevin N., 185–6n
learning, 36, 44, 53, 54, 57, 82, 116, 127, 154, 166, 187n; see also culture; teaching
Lestel, Dominique, 5–6, 22–4, 29–31, 33, 51–2, 55–9, 87–9, 105, 154, 170–1n, 175–6n, 185n, 186n, 213n
Levinas, Emmanuel, 2, 14–15, 62, 76, 169n, 173n, 190n, 202n
life (the living)
  animal, 33–4, 64–5, 90–1, 95–6, 100, 102, 105, 170n, 177n, 178n, 210n
  artificial, 25, 27–8, 30, 59, 127, 138, 148, 151–3, 154
  bare, 63–5, 78, 95
  biological (ecological), 24, 63, 95–7, 100, 120, 122, 127–30, 133–4, 136–41, 151–3, 156–7, 159, 207n, 212n
  culture, 24, 30, 39, 42, 48, 51–4, 56–7, 59, 126, 182n, 185–6n, 210n
  everyday, 42, 98, 102, 114–15, 119
  as institutional, 9, 24, 27, 51–2, 54, 74–5, 126, 138–42, 148, 151–2, 163, 167, 217n
  normative logic (metaphysics) of, 133–8, 140, 145, 149, 151, 153, 212n
  political, 26–8, 39–40, 63–5, 72, 76–7, 80, 93, 94–100, 117, 119–20, 126–7, 134–5, 158, 163, 217n
  reproductive (subsistence), 63, 95–7, 100, 120, 186n, 189n
  wildlife, 56, 59, 114–15
    see also animality; death; survival; zoē and bios
limit, 3–4, 19–24, 67–8, 107, 132, 134, 139, 178n, 205n
  abyssal, 19–21, 23–4, 29, 32, 141, 170n
  natural limits, 50, 139–40, 141–3, 208n
    see also human-animal distinction; limitrophy
limitrophy (feeding limits), 3–4, 19, 24, 29, 34, 92–3, 136, 161, 178n
living together (cohabitation), 30, 72, 87, 116–17, 196; see also domestication; hybrid communities
Llored, Patrick, 184n
Lovelock, James, 145, 149–50
Lucy, Niall, 48, 184n
Lynes, Philippe, 216n
Lyotard, Jean-François, 159–60, 211n

McGrew, William Clement, 37–8, 41, 42–3, 46, 47, 49–50, 56, 183n, 187n
McHoul, Alec, 39, 41–3
'man', 7–8, 21–2, 26–9, 31, 87, 91–2, 93, 122, 127–9, 132–5, 137, 147, 159–62; see also humanism
Marchesini, Roberto, 171n
Margulis, Lynn, 145, 149–50
meaning, 13, 20, 67, 69–70, 72, 76, 86, 93, 98, 113, 116, 117, 128, 132, 133–4, 137–9, 148, 149, 157, 175n, 201n, 206n
media, 34, 109–19, 163, 200n, 201n, 203n; see also teletechnology
metaphysics, 2, 13, 17, 23, 101, 124, 128, 130–4, 180n, 194n, 202n, 204n, 205n
  of animality, 18, 153, 169n
  of interiority (internal law), 25–6, 27–8, 51–2, 140, 151, 153, 178–9n
  of life, 133–4, 137–8, 140, 145, 149, 151
  metaphysico-anthropocentric axiomatic, 15, 170n
    see also animal-machine; Descartes; humanism
Moore, Jason, 130

Morozov, Evgeny, 203n
mortality, 29, 97, 99, 101, 103, 115–16, 205n; *see also* death
Morton, Timothy, 130, 132–3
mundane world *see* everydayness

Naess, Arne, 168n
naming, 16, 17, 19–22, 27, 110, 114, 176n, 211n, 214n, 215n, 217n
  animal-to-come, 33, 59–60, 174n
  Anthropocene, 122, 128–31, 147–8
  culture, 37, 39, 45, 51, 58
  Gaia, 144–6, 148, 153–4
  man (the human), 8, 19–22, 24, 122, 131–2
  nonpower, 4, 70–1, 73
  politics (action), 27, 77–8, 101, 103, 116–17
  species, 105, 124, 128, 130–1, 133, 146–9
  zoopolitics (*zoon politikon*), 4, 7, 27, 101, 119–20, 148, 163–4, 167
natality, 97–8, 102, 115–16, 118, 120, 163, 166, 170n, 202n; *see also* action; initiative
Negri, Antonio, 78–9, 194n
Nietzsche, Friedrich, 2, 69, 194–5n
non-normative approach, 3, 4, 9, 61, 153
nonpower, 4, 66–76, 78–80, 85, 90, 91, 94, 102, 118–19, 124, 126, 136, 148, 154, 161, 163, 190–1n, 194–5n
normativity, 44, 117, 158
  of concept of culture, 42–3, 47, 48, 50, 184n
  logic of life, 133–8
  see also ethics

Oliver, Kelly, 189n, 202–3n
ontology, 1, 3, 19–25, 28, 32, 80, 130, 134, 201n, 207n, 208n
  ontological priority, 13–14, 17, 21, 101, 109–10, 112–13, 123, 205n
  see also following; institution; writing
openness (opening, gap), 3, 130, 137, 149, 167, 175n
  death (destruction), 135, 138, 161–3
  events (to-come), 3, 15–17, 29, 32–3, 45, 53, 85–6, 101, 135, 140, 144, 166–7, 174n
  outside (environment), 45, 51, 55, 138–41, 151–3
optimism, 79–80, 158–9, 164; *see also* hope
otherwise, 16, 34, 44, 51–2, 53, 58, 60, 94–5, 105, 119, 142–3, 149–51, 162, 164; *see also* transformation
outside *see* exteriority

Parks, Lisa, 188n
passivity *see* nonpower
pessimism, 77–80, 90–1, 92–3, 101, 119, 161–2; *see also* fear
Pfungst, Oskar, 103–5
philosophical ethology, 5, 105–6, 171–2n
Plessner, Helmut, 161
politics
  animality, 7, 13, 26–9, 80, 34, 53, 80, 90–1, 92–3, 95, 102, 121, 128–9, 154, 162
  environmental (climate change, Anthropocene), 124–8, 130–1, 133, 134–6, 139–55, 159–60, 163–4, 206–7n
  fear, 27–8, 77–8, 80, 94
  global, 109, 113–14, 118, 131, 133, 135, 140, 146–7, 202–3n
  hope, 16, 133, 141, 157–67
  original meaning, 95–101, 116, 117, 118–19, 201n
  progressive, 130, 158–60
  protection, 39–40, 63–4, 76–80, 85, 90, 91, 92, 94, 114–15, 117, 151, 161–2, 163, 164–5, 193n, 208n
  space of (*polis*, public), 63, 94–7, 99–101, 109–20, 121, 158, 163, 200n, 201n
  state institutions (government), 18, 26–7, 63–4, 78, 90–1, 95, 96–7, 98–9, 101–2, 110, 113, 117–18, 143, 158, 161–2, 165, 193n, 217n
  see also action; Agamben; Arendt; biopolitics; democracy-to-come; Hobbes; power; sovereignty; transformation; zoopolitics
Porcher, Jocelyne, 82–3, 195n
posthuman(ism), 6, 7, 133, 137, 139, 145, 159–60, 162, 163, 171n, 172n
potential animal (indefinite animal), 64, 78, 119–20, 124–6, 128, 135–6, 141–2, 154, 206–7n
potentiality, 29, 33, 56–7, 60, 72–3, 87, 89, 121, 124, 126, 135, 141–2, 148, 154, 156, 166; *see also* power
power, 20, 62–91, 124, 134, 148, 158, 160, 164, 190n, 195n, 214–15n
  appearance, 94, 100, 106–7, 119–20
  biopower, 63, 77, 179n, 194n
  concept (meaning), 3, 4, 7, 61, 68–75, 86, 95, 191–2n

disciplinary, 73, 81–6
discourse (language) of power, 72, 75–9, 177n
 naming, 19–21, 24
 of speech (language, writing), 24, 62, 63, 66–8, 71–2, 87–9, 124, 137, 175n
 see also affect; agency; force; nonpower; potentiality; sovereignty; sway; zoopower
promise, 15–17, 33, 131, 132, 139, 153–4, 156–7, 159, 163–4, 165, 173–4n, 215n
prostheticity, 26–8, 29, 31, 60, 74–5, 81, 83, 89, 120, 138–40, 167, 170n, 185n, 194n
protection, 5, 92–3, 94, 114–15, 117, 142, 207n
 animal, 5, 64–5, 114–15, 164–5
 biopolitical focus on, 76–80, 85, 90–1, 92
 environmental, 142–3, 145, 151
 politics of, 39–40, 63–4, 94, 114–15, 151, 161–2, 163, 164–5, 193n, 208n

question(ing), 1–2, 11, 13–15, 46–7, 59–61, 62, 65–6, 73, 81, 91, 93, 106–7, 119–20, 135, 143–4, 145, 146, 149–50, 154–5, 156–67, 216–17n; *see also* deconstruction; speculation

reaction, 25–6, 28, 73–4, 118, 136, 149–50
Read, Jason, 126–7, 208n
reading (interpretation), 7–8, 20, 32–3, 65–6, 69–70, 75–6, 81, 101, 111–12, 132, 137, 156, 167, 196–7n, 209n
 nonhuman, 103–5, 137–8, 142–3, 209n
response
 coordinated (political), 131, 133, 140, 147–8
 ethics, 4–5, 14, 33, 66, 75–6
 nonhuman (animal), 33, 54, 74–5, 82–3, 103–8, 136–7, 144–5, 148–55, 163, 195n, 212–13n
 problem, 123, 142–9
 reaction, 25, 73–4, 118–19, 149–51
 see also action; responsibility
responsibility, 4, 14, 65, 121, 130–1, 133, 140, 143–6, 157, 159–60, 182–3n, 213n
 nonhuman, 104, 148–55, 163, 212–13n
 see also animal other; ethics; justice

rights
 animal, 1, 6–7, 18, 31, 64–5, 76
 human (political), 28, 63–5, 71–2, 94, 95, 101, 135, 169n, 189n
risk, 21, 70, 82, 132, 158, 162, 216n

Sapolsky, Robert, 49–50, 183n
Schmitt, Carl, 77–8, 90, 161–2, 193
science, 30–1, 37, 42, 45, 49, 60, 74, 87–8, 106–7, 109, 114–15, 124, 187n, 198n, 199–200n
 biology, 29, 124, 142, 152, 166, 196–7n, 207n, 209n, 212n
 of culture, 36–8, 40, 42, 49–50, 53, 134, 184n
 ethology (behavioural), 103, 106–9, 199–200n
 primatology, 35–8
 social (human), 40, 73, 134, 183–4n
 see also anthropology
Shepard, Paul, 176n
Shukin, Nicole, 209–10n
signification *see* meaning
Sloterdijk, Peter, 87, 196n
Smith, Mick, 173n, 180n
sociality, 37, 53–5, 114, 137–8
sovereign(ty)
 decision, 39, 63, 95, 78, 95, 119
 human, 29, 29–40, 79, 81, 90–1, 122–5, 128–9, 131–3, 136, 140–1, 144, 150, 153, 159, 189n
 over self (action, response), 27–8, 39, 72–4, 131, 134–40, 144, 149–50, 153, 163, 211n, 216n
 political (state), 26–8, 39–40, 63–5, 72, 77–9, 90, 95, 101, 193n
 see also ipseity; power
species
 autonomy (autopoiesis), 29, 50–1, 53–4, 61
 biological character (behaviour), 36, 56–9, 102, 105–8, 120, 123–4, 127–9, 133, 136, 138, 164, 166–7, 185–6n, 205n
 endangered, 57, 114, 127–8, 134–5, 164–7
 human, 22, 31, 40–1, 47, 56, 73, 121–55, 206–7n
 logic (name), 52–4, 105–8, 114–15, 128–31, 133, 146–9
 see also animality
speculation, 2–4, 9, 31, 53, 92–3, 157, 178–9n, 210n; *see also* deconstruction; hauntology; question(ing)

Stengers, Isabelle, 6, 144–8, 150
Stiegler, Bernard, 110, 185n
subject(ivity), 11, 20, 25–8, 30, 51–2, 53–4, 57–8, 65, 72–3, 77, 78, 80, 81, 94, 111, 122, 149–50, 154–5, 159, 169n, 178–9n, 185n, 194n, 203n
suffering, 4, 14, 32–3, 62, 65–6, 74, 76, 79, 91, 118, 121, 152, 190n
survival (survivance), 34, 57, 127–8, 133–5, 140, 158, 159–60, 163, 164–5, 166, 186n, 216n
sustainability, 75–6, 135, 138, 140–1, 163; *see also* bearing
sway, 122, 153, 162

teaching, 50, 57, 108, 115, 186n, 187n; *see also* learning; training
technology (technicity), 13, 21–2, 26, 30–2, 44–5, 47, 60, 71, 80, 84, 89, 112, 124, 138, 151, 167, 172n, 194n, 198n, 203n; *see also* teletechnology; writing
teleology, 12, 32, 97, 130, 141, 180n, 205n
eschato-teleological situation, 8, 131–3
teletechnology, 110–13, 116, 119–20, 201n; *see also* media
terror *see* fear
textuality (texturity), 3, 22–4, 29, 32, 58, 89, 176–7n
Thompson, John B., 200n
to-come (future-to-come, *a-venir*), 2–3, 7, 15–18, 28, 32–4, 60, 91, 122, 139, 151, 156–7, 160–1, 162–4, 174n, 214–15n; *see also* democracy-to-come; future; hauntology; invention; justice
trace (tracing), 16–17, 20, 29, 39, 67, 70, 86, 153, 154–5, 194n
training, 12–13, 57, 84–7, 104, 109, 178n, 181n; *see also* learning; teaching
transformation, 3, 15–17, 29, 31, 33, 44, 58, 59, 60–1, 63, 81, 84, 86, 87, 89–90, 96, 105, 110–11, 113, 114–15, 116–17, 122, 132, 140, 148, 152–3, 158, 174n, 188n, 200n, 204n
Tylor, Edward Burnett, 38, 39, 183n

unpredictability (unexpectedness), 85–6, 98–9, 102, 108, 109, 119, 150–1
of animal action, 103–5, 108–9, 114–15, 120, 150–1
see also invention

van Dooren, Thom, 164–7, 218n
Vico, Giambattista, 39–41, 42, 184n
violence, 17, 51, 62–5, 75–7, 78, 80, 91, 121–2, 140–1, 148, 157–8, 167, 193n
Virno, Paolo, 123–7, 128–9, 135–6, 141–2, 147, 154, 204n, 206n
vitalism, 137–8, 140
vulnerability, 4, 62–6, 68, 70, 74–80, 86, 90, 91, 92, 94, 118, 190n, 194–5n; *see also* nonpower

war *see* conflict
'we', 24, 118, 133, 144, 147, 153–5, 205n
Weinstein, Jami, 122, 159–60
wildlife (wild animals), 54, 56, 57, 59, 114–15, 183n, 210n
Wills, David, 11–12, 13, 198n
Wolfe, Cary, 62, 64–5, 77–8, 80, 91, 93, 143, 172n, 185n, 194n
Wood, David, 217n
world *see* environment
writing (inscription), 3, 9, 16, 20–4, 52, 67–8, 71–2, 79, 89, 101, 119, 122, 125, 139, 157, 163, 174–5n, 207–8n

Žižek, Slavoj, 130
zoē and bios, 23, 95–6, 98, 119, 177n; *see also* Agamben; Arendt
zoopolitics, 4, 7, 24–5, 28–9, 80, 90–1, 94–5, 101–2, 117–18, 119–20, 121, 123, 139–40, 148, 161, 163–4, 166–7, 189n, 202–3n, 217n
zoopower, 4, 52, 62–91, 94, 102, 107, 118, 141, 163, 211n; *see also* power

EU representative:
Easy Access System Europe
Mustamäe tee 50, 10621 Tallinn, Estonia
Gpsr.requests@easproject.com

www.ingramcontent.com/pod-product-compliance
Lightning Source LLC
Chambersburg PA
CBHW070344240426
43671CB00013BA/2395